INDIAN KNOWLEDGE SYSTEM

UNVEILING TRADITIONS PERSPECTIVES AND NARRATIVES

Editor

Dr. Anshul Saluja

Assistant Professor,

School of Education

K. R. Mangalam University

BOOK RIVERS

WE CREATE READERS

Published By: Book Rivers

Website: www.bookrivers.com

Email: publish@bookrivers.com

Mobile: +91-9695375469

1ST Edition: -2023

MRP: 399/-INR

ISBN: 978-93-5842-838-4

[PRINTED IN INDIA]

Foreword

Understanding, touching lives, expanding the circle, working hard and smart, and always open to receiving and giving- that is a fair description of many of the amazing people we encounter. And where these people live and work in different spheres and different parts of the world, they all share a similar core philosophy of "*working hard*". This book is a culmination of all those efforts, dedication and hard work which the authors of seventeen chapters of this book have shown. I feel privileged to write the foreword for this book on the Indian Knowledge System written by Dr. Anshul Saluja, who has been an enthusiastic learner and a dedicated faculty member of my university. I have always admired her dedication and passion for exploring avenues.

The theme of this book has been very central to my heart. The book targets several aspects of the knowledge system of India prevalent from the historic times; the aspects which are interconnected and interwoven to shape India's rich heritage. The knowledge accumulated by Indian society over thousands of years has been expressed in the shape of arts, literature, traditions, customs, languages, architecture, etc. The foundation of Indian knowledge is the long tradition of unhindered knowledge acquisition, maintenance, and transmission. Indians established ancient practices over centuries, passing them down from one generation to the next. That establishes our capacity to think and reason critically or otherwise in a way that harmonises the mind, body, and soul with the justification of the applicability and power of Indian Knowledge heritage. Thus, it would be apt to compare this system with the perennial and pious river Ganga, "*bharatiya jnana parampara sanatana ganga pravah*", whose flow is continuous and unhindered like our knowledge system.

Though the country witnessed foreign invasions and changes in structure and policies, despite that the rich knowledge, traditions and cultural practices have been passed on from generation to generation. Due to British rule, this gem was lost somewhere behind the doors, in the almirahs, but of late, the policymakers realized that this Indian treasure should be revived, secured and should be introduced to the entire world. This we get to see in the NEP (2020) which lays special emphasis on the promotion of Indian languages, arts, and culture and on removing the discontinuity in the flow of IKS by integrating it into curriculums at all levels of education. Being from a science background, I always look forward to the contributions IKS have been making for inventions so the chapters which specifically have spoken about the IKS in science and technology have managed to get my extreme attention. Besides, I was fascinated to see how the contributors have comprehensively thrown light on women and their evolution in Indian society.

This book features the extensive application of IKS in varied arcas which will bc of grcat usc to thc rcadcrs: India's philosophical system, scientific methods, social organization, women in Indian literature, Indian psychology, Buddhist traditions, traditional architecture etc. The readers can relate, appreciate and explore the various dimensions which have been presented in the book. The seventeen contributors, many of which are my young-spirited students have made their contributions to revive and revitalize IKS in academic and public spheres. I commend all the contributors and Dr. Anshul Saluja, the editor of the book for their remarkable work and I really hope that this book will inspire many readers to explore and experience the wisdom and beauty of the Indian Knowledge System.

Prof. Chandra Shekhar Dubey

Prefatory Note

"We owe a lot to the ancient Indians, teaching us how to count. Without which most modern scientific discoveries would have been impossible"

~ Albert Einstein

The above quote is true to every extent since Indian civilization has long placed a high emphasis on knowledge, its development and dissemination. As evidenced by the incredibly enormous corpus of intellectual texts, India has the greatest collection of manuscripts in the world, and its well-documented heritage of texts, thinkers, and schools in a wide range of fields makes this country a hub of knowledge. India's knowledge legacy is ancient and unbroken and has been at the heart of all rational and speculative investigations. The Indian Knowledge System includes all established disciplines of knowledge that have been extensively developed in India from ancient times as well as all customs and practices that various communities of India, including the tribal people, have adopted. These traditions are still alive in the practices and learnings of Indian people.

This book is a result of my fascination with India's rich and diverse culture, history and wisdom. My curiosity about the origins and meanings of various traditions, customs and practices that have shaped the Indian systems has led to the emergence of this book. My aim in writing this book is to acknowledge and appreciate the achievements and future prospects of the vast knowledge system of India so that people can apply these in their lives and live with them. This book consists of seventeen chapters dealing with different themes. The major themes covered in this book are the nature and philosophical system of IKS, India's scientific methods, the social organization of knowledge in India, women in Indian society, Indian psychology, Buddhist traditions and knowledge, state and society in India.

Chapter 1 deals with the nature and philosophical system of the Indian knowledge system. The chapter discussed various Indian schools of philosophy and their relevance to the present-day education system. It also focuses on various aspects of education, such as teaching and learning, management and how various disciplines are interconnected. In India, mathematics, astronomy, technology and chemistry find their special place. Various sophisticated concepts have evolved in history which hold relevance and practical utility in today's time too. Chapter 2 of the book deals with this aspect only and discusses how India has been instrumental in contributing globally to the fields of mathematics, physics, chemistry, geography, astronomy, engineering, medicine and surgery, music, and arts.

Chapter 3 discusses the fascinating background of Indian traditions and their impact on modern society. This chapter will take the readers on a beautiful journey to understand the depth, diversity and enduring legacy of different faiths, practices, food, clothing and languages. Chapter 4 deals with identifying the Chakma community, their interaction with nature and society and the associated pedagogical dimensions. It depicts how the knowledge, know-how, practices and representations are developed and maintained by the members of the local community and how the indigenous knowledge holders are constantly observing, experimenting and adapting their practices to ensure their survival and well-being. Most importantly, this chapter gives insights into knowledge transformation strategies which can be incorporated into the formal teacher education curriculum that could have valuable implications for the pedagogical diminutions.

Chapter 5 speaks about the portrayal of women in traditional Indian literature including the scriptures, epics, poetry and prose.

Since Indian literature spans across different languages, genres, periods and regions, it reflects the diverse and complex realities of Indian women. In the forthcoming three chapters also, chapters 6, 7 and 8, the contributors discuss some of the prominent works of the ancient period including the Vedas, Upanishads, Ramayana, Mahabharata and various folklore and folktales. They demonstrated how the role of women was shaped by a complex network of social norms, traditions and religious doctrines and were revered as the stewards of family honour, upholding the rituals and conventions inside their homes and families. However, some women personified their ambitions challenged injustice and social structures and transformed themselves into a figure of determination and virtue. They were known warriors, poets, mystics, saints, scholars, intellectuals, politicians, and administrators.

Buddhism originated in India and is primarily based upon the principles of wisdom, compassion and ethical conduct and aims to liberate from the cycles of rebirth and suffering. The concept of karma, mediation, non-violence and compassion, creation of stupas, caves, statues, paintings and manuscripts etc. reflects the rich cultural heritage and diversity of Buddhism. Chapter 9 gives a comprehensive picture of the traditions of Buddhism and its influence on Indian philosophy, literature and art. It discusses how the Indian school of thought were influenced by Buddhist logic and epistemology; the creation of art and architectures like stupas, caves, statues, rituals and festivals, jataka tales, Zen literature, Nalanda University etc. are some of the prominent results of the Buddhist traditions. Chapter 10 exposes characteristics of architecture during Buddhism by emphasising the three major types of structures: stupas, chaityas and viharas, each with special kind of architectural details. Chapter 11 explores the inclusion of the norms of Vaastu shastra in present-day modern architecture. Vaastu Shastra, as derived from the Vedas, is based on the concept of five elements (panchabhuta) - earth, water, fire, air and space - and their balance and interaction with the human body, mind and spirit. Modern architecture forms a basis for the creation of such buildings which are conducive to the physical, psychological and spiritual well-being of the occupants while optimizing the use of natural resources.

Chapter 12 speaks of the rich and distinct body of knowledge of Indian psychology and the implications it has in various domains of life such as education, health, management, leadership, governance, law, art etc. To further this, chapter 13 of the book deals with the origin and effect of polytheism in Hindu society and its belief system. Polytheism is the belief system in many gods, each with distinct names, attributes, functions and domains. It helps people understand the nature of human identity, diversity, morality and spirituality and allows Hindus to relate to different aspects of divinity that resonate with their personal needs, preferences and aspirations. Chapter 14 looks at Indian psychology from the purview of yoga, ayurveda and homeopathy. The chapter discusses how since ages, yoga and meditation have been used as tools for self-awareness and spiritual development and their potential benefits in treating many health conditions.

We all must have heard the story of Newton regarding his discovery of gravity at one or the other stage of our life. But we seldom know that Bhaskaracharya discovered gravity around 500 years before Newton. His contributions in fields like calculus, trigonometry, algebra, geometry etc. remain unknown and unacknowledged by this world. In Chapter 15, the contributor throws light on some of the greatest achievements of India in astronomy and mathematics. By mentioning the shlokas from Bhaskaracharya's book *Surya Siddhanta*, the chapter recognizes the significant contributions made by him in the fields of astronomy and mathematics.

Chapter 16 discusses the relationship between the state and society and delves into the political system that persisted in ancient

India. It focuses on the discourses and ideological frameworks and India's quest for effective governance. India is driven by social, linguistic, religious, and regional diversities and it is important to develop such a system which works towards developing a better relationship between the state and its citizens. Chapter 17 explores the intricate relationship between the Indian state and society. It explores the dynamics, social structure, and historical backdrop of Indian society, highlighting potential problems in the interactions between the state and society. For India to advance, emphasis is placed on effective government, social inclusion, and sustainable development. In order to achieve an equitable future, the paper promotes strengthening democratic institutions, lowering inequality, managing communal conflicts, and promoting sustainable development. In the end, it seeks to fully comprehend state-society relations in India and offer suggestions for a diverse, sustainable country.

Anshul Saluja

Acknowledgement

This acknowledgement goes beyond a simple "thank you"; rather, I see it as the best way I know how to show the people who were instrumental in the completion of this work my respect and sincere gratitude. Writing this book continued to be an interesting journey. It was a long process, and I feel really fortunate to have gotten the necessary help from so many individuals.

First and foremost, I want to express my sincere gratitude to Prof. Chandra Shekhar Dubey, Hon'ble Vice Chancellor, K. R. Mangalam University for giving me the chance to take on this assignment. His invaluable enlightenment, guidance, encouragement and constant feedback have helped to make this work a better one. I would like to express my sincere respect and thanks to Prof. Pushplata Tripathi, Hon'ble Pro-Vice-Chancellor, K. R. Mangalam University for consistently inspiring me and providing me with insightful feedback. I have been fortunate enough to have supportive colleagues who have helped me now and then. Their support has been invaluable to me. I also extend my deepest gratitude to all the contributors to this book, especially my own students, for showing interest in this work, contributing their chapters and being timely available. I am grateful to my publishers for their enthusiasm and professionalism.

I also extend my deepest gratitude and love for the most important part of me, my son Aakanksh, for being so understanding, patient and supportive of me throughout my journey. He made countless sacrifices, and I greatly appreciate the love he showed me during all the changes. I want to express my gratitude to my parents for always being supportive, helping, and caring for my son and me while I overindulged at work. Without their help and trust, it would have been difficult for me to complete the assignment. They have all been a wonderful godsend for me.

Finally, I want to thank you, the readers of this book, for picking up this book and giving it a chance. "I wish you enjoy it as much as I enjoyed writing it."

Anshul Saluja

Contents

INDIAN KNOWLEDGE SYSTEM: NATURE AND PHILOSOPHICAL SYSTEM

Ritu Jain

Assistant Professor, School of Management and Commerce, K. R. Mangalam University, Gurugram

Manisha Rani Sahu

Student, School of Medical and Allied Sciences, K.R. Mangalam University, Gurugram

Shanvi Mathuria

Student, School of Engineering and Technology, K.R. Mangalam University, Gurugram

Abstract

This chapter explores the various advantages of the Indian Knowledge System, which includes its culture, philosophies, and teachings. The article addresses the profound wisdom ingrained in Indian culture by drawing on a vast heritage of ancient texts, scriptures, and practices. It draws attention to the variety of fields in which people can use this method to get insightful knowledge that can change their lives. Furthermore, it explores the practical applications of the Indian Knowledge System in various aspects of life, including education, psychology, health, and well-being. It investigates how concepts such as meditation, mindfulness, Ayurveda, and yoga have gained global recognition for their potential to promote physical and mental health, stress reduction, and overall holistic well-being. Overall, this research paper highlights the immense value of the Indian Knowledge System, offering a comprehensive understanding of the manifold benefits it provides across personal, societal, and cultural dimensions. It underscores the significance of integrating these learnings into contemporary contexts to promote personal growth, well-being, and a deeper appreciation of shared humanity.

Keywords: Indian Knowledge System, Indus Valley Civilization, Mindfulness, Meditation, Indian Philosophy.

Introduction

The "Indian Knowledge System" encompasses the extensive body of knowledge accumulated over a significant period. When referring to "India" in this context, it pertains to Ancient India, which encompassed regions like Nepal, Pakistan, and other neighbouring nations. This wealth of knowledge is preserved in ancient texts such as the Upanishads and palm leaf scrolls. These texts serve as repositories of wisdom, covering diverse subjects and disciplines. Moreover, the Indian Knowledge System is also transmitted orally across family generations. Through rituals, traditions, and cultural beliefs, valuable knowledge is passed down, ensuring its continuity and relevance in contemporary times.

The Indian Knowledge System encompasses a wide range of subjects, including philosophy, spirituality, metaphysics, ethics, governance, social sciences, mathematics, astronomy, linguistics, medicine, and more. It offers profound insights into the human experience, the nature of reality, and the pursuit of knowledge. The system has a rich cultural and spiritual heritage that continues to influence contemporary Indian society. It has inspired great thinkers, scholars, and practitioners throughout history and remains a source of wisdom, guidance, and inspiration for individuals seeking personal growth, intellectual exploration, and spiritual enlightenment.

The present study aims to explore and understand the various advantages and practical applications of the Indian Knowledge System in different aspects of life. An in-depth examination of the subject matter allows for a conceptual understanding of the subject, capturing the richness of experiences, perspectives, and insights related to the Indian Knowledge System.

Historical Development of the Indian Knowledge System

One of the most significant facets of Indian culture and civilization is thought to be knowledge. Indian knowledge development and transmission have a long history that dates to prehistoric times. Several educational institutions were founded in India throughout the mediaeval era, including Nalanda, Taxila, and Vikramshila, which drew academics from all over the world. These organizations made major contributions to the advancement of knowledge and the dissemination of ideas.

i) Indus Valley Civilization:

The first known urban civilization on the Indian subcontinent was the Indus Valley Civilization, often known as the Harappan civilization. Although the southern sites may have persisted later into the second millennium BCE, the civilization's nuclear dates appear to be between 250 to 1700 BCE. The Indus civilization was the largest of the three early civilizations in the world (the other two are those of Mesopotamia and Egypt). It is known that the Indus civilization included more than 100 towns and villages, many of which were quite small, in addition to the two major cities of Harappa and Mohenjo-Daro. The two cities were roughly one mile (1.6 km) square in total dimensions, and their extraordinary size suggests political centralization, either in two big states or in a single great empire with alternate capitals, a practice with historical precedent in India. It's also conceivable that Harappa replaced Mohenjo-Daro, which is known to have been severely damaged by unusual flooding more than once (McIntosh, 2008).

ii) Vedas and Upanishads:

The Vedas, which are regarded as Hinduism's earliest sacred books, are thought to have been written between 1500 and 500 BCE. They consist of several hymns, customs, prayers, and philosophical teachings. In Sanskrit, the word "Veda" denotes wisdom or understanding.

- **Rigveda:** It is a collection of hymns to many gods that is rich in knowledge about the cosmology, rites, and civilization of ancient India.
- **Samaveda**: This text, which primarily serves as a chanting guide for religious rituals, comprises melodies and musical notations taken from the Rigveda.
- **Yajurveda:** It is a Veda that concentrates on the steps and rituals of yajnas (sacrifices) and offers guidance to the priests who carry out these rites.
- **Atharvaveda**: It consists of songs and ceremonies about domestic, magical, and therapeutic practices as well as daily living (Frauwallner, 1973).

The Upanishads are a body of prehistoric philosophical writings that are fundamental to the Indian knowledge system. They are frequently referred to as Vedanta, which translates as "the end of the Vedas" and are deemed to be the pinnacle of Vedic thought. The Upanishads were written between the years of 800 and 200 BCE. The word "Upanishad" is a Sanskrit word that means "sitting near" or "sitting down near." It alludes to an intimate teaching session between a teacher (guru) and a student (shishya), during which profound philosophical lessons are conveyed.

iii) Influence of Bhagavad-Gita

The Bhagavad Gita, often known as the Gita, is a revered Hindu scripture that is recognized as one of the most significant works of spiritual and philosophical literature in India. Philosophy, spirituality, ethics, and psychology are just a few of the areas of Indian knowledge that have been profoundly impacted by it. Indian knowledge has been influenced in the following ways:

- **Philosophy:** The Gita offers a synthesis of numerous intellectual theories and schools of thought. The nature of existence, the self, consciousness, and the meaning of life are among the topics that are covered. It introduces philosophical ideas like karma (activity and its results), yoga (spiritual practice), and dharma (duty/righteousness). Vedanta, Yoga, and Samkhya are just a few of the Indian intellectual systems that have been impacted by Gita's teachings.
- **Spirituality:** The Gita offers instructions on how to advance spiritually and find self-realization. It describes several forms of yoga, such as jnana yoga (the path of knowledge and wisdom), bhakti yoga (the road of devotion), and karma yoga (the path of selfless action). These routes have influenced many seekers on their spiritual journeys and are now an essential part of Indian spiritual practices.
- **Ethics:** The Gita provides insightful analysis of moral decision-making and ethical conundrums. It emphasizes the value of carrying out one's obligations with honesty and objectivity while being disinterested in the outcomes. Gita's explanation of justice and ethical behaviour has left a long-lasting impression on Indian society's moral foundation.
- **Psychology:** The Gita delves into the human mind and explores the nature of desires, emotions, and the challenges of controlling one's thoughts. The idea of the "inner battle" or the conflict between the higher and lower selves is covered. The Gita's lessons on controlling the mind and reaching mental equilibrium have affected Indian psychology and given important new perspectives on how people behave and feel about themselves.
- **Literature and Arts:** The Gita's profound wisdom and poetic verses have inspired numerous writers, poets, and artists

throughout history. It has served as a source of inspiration for literary works, including poetry, novels, and dramas. The themes and teachings of the Gita have also been depicted in various forms of Indian art, such as paintings, sculptures, and dance performances.

Philosophical Foundations of the Indian Knowledge System

A rich and varied history of thought that has evolved over thousands of years is included in the Indian knowledge system, often known as Indian philosophy or Darshans. A holistic approach that incorporates numerous facets of life, such as nature, spirituality, ethics, and philosophy, is what distinguishes it. Ancient literature like the Vedas, Upanishads, Bhagavad Gita, and other texts have a significant influence on the Indian knowledge system.

Indian philosophy refers to the thought and reflection processes that the civilizations of the Indian subcontinent created. They comprise both orthodox (astika) and non-orthodox (nastika) philosophical traditions, such as Buddhism and Jainism. Orthodox systems include the Nyaya, Vaisheshika, Samkhya, Yoga, Purva-Mimamsa (or Mimamsa), and Vedanta schools of thought. Numerous philosophical issues have interested Indian thinking, chief among them the nature of the universe (cosmology), the nature of reality (metaphysics), logic, the nature of knowing (epistemology), ethics, and the philosophy of religion.

Constituents of Indian philosophy

The self or soul (atman), works (karma), and salvation (moksha) are the three fundamental ideas that constitute the basis of Indian philosophy. All Indian philosophies, except the Charvakas, are concerned with these three ideas and how they relate to one another, though this does not mean that they all accept the notions' objectivity in the same way. The idea of karma, which denotes the moral effectiveness of human deeds, appears to be the most characteristically Indian of them.

i) Dharma:

Dharma is a central idea in Indian philosophy and has a significant impact on India's system of knowledge. It covers a broad spectrum of concepts, such as duty, righteousness, moral and ethical standards, cosmic order, and spiritual path. Dharma is well ingrained in Indian culture and has influenced a number of areas of Indian knowledge, such as philosophy, social organization, and education.

- **Religion and philosophy:** Indian religions including Hinduism, Buddhism, and Jainism all place a strong emphasis on dharma. It gives people and societies a moral and ethical basis for living good lives. Dharma serves as the foundation for ideas such as karma (the law of cause and effect) and moksha (freedom from the cycle of birth and death). Dharma affects religious customs, rites, and moral standards, directing people in their spiritual exploration and social interactions.
- **Social Structure:** Dharma has had a big impact on India's social structure. The caste system, commonly referred to as the varna system, has a close relationship with dharma. Depending on their caste or social standing, people are assigned certain jobs and responsibilities under this system.
- **Ethics and Morality:** Dharma provides a moral compass for individuals, guiding them in making ethical choices and actions. It emphasizes virtues such as honesty, compassion, righteousness, and non-violence. The teachings of dharma encourage individuals to fulfil their responsibilities towards family, society, and the environment, fostering a sense of duty and social welfare.
- **Education:** Dharma's emphasis on the value of education has had an impact on the Indian knowledge system. An integral component of one's dharma is the pursuit of knowledge,

especially spiritual and moral knowledge. Ancient Indian educational institutions, such as gurukuls (ancient schools), placed equal emphasis on the building of moral character and the dissemination of knowledge.

ii) Karma and Law of Effect and Cause:

The ideas of karma and the law of cause and effect have their origins in many different religious and philosophical traditions, especially in Jainism, Buddhism, and Hinduism. These traditions typically pertain to the belief that one's acts have consequences and that those repercussions will eventually appear in one's life, but there may be some discrepancies in their interpretations.

In its simplest form, the Sanskrit word for karma is "action". It implies that every action one takes, whether it be verbal, mental, or physical, leaves a mark or releases energy that affects the experiences in the future. According to the idea of karma, one's current circumstances are the outcome of her/his past behaviour, and the current behaviour will determine the circumstances in the future. In general, all occurrences in the cosmos, including human behaviour, are subject to the law of cause and effect. Understanding karma is meant to help people develop good thoughts and behaviours, as well as a sense of responsibility for their acts.

Overall, karma and the law of cause and effect are concepts that highlight the interconnectedness of one's actions and experiences, suggesting that choices and behaviours have far-reaching consequences that shape her/his life (Humphreys, 2005).

iii) Pursuit of Moksha (Liberation):

One of the main objectives of several religions and philosophical systems, particularly Hinduism, Jainism, and some schools of Buddhism, is the pursuit of Moksha, often known as emancipation. The highest level of life, moksha is the ultimate escape from the cycle of birth, death, and reincarnation (samsara).

In this condition, one is free from pain and achieves eternal bliss and unity with the supreme reality. However, Moksha is thought to be the ultimate goal of life, surpassing the pursuit of materialistic ambitions and successes. One is said to be able to escape the cycle of life and death and achieve unity with the divine through self-realization, education, and spiritual practices. Hinduism offers a variety of Moksha pathways that can be followed according to one's temperament and abilities. The most well-known paths are:

- **Jnana Yoga:** The path of knowledge and wisdom is known as jnana yoga. It entails in-depth reflection, self-examination, and the realization of one's actual essence as the divine, eternal self (Atman), who is one with the ultimate reality (Brahman).
- **Karma Yoga:** Selfless activity is the way of Karma Yoga. It places a focus on carrying out one's obligations without becoming emotionally invested in the outcomes. One can purify the mind and ultimately arrive at liberation by engaging in detachment practice and offering the benefits of one's activities to a higher power.
- **Bhakti Yoga:** The devotional path is called bhakti yoga. It requires growing a strong, unwavering love and devotion for a particular deity or the divine. One seeks connection with the object of devotion through prayers, rituals, chanting, and submission to the divine.
- **Raja Yoga:** The practice of meditation and mind control. Asanas (physical postures), pranayama (breath control), and dhyana (meditation) are some of the techniques used. One can experience the true essence of reality and find liberation by calming the mind and experiencing intense states of concentration and absorption.

The quest for emancipation has a high priority in Jainism. According to Jain's philosophy, Moksha—the release from all karmic bonds—is the ultimate aim of existence and can only be accomplished by doing so. To purify their souls and finally attain Moksha, Jains follow the path of non-violence (ahimsa), honesty, non-possessiveness, and stringent ascetic practices. Liberation from the cycle of life and death is one of the goals of Buddhism too, especially in the Theravada and Mahayana branches. The Buddhist way of life includes exercises in mindfulness, meditation, moral behaviour, and wisdom. Nirvana, or enlightenment, and dukkha, or freedom from pain, are the desired outcomes.

It's crucial to remember that the quest for Moksha is an intensely particular and personal path. The fundamental goal is to overcome the constraints of earthly existence and achieve emancipation, peace, and ultimately connection with the divine or the true nature of reality. The methods and practices may differ, but the fundamental goal does not (Chalise, 2022).

Indian Philosophical Schools

A variety of philosophical schools can be found in the rich and diverse legacy of Indian philosophy. Some of the most significant schools of Indian philosophy are listed below:

- **Nyaya:** It is an epistemological and logical school. It focuses on the research of reliable knowledge (pramana) and logical reasoning techniques. The Nyaya philosophers developed trustworthy sources of knowledge by examining the nature of perception, inference, and testimony.
- **Vaisheshika:** Atomism and metaphysics are the two main tenets of this school. The cosmos is assumed to be made up of distinct atoms (paramanu), and it explores the nature of reality, causation, and the categories of existence.
- **Samkhya:** Samkhya is a dualistic school that investigates the nature of existence by dissecting principles (tattvas). It assumes the presence of two fundamental beings, known as Purusha (consciousness) and Prakriti (matter/energy), and works to free Purusha from Prakriti's control.

- **Yoga:** Yoga is a school that emphasizes self-realization and practical approaches to spiritual practice. It involves physical positions called asanas, breath control called pranayama, concentration called dharana, meditation called dhyana, and moral guidelines called yamas and niyamas.
- **Mimamsa:** Mimamsa is a school of ritualistic exegesis and Vedic exegesis. Its main objectives are the study of dharma (duty/righteousness) and the proper execution of Vedic rituals.
- **Vedanta:** The Upanishads, which are regarded as the pinnacle of Vedic wisdom, are interpreted by the school of Vedanta. It places a strong emphasis on researching Atman—the self and Brahman—the supreme reality. Different sub-schools of Vedanta are included, such as Advaita (non-dualism), Dvaita (dualism), and Vishishtadvaita (qualified non-dualism) (Mohanty, 2023).

Scientific Contributions to the Indian Knowledge System

Throughout history, the Indian knowledge system has significantly advanced science in several domains.

i) Calculus

- **Mathematics in ancient India:** The mathematicians of ancient India made significant contributions to the subject. The Sulba Sutras, one of the earliest mathematical writings from India, offers geometrical techniques for building altars and fire pits. Early notions of irrational numbers and square roots are also included.
- **Algebra and the numerical system:** The Hindu-Arabic numeral system, also known as the Indian numerical system, was a revolutionary invention that introduced the idea of zero and decimal place values. Together, this numerical system and the idea of positional notation revolutionized mathematics and greatly simplified even the most difficult calculations. Indian

mathematicians also created algebraic strategies, such as how to solve quadratic equations.

- **Advancements in trigonometry:** Advancements in trigonometry have advanced significantly from the time of ancient India, according to mathematicians. The terms sine, cosine, and versine were first used in mathematics in the fifth century CE by the Indian mathematician Aryabhata. Other Indian mathematicians like Bhaskara I and Bhaskara II went on to develop these trigonometric functions in the future. Additionally, Indian mathematicians created trigonometric tables and used trigonometry to resolve astronomical puzzles.

ii) Astronomy

- **Ancient Indian astronomers:** India has a long history of astronomy that dates to the beginning of time. Aryabhata, Varahamihira, and Brahmagupta were well-known astronomers who made major contributions. To build mathematical models to forecast astronomical events, they researched celestial bodies, determined planetary locations, and investigated celestial bodies.
- **Understanding celestial bodies:** Indian astronomers produced significant observations and theorized about celestial bodies, which is useful today. Aryabhata correctly hypothesized that the Earth revolves on its axis and that this rotation is what causes the stars to appear to move. Additionally, they presented theories for eclipses and acknowledged that the Moon reflected sunlight.
- **Calendars and astrology:** Indian astronomers created sophisticated calendars, such as the Surya Siddhanta and the Jyotisha Vedanga, which assisted in choosing auspicious dates, forecasting the seasons, and planning religious holidays. Ancient Indian astrologers began establishing links between celestial activities and human situations as the science of astrology developed.

iii) Medicine

Significant scientific advancements in many areas of healthcare have been made possible by the Indian medical knowledge system, particularly Ayurveda. The term "knowledge of life," or "ayurveda," refers to a conventional medical system that has been used in India for countless years. With a focus on the harmony and balance of the body, mind, and spirit, it encompasses a holistic approach to wellness.

- **Ayurveda (principles and practices):** Doshas, or the three primary forces that control the human body—Vata, Pitta, and Kapha—are the foundation of Ayurveda. These doshas are thought to affect a person's physical, mental, and emotional traits. To reestablish balance, ayurvedic practitioners evaluate a patient's doshic constitution and offer customised remedies. The personalised medicine movement is comparable to how this strategy is tailored to each person.
- **Herbal treatments:** Ayurveda uses herbal treatments extensively for a variety of diseases. Generation after generation has passed down knowledge of medicinal plants and their therapeutic characteristics. Scientific research has demonstrated the pharmacological activity of several Ayurvedic medicines, including their anti-inflammatory, antioxidant, antibacterial, and immunomodulatory actions. Some well-known Ayurvedic herbs are Triphala, Brahmi, Turmeric, and Ashwagandha.
- **Herbal remedies and preventive healthcare:** Preventive healthcare is stressed in Ayurveda, which also places a strong emphasis on sustaining general health. It emphasises the value of leading a balanced lifestyle, which includes making changes to one's nutrition, developing daily routines, and engaging in seasonal activities. Global acclaim has been given to ayurvedic practises including yoga, meditation, and pranayama (breathing

exercises) for their potential to improve mental health, lower stress levels, and improve general wellness.

- **Holistic approach to wellbeing:** Ayurveda's holistic approach to well-being is one of its major accomplishments. It takes into account the interdependence of the body, mind, and spirit and seeks to treat the underlying causes of illness as opposed to only its symptoms. Ayurvedic treatments may include nutritional advice, lifestyle changes, herbal remedies, detoxification therapies, and rejuvenation techniques, all of which are adapted to the individual's particular needs.

Contemporary Relevance of the Indian Knowledge System

i) Integration in Psychology and Education:

- **Mindfulness and meditation:** The ancient wisdom traditions of India, especially those connected to yoga and Buddhism, place a strong emphasis on these practices. In the modern world, these practices are well known for their positive psychological and educational effects. According to research, mindfulness and meditation can help with stress reduction, cognitive improvement, emotional well-being, and general mental health. These ideas are currently being applied globally in a range of educational contexts and psychiatric therapies (Sinha, 1965).

- **Holistic approach to education:** The Indian knowledge system acknowledges that education should take into account all aspects of a person's growth, including their physical, mental, emotional, and spiritual well-being. This all-encompassing strategy encourages a more balanced and thorough understanding of education, extending beyond academic success to concentrate on students' general well-being and character development. Indian philosophical traditions place a strong emphasis on the importance of values, ethics, and self-realization in education, all of which are pertinent when addressing current issues like student well-being, mental health, and character education (Choudhary, 2008).

- **Individual differences and personalized learning:** The Indian knowledge system values and respects each person's individuality. It recognizes that everyone has unique learning preferences, skills, and capacities. This understanding is consistent with modern educational strategies that prioritize inclusive education, personalized learning, and individualized instruction. The Indian knowledge system can aid in the creation of more effective educational interventions and techniques that are tailored to varied learners by recognizing personal differences (Varma, 2020)

ii) Management and Leadership Principles:

The Indian knowledge system also provides helpful principles and insights for leadership and management in modern organisational environments.

- **Ethical leadership:** Indian philosophies, such as those found in the Arthashastra and Chanakya Neeti, place a premium on ethical leadership. Dharma (righteousness) and karma (action) are concepts that give leaders a foundation for making moral decisions and taking into account the overall well-being of their organisations, employees, and society. Addressing current difficulties with corporate governance, social responsibility, and sustainable business practices requires the application of these concepts.

- **Self-management and self-development:** The Indian knowledge system places a strong emphasis on the value of self-management and self-development as crucial components of successful leadership. Indian philosophical traditions like Yoga and Vedanta contain ideas like self-awareness, self-discipline, and self-transformation. These guidelines are especially pertinent in today's leadership development programmes that emphasise the improvement of leaders' self-awareness, emotional intelligence, and personal development.

- **Collaboration and teamwork:** Collaboration and teamwork are recognised as having great power in the Indian knowledge system. The Ramayana and the Mahabharata, two ancient Indian writings, emphasise the value of teamwork, happy relationships, and utilising the individual strengths of team members. The concepts of the Indian knowledge system can provide useful insights into effective collaboration and teamwork, which are essential for organisational success in today's globalised and linked world (Dasgupta, 2014).

iii) Sustainable Development and Environmental Ethics:

The roots of sustainable development and environmental ethics in ancient India can be found in numerous ancient books and ideologies.

- The idea of "Dharma" was essential in directing people towards living in harmony with nature. The need to carry out obligations while taking into account the welfare of all living things and the environment was emphasized by Dharma.
- Indian culture had a strong foundation in the "Ahimsa" (non-violence) practice, which encouraged compassion for all living things. The exploitation of natural resources was prohibited by this idea, which promoted environmentally friendly behaviour.
- The Vedas, a collection of prehistoric Hindu teachings, included hymns to nature that emphasised the environment's purity. They supported their preservation because they understood how linked all of nature's components are.
- Kautilya (Chanakya), in his treatise on governance known as *The Arthashastra*, emphasised the significance of sustainable

resource management. It promoted the preservation of forests, the safeguarding of wildlife, and the use of sustainable farming methods.

- Ancient Indian towns were planned with the environment's sustainability in mind. For instance, the idea of "Vastu Shastra" served as a blueprint for creating energy-efficient structures that used natural light and air, and were in tune with the environment.

iv) Yoga, Meditation and Mindfulness Practices:

Yoga, meditation, and mindfulness techniques have their roots in ancient India and have become incredibly popular worldwide in recent years. These techniques' value comes from their capacity to advance bodily, mental, and spiritual well-being. Strength, flexibility, relaxation, and inner calm are encouraged by yoga, which blends physical postures, breathing exercises, and meditation practices. It is widely used all over the world as a method to lessen stress, promote mental health, and improve general wellness. Similarly, mindfulness and meditation techniques aid in the development of attention, self-awareness, and emotional resilience and provide useful skills for managing stress, anxiety, and other mental health issues. These practices are now being included in numerous wellness initiatives, therapeutic approaches, and routine activities because the scientific community is still investigating and validating their advantages.

v) Art, Music and Dance:

Indian culture has long included art, dance, and music, and its significance is still very strong now. Indian art genres, including painting, sculpture, and architecture, serve as a medium of expression and narrative as well as a window into the country's rich cultural legacy and aesthetic sensibility. Deeper insights into the Indian knowledge system can be gained from the numerous spiritual and philosophical topics that were frequently present in ancient Indian art. Traditional Indian dance styles like Bharatanatyam, Kathak, Odissi, and Kathakali combine rhythmic movements, nuanced gestures, facial expressions, and storytelling to transmit emotions, narratives, and cultural values. These dance styles are still practised, taught, and performed today, conserving cultural history and incorporating modern elements into their development.

In a nutshell, from the context presented above, the following are the major takeaways of the Indian Knowledge System from the perspective of the Indian philosophical system:

Cultural dialogue and interfaith harmony: The Indian knowledge system, which is based on ancient wisdom, has stressed the value of tolerance, respect, and understanding between many cultures and religions. Hinduism, Buddhism, Jainism, Sikhism, and other varied religious and philosophical traditions are part of India's rich cultural legacy, which has encouraged interfaith communication and harmony. Indian philosophy has a strong foundation in the idea of pluralism, which promotes coexistence and acknowledges the worth of other viewpoints. This has aided in fostering interfaith harmony and cross-cultural communication both within India and outside its boundaries, encouraging people to have deep discussions and discover points of commonality amongst various communities.

Contributions to peacebuilding and conflict resolution: The Indian knowledge system provides insightful information about promoting peace and resolving conflicts. The teachings of famous philosophers like Mahatma Gandhi and Swami Vivekananda, as well as ancient Indian literature like the Vedas, place a strong emphasis on the virtues of nonviolence, compassion, and understanding. These ideals were a major influence on the Indian independence movement and served as an inspiration for peace movements around the world. Peaceful resistance movements around the world have benefited from the teachings of Satyagraha (nonviolent resistance) and the philosophy of Ahimsa (nonviolence). India's dedication to coexistence and participation in international peacekeeping initiatives serve as evidence of the impact of Its knowledge system on peacebuilding on a global scale.

Addressing societal challenges: The Indian knowledge system comprises a wide range of academic fields, including philosophy, Ayurvedic medicine, Vedic mathematics, astronomy (Jyotisha), and environmental sciences (Vrikshayurveda). To address societal difficulties, these disciplines have offered distinctive viewpoints and workable solutions. For instance, the traditional Indian medical system known as Ayurveda places a strong emphasis on prevention and a holistic approach to illness. Its tenets and procedures have attained widespread acclaim and aided alternative and complementary medical systems all over the world. Insights into ethical behaviour, ecological preservation, and sustainable living are also provided by the Indian knowledge system. These concepts are essential for tackling science, art, and other fields. It has influenced India's intellectual landscape, from its historical beginnings in the Indus Valley Civilization to the philosophical pillars of dharma, karma, and moksha. The system's contributions to science in the fields of mathematics, astronomy, and medicine show just how far it has come. In industries including psychology, education, management, and wellness procedures, it is still relevant today. The Indian knowledge system also promotes inclusion, peacemaking, and intercultural communication. Overall, it is a deep legacy that advances the knowledge of the various intercurrent societal and environmental problems.

Promotion of inclusivity and compassion: The Indian knowledge system places a strong emphasis on the ideals of inclusivity and compassion. Indian philosophical traditions place a strong emphasis on the interconnection of all living things as well as the intrinsic value and dignity of every person. No matter a person's social standing, religion, or caste, this viewpoint encourages empathy, kindness, and compassion for others. The teachings of historical leaders like Gautam Buddha and saints like Kabir and Rumi, who emphasized love, service, and the unity of humanity, have struck a chord with people all across the world and have helped to develop a more diverse and compassionate international society.

Conclusion

In summary, it can be concluded that the Indian knowledge system has a rich and profound history that has influenced Indian culture, philosophy, science, and the arts, as well as having a long-lasting influence on the world stage. A great deal of learning has been made about the depth and scope of this ancient knowledge system by investigating its historical evolution, philosophical underpinnings, scientific contributions, and present relevance. The Indus Valley Civilization and its succeeding Vedic literature, which established the groundwork for the profound spiritual and philosophical principles found in the Upanishads and the Bhagavad Gita, are the historical origins of the Indian knowledge system. The idea of dharma, pursuing moksha, and the numerous schools of Indian philosophy have offered a framework for moral behaviour, self-realization, and investigation into the nature of reality. In addition, the Indian knowledge system has significantly advanced science, particularly in the disciplines of mathematics, astronomy, and medicine.

While astronomers made outstanding advances in comprehending celestial bodies, creating calendars, and investigating astrology, ancient Indian mathematicians devised advanced numerical systems, algebraic approaches, and innovations in trigonometry. Ayurveda continues to influence current medical practices with its emphasis on preventive healthcare and a holistic approach to wellness. The Indian knowledge system is still relevant today in a variety of societal spheres outside of academics. Its incorporation into psychology, education, management, and leadership has aided in the improvement of instructional methods and the development of successful organizational tactics. Additionally, Indian knowledge-based practices like yoga, meditation, and mindfulness have acquired popularity around the world for their potential to promote inner calm and improve well-being. Beyond academia, several facets of society are affected by the contemporary relevance of the Indian knowledge system. A greater comprehension of human behaviour, enhanced pedagogical methods, and successful organizational tactics have resulted from its integration into psychology, education, management, and leadership. Additionally, Indian knowledge-based practices like yoga, meditation, and mindfulness have become well-known worldwide for their capacity to promote well-being and inner peace.

References

Chalise, K. R. (2022). Pursuit of moksha through existential anxiety and karma in Ghanashyam Khadka's nirvana. *Outlook*, 56–67. https://doi.org/10.3126/ojes.v13i1.46694

Choudhary, S. K. (2008). Higher education in India: A sociohistorical journey from ancient Period to 2006–07. *Journal of Educational Enquiry*.

Dasgupta, S. S. (2014). Managerial communication practices and employees' attitudes and behaviors: A qualitative study. *Corporate Communications: An International Journal*. ISSN: 1356-3289.

Frauwallner, E. (1973). *History of Indian philosophy*, *1* p. 665.ISBN 8120809874, 9788120809871.

Humphreys, C. (2005). *Karma and rebirth: The karmic law of cause and effect*, *110*.ISBN 9780700701636.

McIntosh, J. (2008). *The ancient Indus valley. New perspectives*. ISBN 1576079074, 978157607907.

Mohanty, J. N. (2023, May 29). *Indian philosophy. Encyclopedia britannica.*

Sinha, D. (1965). Integration of modern psychology with Indian thought. *Journal of Humanistic Psychology*, 5(1), 6–17. https://doi.org/10.1177/002216786500500102

Varma, S. (2020). Culture and mental health. Pages 387–398. *Publisher Routledge*. ISBN 9781138280007.

***

INDIA'S SCIENTIFIC METHOD: A HISTORICAL AND CONTEMPORARY PERSPECTIVE

Anshika Prakash

Associate Dean, School of Management and Commerce
K.R. Mangalam University, Gurugram

Ayushi Shah

Student, School of Management and Commerce
K.R. Mangalam University, Gurugram

Abstract

This chapter reflects on the Indian scientific method and its emergence in the ancient period time. The contribution of the enlightened time of the scholar to science (mathematics, astronomy, biology, and medicine) is prevalent till the present age. Over time the use of ancient techniques, quality, skills, and influence of the intellect has evolved and progressed. It analyzes the historical events in the era of pre-colonial rule and the scientific methodology which emerged during the colonial period, the influence of British learning and how they interfered in the Indian science institution. Post-colonial circumstances and advancement in the present under the government law and situation. This concludes the journey of Indian scientific knowledge and its influence in the present world. The circumstances and factors influencing the decline in the medical field and India's emergence in the new age of biotechnology.

Keywords: India, Scientific Method, Ancient Indian Science, Philosophy, Scientific Heritage, Colonialism, Contemporary Science.

Introduction

The course of Ancient Indian knowledge traces back to the 6th and 7th centuries in the fields of medicine, mathematics, and astronomy. The under-appreciative effort of scholars like Surstra and Charak in the field of medicine has seemed to be dismissed and limited. Their book in the field and the relevance of today's knowledge made the Indian knowledge system during those times rich. The methodology used by scholars to signify and evaluate knowledge was also developed from the diversity of Indian culture. The Buddhists contributed a well-defined system of inference that checked the validity and nature of the subject matter. With time and extensive knowledge exchange from sub-countries of India, the knowledge in Asia became versatile in its own way. The changes in the colonial era were made using this diversity as weapons to cause disintegration which changed the traditional course. But, with the rise of countryside scholars for translation of old text emerged a new social group. Also bagged a Noble Prize in 1930 by C. V. Raman (a Tamil Brahmin). This showcases the combination of modern or Western skills with the traditional background established a new Indian science branch. During the independence, the science sector suffered but after independence, the research and technological industries gained foreign support. At present the biotechnology of India has served as massive significance globally after the Covid-19 outbreak.

Literature Review

Sanathanan in his paper sheds light on the notable contribution of India in the fields of Mathematics, Physics, Chemistry, Geography, Astronomy, Engineering, Medicine and Surgery, Music, Arts, and Philosophy. Many wise noblemen like Aryabhata, Brahmagupta, and Bhaskara II made significant contributions to trigonometry and geometry. Indian astronomers are also respected for their wisdom like Varahamihira and Aryabhata who made important discoveries in the field. The authors describe the Indian legacy of knowledge and wisdom by highlighting the key lessons from India's ancient history in terms of spirituality and mindfulness, communities and family ties, and orthodox practices in health and well-being.

Haldipur(2022) analysis when it comes to ancient Indian medicine, there is limited information available about the individuals who played significant roles, unlike in the Western world of medicine where figures like Hippocrates are widely recognized and familiar to the world. This paper walks upon the road to explore and appreciate the ancient Indian Medicine techniques and the role they played during ancient times. The author (Haldipur, 2022), looks into the curriculum, response, training, and approaches in medicines of physicians and psychiatrists. The primary objective of this paper is to enhance the understanding of ancient Indian physicians and appreciate the foundation of the Indian medical heritage.

Singh (2013) states that ecology in India remains a less viable career option but the significance of the career in the present world of sustainability is very important. According to Singh (2013), 'However, there is great uncertainty regarding the roles scientists, educators, and policymakers, among others, must play to arrest, if not reverse, this unabated environmental decline'. Even in ancient India, the importance of these was valuable but it was during the British colonial rule that the resources of India went under a lot of stress.

Bandyopadhyay (2023) mentioned that Susrata was one of the most well-known people in the field of surgery who combined Ayurveda and surgery in his book with 6 volumes. He has mentioned the management, instrument, stitching and other performance to be carried out in the process. 8 types of surgical procedures were described in the Suśruta-saṃhitā and the book remains valid in the present time.

Now, to examine and analyze India in the field of science and research, this chapter studies the growth of India in the field of intellectual knowledge and the journey the medical industry has paved in the present. The study examines the new-age representation of biotechnology and automobile advancement in the global sphere. Ancient India contributed to the present world's knowledge wealth and notable scholars' contribution to knowledge in the medicinal field. It aims to focus on the technological growth India might see in the future and the obstacles it faces to obtain the same.

Methodology

The study relies on analysing the already available data on the concerned topic. This chapter puts special emphasis on the ancient knowledge bank and its contributor's name and recognition. The art and institutions which have revived the knowledge and its significant use in the present times are reflected. This research article intends to add to the body of knowledge regarding the science present in India before the colonial rule and its rich culture carried till today.

Findings

This paper looks to reflect on the historical techniques and structure of ancient Indian science. Looking primarily into the objective of the key scholar and their prior setup with lead to a massive impact on the fields of astronomy, mathematics and science. Indian scholar and the scientific enquires they used is also identified and noted in research. A brief on the impact of ancient India on the outside world is also counted. The interaction during the colonial rule is studied in this paper, and its effect on the countryside as well as urban colonised India. The achievement of the traditional and Western techniques combine in present contemporary India. Present India and its highly respected biotechnology especially during the Covid-19 has brought focus to the ancient techniques which build the present-day system.

Historical Perspective

Rao (1997) presented a comprehensive overview of India's rich history of science and technology, from ancient times to the present day. He highlighted various intellectual feats and pioneering technological processes that have shaped India's civilization over the millennia. One of the key takeaways from the paper is that India has made significant contributions to various fields, including astronomy, medicine, and geometry. For example, Lagadha's Vedanga Jyotisba (circa 400 BC) described astronomical discussions relating to the solar system, while Sulbba Sutra (circa 400 BC) presented geometrical ideas. Additionally, Charaka and Sushruta Sambitas covered medicine and surgery in the pre-Christian era. He also noted that India has excelled in fine arts such as sculpture, painting, music, and dance throughout its history. He further mentioned that "In its philosophical literature and the practice of fine arts, India has excelled down through the millennia." He mentioned that "India is now recognized as a major player in software development," with companies like Infosys and Wipro leading the way.

Ancient Indian Science

The progress of ancient Indian medicines and science is not limited to the scientific progress they made over time with limited resources but goes beyond touching the boundaries of many different spheres. The Ayurveda, the surgical practice, the invention of zero, and calculus have stood the test of the times but the wisdom bearer who established them is not so well known. Other than yoga, mindfulness, and spirituality, inference has been focused on the mental aspect of the human body with proper science and explanation. "The fundamentals on which the Ayurvedic system is based are essentially true for all times and do not change from age to age. These are based on human actors, on intrinsic causes. The origin of Ayurveda is attributed to Atharva Veda where mention is made several diseases with their treatments. Later, from the 6th Century BC to the 7th Century AD there was systematic development of the science and it is called the Samhita period, when some classical works were produced by several authors and during this period there is evidence of organized medical care" (Narayanaswamy, 1981).

The science in the ancient Indian Ayurveda, the ancient Indian system, emphasizes the holistic approach to health and mental well-being. Ayurveda uses plants and nature to heal the within which works effectively but is limited to only certain areas. The contribution to math and astronomy in India is well-known and appreciated. The existence of zero, calculus, negative numbers, and expression have been used by Europeans and Americans to create modern equipment from time to time. It was during the 3rd century when the Brahmi numerical shreds of evidence were traced, after the significant discovery of the zero, the mathematical mechanism was on the height of higher expression.

Vahia (2011) presents a comprehensive model for the evolution and growth of astronomy in a culture, which consists of four distinct phases: initial, settlement, civilization, and technology-based. Using examples from Indian prehistory and history, the author shows that these phases mark distinct steps in the growth of astronomy in a culture.

Scientific Methodologies in Ancient India

The scientific inquiry conducted in India was based on experimentation, documentation, analysis, observation, and collaboration of knowledge through text and debate with discussion. They adapted logic and deduction, used deduction reasoning, and inference to draw hypotheses and conclusions, formulate ideas, and further conduct experiments and observations to understand the logical approach. Scholars used mathematical calculators, and measurements to understand natural phenomena, resulting in a symbolic relationship between scientific inquiry and mathematical investigation.

Key Scholars and their Contributions

The history of mathematics in India, tracing its roots back to Vedic literature, dates between 1000 B.C. and 1000 A.D. Author of various treatises on Mathematics, who introduced the concept of zero given by the ancient Indian astronomer Brahmagupta is credited with having put forth the concept of zero for the first time. Brahmagupta is said to have been born in the year 598 A.D., further, the techniques of Algebra and algorithm, square root and cube root were also created subsequently. The success of Indian Mathematics was due to their clear conception of abstract numbers as distinct from numerical quantities of objects or spatial extension. This allowed them to take mathematical concepts to an abstract plane and devise rudimentary Algebra with a simple numerical notation. This was in contrast to the Greeks or ancient Egyptians who remained confined to mensuration and geometry due to their concern with the immediate measurement of physical objects (Gupta, 1987).

Ancient math, Ganit, consisted of arithmetic, geometric, algebraic, astronomy, and astrology as the foundation. The most notable in the field of mathematics are Aryabhatta, Brahmagupta, and Bhaskarachrya. The discovery of algebra by Aryabhatta who was the 5th century mathematician, astronomer, and physicist to find the distance between the moon and the earth. This discovery was seen as a huge mathematics and astronomical progress in the world.

The Jyotishvedanga text deals with systematic categorization which helps in the study of astronomy. Additionally, the Aryabhattiya is a short text of 121 verses, which carries the knowledge of the planet, sun, moon earth rotation, axis, orbit, and other traditional beliefs of those times. Aryabhatta's astronomical and mathematical viewpoint led to the exploration of present-day technology and scientific progress. Brahmagupta's Bharmaputa Siddhanta was the first book to mention "zero", the use and explanation of the zero were also mentioned in the book.

Ayurveda was one of the first books to mention the cure and the disease of fever, cough, dropsy and sores, and other common diseases of those times. Rational science began in 600 BC before that diseases and cures were named demons spells and magic. In 600 BC the Charakhsamihita by Charak and Sushrusamhita by Sushruta was a major Ayurvedic and medical book in the field, which further went beyond geographic boundaries to China and the centre of Asia and got translated only to emerge as a widely accepted medium in use. The cure contained remedies from plant and natural herbs available in basic households. Sushrutha was considered the 'father of plastic surgery' whose methods and techniques are still prevalent in the present.

Charak Samhita is a famous accomplishment in the field of Ayurveda which is published by Charak, who was considered as the rishi- scientist and profound person in Indian medical history. The book "Charaksamhita" is considered a complete encyclopedia of Ayurvedic science based on "non-surgical techniques". This book gives brief knowledge about Ayurveda with proper logical reasoning and philosophy behind the action performed.

Champaneria (2014) focused on the "Father of plastic surgery" Sushruta and his contributions to the field of medicine in ancient India between 1000 and 800 BC. One of the notable developments is the nasal reconstruction technique with the use of the cheek flap which has left a lasting impact in the surgical field being used even in the present technique. Despite the limited resources and knowledge of that time the technique and teaching of anatomy, path physiology, and therapeutic strategies of India are some of the most advanced at present. The technique of Sushruta crossed boundaries of countries and knowledge of timcs but in the contribution of history, his name is still not evident. This paper aims to appreciate the contribution of Sushruta and explore the knowledge relevance in the present world.

Philosophical Influences

Ancient India has rich traditional philosophical influence in the examination and validity of the knowledge raised from diverse knowledge systems and served as a systematic approach for fundamental research in those times. The observation was considered the first and foremost action similar between all fields of study. Scholars observed the behaviours of plants, animals, and celestial bodies with context to their research field and then decided to involve or exclude them. Further, they would classify and categorize their complex formulas. The logic and epistemology of the experiment conflict ideas with induction and deduction, the Nyaya and Mimamsa formulated inference studies for the systematic absorption of knowledge.

Vedanta and Scientific Inquiry

Tathagatananda emphasized the philosophical and spiritual aspects of Vedanta, highlighting its universal and enduring nature. It claims that Vedanta's impersonal approach makes it universal in spirit, and credits the philosophy with inspiring scientific tradition in ancient India. The author discusses the relationship between Vedanta and science. It states that Vedanta encourages science and critical questioning, and it suggests that the two fields can harmoniously coexist and contribute to a better world. In the present world, people look at things with a subjective opinion. They think the brain exists alone but Vedanta Swami Vivekananda, a prominent Vedantic philosopher, acknowledges the importance of both external and internal approaches to seeking truth. Furthermore, the author addresses the limitations of science and dogmatic religion in providing a comprehensive understanding of reality. He further argues that Vedanta, as a profound philosophy and science of religion, reconciles the weaknesses of both science and creed-based religions. It emphasizes the importance of consciousness in Vedanta and highlights how modern physicists have recognized the role of the observer and consciousness in their scientific inquiries.

Nyaya and Systematic Analysis

Nyaya (anumāna) is a means of valid knowledge (pramāṇa). In Indian philosophy, there are diverse perspectives which are surrounded by debate on its nature and structure within different systems. The Naiyāyikas and Buddhists have made significant contributions to the understanding and approaching with systematic knowledge towards the Inference. The inductive and deductive approach towards any study was the basic methodology but was rather unreliable. So, the Nyaya focused on reaching a conclusion based on evidence and fact with the help of logical reasoning examination leading to the least fallacies. The Nyaya philosophy recognizes four primary means: Perception (pratyakṣa), inference (anumāna), comparison (upamāna), and testimony (śabda). They used these systematic processes to validate the data, which helped scholars to give brief debates in favour of their ideas and intellect. This concept intervenes in many philosophical systems of Buddhism, Jainism, Nyāya-Vaiśeṣika, Mīmāmsā, and Vedānta. Each system has its diverse understanding of the concept of inference and validity.

Integration of Philosophy and Science

The ancient scholars of India intersected the interaction of philosophy and science. They collaborated on both the aspect of science as a systematic study and philosophy as a study of allied study of the human mind, body, and nature creating a mutual agreement by the ancient Indian research. The philosophical idea included the systematic, ethical, conceptualization of scientific inquiry and created a synergy. Science used the philosophical perspective of thc alliance of nature and everything together to create new ideas. Physiologically, the Gukhuls of Vedanta and Samkhya explored these studies. As a result, Philosophy and science in ancient India fostered a rich and holistic approach to parallel study.

Colonial Era and Integration of Western Scientific Method

India has a huge treasure of knowledge and intellectual learning, the diversity of India and its sub-continent was the strength to combine vivid distinct learning, but the diversity is the cause of decline as one institution fell the other could not cope with the circumstances and everything feels part. The political and cultural disintegration worked in the favour of the British too. (Arnold, 2000). From the British perspective, India was a technologically backward country due to India's (society) selective adaptation of print technology in the Indian society. After the shift in technology and ideology, the Mughals adopted the new warfare technology during the early colonial period. (Arnold, 2000)

Even if the times in Indian science were tense it gave rise to metropolitan cities like – Calcutta, Bombay, and Madras as rising ground in invention and knowledge. Other parts of India specially the countryside and rural emerged as a site for the translation of old texts (also known as middle–class intelligentsia). Their community also bought India's 1st noble prize before independence by C. V. Raman in 1930 who was a Tamil Brahmin. This intelligentsia combines the traditional background with modern skills, insight, and inspiration (Arnold, 2000).

Contemporary Science in India

The expansion of Western influence with Indian creative roots has been seen as an opportunity to rule out poverty and drive economic growth. However, the oil crisis in the 1970s led to a critical situation in the role of science and technology in achieving development. The contemporary motive of globalization, commercialization, and modernity has influenced the orthodox style of ancient Indian research with time. India's contemporary science in the present world has changed. Contemporized science also involves sides of politics. In the midst of all this, India as a country in the new time has emerged as a hub for space research, biotechnology advancement, skilled software workforce, and other vibrate fields necessary for present world technology. Scientist in India dives into nanotechnology, health science, and renewable energy techniques for future sustainability.

Post-Independence Scientific Advancements

Since the independence advancement in India has seen a rise. The aim of government and change in the laws have helped in the evolution of the space sector, automation sector and funding in this sector. In space research, the Indian Space Research Organization (ISRO) has achieved many headlines. India has used its ancient text of Vedas and their references to astronomical knowledge, in the present. Konde (2008) studied the biotechnological brand in India in collaboration with the public and private sectors which yielded mutual benefits in developing India after the post-independence era. The Indian government plays a significant role in the development and exploration of the R&D institutions (scientific, medical, industrial, and agriculture) that have been initiated by the government over the past 2-3 years increasing the performance in this sector. The collaboration between the two parallels has been seen as a massive opportunity to boost the capacity of biotechnology in food, health, and environmental stability. The public-private alliance has been good for developing India's future and research opportunities.

Pillai (2023) examined the present staging of India in the effort of 8 decades in the IT field due to its political minister and leader shaping the law and rule for the boost of this country. These laws gave safety to the sector in terms of social, cultural, and historical factors and were magnified by public policy. These factors together strengthen the technological – infrastructure and self-reliance aim of India.

Indian Scientific Institutions and Organizations

Ramnath (2018) studied the efforts of Mahendra Lal Sircar who is not so well–known in the world of scholars in post-independence. Mahendra Lal Sircar (1833- 1904) is a well-known homoeopathic doctor who established the Indian Association for the Cultivation of Science (IACS) in 1876. The IACS changed the course of Indian scientific research and practice, which produced reliable sources of scientists for post-independent India. This was due to the shift in the Sircar perspective of science, involving both theoretical and practical knowledge. The author found that 'Sircar wanted the institute to be funded and managed by Indians during British governance; the main idea was to produce science-literate natives, making it a nationalistic endeavour that promoted the growth of the country' which shows the nationalism recipient for a new future of India.

Collaboration with the Global Scientific Community

The prior contact of India with outside countries during ancient India had given massive knowledge. Ancient Indian mathematics, chemistry, medicine, and a few branches of biology led to massive expansion with shared knowledge. The study of science was vigour during the period of Buddha' in the 17th and 18th centuries with interaction with European Sanskrit and Persian as the medium of exchange. Indian contribution to the international market has been recognized as valuable and prestige. India as a market has the size and quality. Indian researchers have received many international awards and honours which highlight the contribution of the contemporary scientific community of India. Indian science collaboration and partnership with the outside world enhance the development and growth of the present quality of science education. The governmental policy helps subsidize the institution for their initiative with technology, science, medicine, and other help to build a community with humanity as a whole.

India and Japan have a formal agreement with the alignment of the SDGs goals. India and Japan's bilateral programs help scientists in both the country in the area of fundamental science physical and chemical systems). This is seen as a move of quality advancement. Similarly, a UK research centre opened in New Delhi, and funded research indexed in Scopus yield research. Indian science fair 'Vigyan Samagram' got the attention of the MEGA science giants, collaborated with India in the fair CERN (European Organization for Nuclear Research), FAIR (Facility for Antiproton and Ion Research), INO (India-based Neutrino Observatory), ITER (International Thermonuclear Experimental Reactor), LIGO (Laser Interferometer Gravitational-Wave), SKA (Square Kilometer Array), and TMT (Thirty Meter Telescope).... In the first decade of this millennium, India built five new science institutions called the Indian Institute of Science Education and Research (IISER), along the lines of India's famous IITs.(htt1)

India has various partnerships and collaborations in the IT and software industries with Microsoft, Cisco, IBM, and Google. In other service sectors, companies like Toyota Motor and Suzuki Motor deepen their roots in India will well-established companies since post-independence.

Challenges and Future Prospects

"Bangalore has emerged as a tech-based start-up, elevating its status and recognition in the world. It is said to have the largest number of start-ups and is considered 3rd largest in the entire world. This reorganization in the field of technology is seen as significant for Indian future prospectus" (Bala Subrahmanya, 2017). But despite the rise of tech- a startup in Bangalore, the funding and the investment of the region is said to be a struggle for the most part. The growth trajectory of the hub can easily be declined if the situation of the funding stays the same. This opportunity can either be a boon or blessing in upcoming India which might be affected by the political turmoil and inflation in the economy.

Varma (2013) analyzed the migration of students in the field of science affecting the country in the social, cultural, economic, and technological progression of society. Brain drain is the phenomenon of migration of students or citizens to developed countries for better growth opportunities; this phenomenon leads to the drain in the primary country population who are capable of building the nation. "A recent survey of nearly 260 undergraduate students from two out of the five original Indian Institutes of Technology (IITs) found that the majority of them have developed an increased interest in staying in India, rather than the decades-old trend of going abroad for education leading to work and permanent stay". This can be seen as a change in the development of Indian society and advancement.

Initiatives, policies and their effect

As per reports floating, the centre has allocated Rs. 16,361cr from the Union Ministry of Science and Technology, making up only 0.36 % of the overall budget which does not seem to be enough for the research and development of the science and technology sector in India. This is also due to unaccountable inflation or fostering research ecosystem instability in the economy. These circumstances might influence the growth and progress in the science and technology sector of India. Translational research has received attention over the guidance of PM guidance. The big problem in the NRF funding channel is also concerning for the growth of investment in the other sector. As per reports if only one funding channel is there the focus drives off from the basic science and into the technology sector only.

Future Prospects and Opportunities

Biotechnology in India has been emerging as a huge space of progress and foreign investment in the course of biotechnology in the time of COVID-19. The world was financially struggling and reliance on their biotechnology industry and Indian development of vaccines and possible repurposed anti-viruses brought the majority focus on the strength of the Indian knowledge which has built from the ancient Indian techniques. This has made India an emerging destination globally for the study and research of biotechnology. According to the Indian Harbor, one of the best medical professions in the world attracts foreign countries for investment through well-developed technology. These opportunities and positive tangents help realize India its potential in the best possible way (Associates, 2021). Kris Gopalakrishnan the Infosys co-founder is investing up to 750 Cr in the medical research study of the human brain and other similar personalities in the same fields are taking the initiative to enhance the growth of research and studies to understand and help the forwarding growth in the country.

Hindustan Aeronautics Limited (HAL) has one of the highest joint ventures among Indian companies. The joint venture of the companies varies from the aeroplane, helicopter, and other aero-based mechanisms. They have had ventures with Roll Royce Holding Ltd. Of the UK, Edgewood Venture of the USA, and other similar projects which evaluated the evaluation of the companies. Other companies which have joint ventures with Indian companies is Tata Starbucks Pvt. Ltd., Mahindra- Renault, and other in the automobile field. In India, there has been enhancement in the field of new technology which give value to AI learner and other jobs contributing to the sector like Blockchain, Robotic and Automation, cyber security, Genomic Medicine, Cognitive computer studies,

Syntectic biology, Robotic and space advancement. In a report of (an Indian company partnering Foreign Company, n.d.)

Conclusion

This chapter explored the ancient Indian historical events happening at the time which led to India as a rich traditional knowledge to be well recognized in the timeline of history. Indian knowledge evidence can be traced from the Bronze Age and the Indus River civilization. The use of Indian knowledge in those timelines has analyzed the potential Indian history carries. The diverse nature of India as a country with the outside world has brought in new establishments in the methodology and research sector of ancient India.

The British impact on the Indian metropolitan and countryside was very different and the accomplishment for those who have combined other modern and traditional knowledge. Indian scientific knowledge has significantly adopted the Western methodology and technique infused with traditional ideology. The Veda and Charaksmhita remain the books of reference in the present day and age. Sushruta's work in the medical field is a footstep for many, He is also called "the father of plastic surgery". Contemporary India is yet to establish a permanent root in the global sphere but, the advancement of the sector in biotechnology and automobile industry set a global mark. The funding and research industry of India still needs the boost to fly to the highest.

References

Arnold, D. (2000). *Science, technology and medicine in colonial India*, *5*. Cambridge University Press. https://doi.org/10.1017/CHOL9780521563192

Associates, S.M.-A. (2021). *Indian Biotechnology Sector: A catalyst for growth opportunities*.

https://www.lexology.com/library/detail.aspx?g=755a9ec6-d4fc-495a-a24d-ba330d0ea142

Bagde, A. (2013). *Charak Samhita-complete encyclopedia of ayurvedic science*. https://doi.org/10.4103%2F0974-8520.158984

Bala Subrahmanya, M. H. (2017). How did Bangalore emerge as a global hub of tech start-ups in India? Entrepreneurial ecosystem—Evolution, structure and role. *Journal of Developmental Entrepreneurship*, *22*(1), 1750006. https://doi.org/10.1142/S1084946717500066

Champaneria, M. C., Workman, A. D., & Gupta, S. C. (2014). Sushruta: Father of plastic surgery. *Annals of Plastic Surgery*, *73*(1), 2–7. http://doi.org/10.1097/SAP.0b013e31827ae9f5

Haldipur, C. V. (2022). Medical education in ancient India. *Asian Journal of Psychiatry*, *72*, 103076. https://doi.org/10.1016/j.ajp.2022.103076

Indian company partnering Foreign company. (n.d.). https://www.lawyered.in/. https://www.lawyered.in/legal-disrupt/articles/indian-company-partnering-foreign-company-how-you-do-it/

Jadhav, A. (ND). *Glimpses of ancient Indian mathematics*. ISSN 2320-8767.

Konde, V. (2008). Biotechnology in India: Public–private partnerships. *Journal of Commercial Biotechnology*, *14*(1), 43–55. https://doi.org/10.1057/palgrave.jcb.3050079

Pillai, R., & Paul, B. (2023). Industry 4.0 and the changing employment relations: A case of the Indian information technology industry. *NHRD Network Journal*, *16*(1), 92–110. https://doi.org/10.1177/26314541221134849.
https://indianhighereducation.com/india-analysis/international-research-collaboration-in-india

Rao, P. R. (1997). India: Science and technology from ancient time to today. *Technology in Society*, *19*(3–4), 415–447. https://doi.org/10.1016/S0160-791X(97)00015-8

Ramanath, S. (2018). Indian Association for the Cultivation of Science: Mahendralal Sircar and his science, morality, and nationalism [Doctoral Dissertation]. http://doi.org/10.1177/025764300101700204

science and technology to get over 16cr in budget2023 experts say not enough for progress. (n.d.). https://www.downtoearth.org.in/news/science-technology/science-and-technology-to-get-over-rs-16-000-crore-in-budget-2023-24-experts-say-not-enough-87443

Vahia, M. N., Yadav, N., … Yadav, N. (2011). The origin and growth of astronomy, as viewed from an Indian context. In *Highlighting the history of astronomy in the Asia-Pacific region: Proceedings of the ICOA*-6 Conference (pp. 61–84). http://doi.org/10.1007/978-1-4419-8161-5_5

Varma, R., & Kapur, D. (2013). Comparative analysis of brain drain, brain circulation and brain retain: A case study of Indian Institutes of Technology. *Journal of Comparative Policy Analysis: Research and Practice*, *15*(4), 315–330. http://doi.org/10.1080/13876988.2013.810376

***

INDIAN TRADITIONS AS THE HEARTBEAT OF A NATION

Shivani Kampani

School of Management and Commerce,

K.R. Mangalam University, Gurugram

Lavanya Aggarwal

Student, School of Management and Commerce,

K.R. Mangalam University, Gurugram

Abstract

This chapter talks about the relevance of Indian traditions, their origination, and the profound impact that is visible on modern society. It explores the values and symbolism embedded within these traditions, highlighting their role in maintaining social cohesion and reinforcing cultural identity. Along with a deeper understanding of various traditions, it provides vivid insights into the ancient traditions that are deeply rooted in the ideologies of the millennials. The traditions form the basis behind which the current value system is elaborated and utilised in the present-day economy. This study further facilitates the various cultures and customs around which religions are practised and festivals are commemorated. It is evident to have at least elementary knowledge of the numerous traditions that are prevalent in the social community. They not only dictate existing beliefs but enlighten individuals about humility, kindness, love, respect, and compassion towards one another. These customs are indeed what ultimately differentiates India, from the rest of the world, which is practising contemporary ways of livelihood.

Furthermore, the chapter provides a detailed account of the infamous and fascinating Indian culture of the widely used greeting of "Namaste," the history behind the battle of Mahabharata and the epic of Ramayana with its valuable teaching about 'Dharma' and 'Karma'. Adding to this, it discusses the Indian cuisine, family structure, religious customs, marriage as well as dances of India and their traditional clothing most exhibited in the past as well as current times. It underlines how crucial it is to integrate rich traditions into this new and woke society through education, art, literature as well as music and dance.

By unravelling the intricate tapestry of Indian traditions, this chapter endeavours to provide a comprehensive understanding of the depth, diversity, and enduring legacy of this ancient civilization. Through the exploration of its origins, evolution, cultural expressions, and contemporary relevance, it illuminates the integral role that Indian traditions play in shaping the collective identity and fostering a sense of unity among its people.

Keywords: Indian Traditions, Cultural Diversity, Religion, Epics and Mythology.

Introduction

India, a land of diversity and cultural richness, is known for its ancient traditions that have shaped its vibrant tapestry of customs, rituals, and beliefs. With a history spanning thousands of years, Indian traditions encompass various aspects of life, including religion, festivals, art, music, dance, cuisine, clothing, and social customs. It is indeed a noteworthy point that Indian culture and tradition teach people kindness, generosity, and tolerance. The overall customs vary from one place to another as it is a multilingual, multicultural, and multi-ethnic society, comprising a satisfactory but, unique blend of Western culture and historical traditions. Some of the primary and infamous Indian culture, traditions and customs that are prevalent in the society are greetings, religious customs, festivals, family structure & marriage, cows as symbols, cuisine & food, traditional clothing, dances of India, epics & mythology, languages and martial arts etc.

Figure 1: Colors of Tradition: Celebrating Indian Heritage

Source: https://www.bhishmaindics.org

Societal Impact of Rich Indian Traditions

One of the key impacts of Indian traditions is undoubtedly on family and social relationships. The increased emphasis on respect for elders, strong family bonds, and the concept of joint family systems promotes unity and cohesion within households, thereby promoting diversity. These traditions foster a sense of responsibility, support, and care for one another, contributing to the social fabric of Indian society. The influence on religious and spiritual practices can be expressed through the diverse beliefs and rituals, such as prayers, festivals, and pilgrimages, that play a pivotal role in the promotion of a sense of community and shared values. They provide a common platform for people to come together, express their faith, and deepen their spiritual connection.

Furthermore, Indian traditions have a significant impact on the arts, literature, and cultural expressions. Traditional dance forms, music, and visual arts are deeply intertwined with cultural practices and religious beliefs, serving as a means of storytelling, celebration, and artistic expression. These traditions help preserve cultural heritage, promote creativity, and contribute to the identity and pride of the society. Indian traditions also shape social norms and etiquette. Concepts such as hospitality, respect for elders, and the importance of modesty influence social interactions and behaviour. These traditions contribute to the sense of community, harmonious coexistence, and social order within Indian society.

Greetings: Namaste

Namaste, a traditional Indian greeting, holds deep cultural and spiritual significance in Indian traditions. Derived from Sanskrit, "namaste" is a combination of two words: "namah," meaning "to bow" or "to honour," and "te," meaning "you." When people greet each other with a namaste, they bring their palms together in front of their chest, fingers pointing upwards, and bow their heads slightly. This simple gesture carries a profound meaning and reflects the core values of respect, humility, and acknowledgement of the divine in others. In Indian culture, it is believed that every person possesses a divine essence or soul, known as the Atman. By bringing the hands together at the heart chakra, the energy centre located in the middle of the chest, individuals symbolically unite their own divine essence with the divinity in others. This gesture signifies the recognition of the interconnectedness and oneness of all beings. The practice of namaste extends beyond formal greetings. It is often used as a gesture of respect, gratitude, and reverence. In India, it is customary to greet elders, teachers, and spiritual figures with a namaste. Beyond its cultural and social aspects, namaste has a spiritual dimension. In yogic philosophy, it is believed that the divine resides in the heart of every living being. By bringing the hands together at the heart chakra, individuals connect with their own inner divinity and pay homage to the divine presence in others. This gesture serves as a reminder of the inherent sacredness within and around us. With its spiritual and cultural dimensions, namaste promotes peace, unity, and respect, transcending borders and fostering a sense of global harmony.

Cow: A religious symbol

The animal, Cow in the Indian culture, is perceived to be a Holy animal. She is assumed and worshipped as a maternal figure having a depiction of the bounty of Mother Earth. Moreover, Lord Krishna is often known by the name of 'Govinda' or 'Gopala', which translates to the 'friend and protector of cow'. Hence, cows have an auspicious significance in Indian Culture and religion. Even Lord Shiva's trusted vehicle is considered to be Nandi- the sacred bull. Thus, feeding a cow or making contributions to cow shelters is of immense religious importance for Indians. The Vedic scriptures, in various verses, have time and again, emphasised the need to protect and care for cows. With its projection as an auspicious animal, killing the cow or consuming cow meat is a common sin. The religion and culture of India appreciate and express their gratitude towards this innocent animal who gives back to Mother Earth and its people in varied forms.

Religious Customs & Festivals

India is a land of diverse religious traditions, with Hinduism, Buddhism, Jainism, Sikhism, Islam, Christianity, and other faiths coexisting harmoniously. Hinduism has a vast array of gods and goddesses. Some of the most popular gods and goddesses in Hinduism include Lord Shiva, Lord Vishnu, Lord Brahma, Lord Ganesha, Goddess Durga, Goddess Kali, Goddess Saraswati, and many more. Each god and goddess has a unique story and mythology associated with them. Each religion has its unique set of customs and practices that are deeply ingrained in the cultural fabric of the country. This essay explores some of the traditional Indian religious customs, highlighting their significance and diversity.

Hinduism, the oldest religion in India, encompasses a vast array of customs and rituals. One prominent custom is the worship of deities in temples and home shrines. Devotees offer prayers, flowers, incense, and light oil lamps to seek the blessings of the gods and goddesses. Pilgrimage is also an essential aspect of Hindu religious practice. Millions of devotees undertake journeys to sacred sites such as Varanasi, Rishikesh, Tirupati, and Amarnath to deepen their spiritual connection and seek purification. In addition to puja, Hindus celebrate numerous festivals throughout the year. Diwali, also known as Deepavali, is the Festival of Lights and is celebrated with great enthusiasm across the country. It involves the lighting of lamps, exchanging of sweets and gifts, and bursting of fireworks, symbolizing the triumph of light over darkness. Other significant Hindu festivals include Holi, Navratri, Durga Puja, Raksha Bandhan, and Janmashtami, each with its own customs, rituals, and regional variations.

Buddhism, which originated in India and later spread to other parts of Asia, has its own set of religious customs. Devotees pay their respects to the Buddha by offering flowers, lighting candles, and chanting sutras. Meditation, a core practice in Buddhism, is undertaken to cultivate mindfulness, concentration, and wisdom. Jainism, another ancient Indian religion, emphasizes non-violence, truth, and asceticism. One of the significant Jain customs is the observance of "Paryushana" or "Daslakshana," a period of intense spiritual reflection, fasting, and self-discipline. During this time, Jains engage in prayer, study of scriptures, and acts of charity. Sikhism, a monotheistic religion founded in Punjab, has its own distinct religious customs. The central place of worship for Sikhs is the Gurdwara, where they gather for congregational prayers and listen to hymns from the Guru Granth Sahib, the Sikh holy scripture. Langar, the community kitchen, is a unique Sikh tradition where free meals are served to all visitors.

Islamic customs and practices are an integral part of the religious life of Indian Muslims. The most significant Islamic tradition is the observance of the five pillars of Islam, which include the declaration of faith, daily prayers, fasting during Ramadan, giving alms to the poor, and the pilgrimage to Mecca (Hajj) for those who are able. Mosques serve as places of worship and community gatherings, where Muslims come together for Friday prayers and engage in communal activities. In India, Christianity is practised by a significant number of people, both in the form of indigenous communities and those who converted during the colonial period. Christianity in India is characterized by its rich cultural and religious customs. The liturgical practices, hymns, and rituals reflect the diverse traditions and influences of different Christian denominations. Indian Christians celebrate religious festivals such as Christmas and Easter with great devotion and enthusiasm.

Marriage and Familial Traditions in India

The joint family structure is a common family structure in India characterised by various generations of a family living together under one roof. The Indian family structure is typically patriarchal and hierarchical. The father is considered the head of the family and is responsible for making important decisions. The mother is responsible for taking care of the children and the household. Children are expected to respect their elders and follow their guidance. Marriage is an important institution in Indian culture. Traditionally, marriages were arranged by the parents of the bride and groom. However, this practice has become less common in urban areas. Marriage is inferred to be a union between two families rather than just two individuals. The wedding ceremony is typically a multi-day affair that involves several rituals and customs.

Wedding rituals and customs in India vary depending on the region and religion. However, some of the most common rituals and customs include:

1. Engagement ceremony: This is the first formal ceremony that takes place after the families have agreed to the marriage. The bride and groom exchange rings during this ceremony.
2. Mehendi ceremony: This is a pre-wedding ritual where the bride's hands and feet are decorated with henna.
3. Sangeet ceremony: This is a musical evening where both families come together to sing and dance.
4. Haldi ceremony: This is a pre-wedding ritual where turmeric paste is applied to the bride and groom's bodies.
5. Wedding ceremony: The wedding ceremony is typically a multi-day affair that involves several rituals and customs. The bride and groom exchange vows in front of a sacred fire.
6. Reception: This is a post-wedding party that is hosted by the groom's family to celebrate the union of the two families.

Indian Cuisine

Indian cuisine is known for its diverse flavours and spices. It varies depending on the region and religion which is undoubtedly deeply rooted in the concept of "unity in diversity." Each region of India has its distinct culinary traditions and specialities, influenced by factors such as climate, geography, history, and cultural practices. Spices play a central role in Indian cooking. The use of spices, such as cumin, coriander, turmeric, cardamom, cinnamon, and cloves, not only adds aroma and flavour but also offers numerous health benefits. Vegetarianism has a strong presence in Indian food culture, influenced by religious and cultural practices. Indian cuisine is also known for its wide range of bread and rice preparations. Roti, naan, and paratha are popular types of Indian bread, while rice is a staple in many regions. Biryanis, pulao and rice-based desserts like kheer are examples of rice dishes that showcase the culinary expertise of Indian chefs. The concept of "thali" is another significant aspect of Indian food culture. Thali refers to a complete meal served on a large platter, typically featuring a variety of dishes including rice or bread, curries, lentils, pickles, yoghurt, and desserts. Indian food culture is not only about flavours and ingredients but also about the art of cooking. Traditional cooking methods, such as tandoor (clay oven) cooking, slow simmering in handis (earthen pots), and tempering of spices, add depth and complexity to Indian dishes. These techniques have been passed down through generations and contribute to the unique taste and texture of Indian cuisine.

Fasting

It is often used as a symbol of devotion and sacrifice and it holds a significant place in Indian traditions and is practised by people of various religions, including Hindus, Muslims, Jains, and Sikhs. Fasting is more than just abstaining from food and drink; it is a spiritual practice that involves self-discipline, purification, and introspection. Fasting in India is characterized by various customs and rituals. Before starting a fast, individuals often take a bath or cleanse themselves, wear clean clothes, and visit a temple or place of worship. Certain foods and ingredients are considered auspicious and are consumed before or after the fast. For example, fruits, nuts, milk, and specific grains are commonly consumed during fasting periods.

Traditional Clothing in India

Traditional clothing in India showcases the country's rich cultural heritage and diversity. Each region has its distinct styles of clothing, reflecting the local customs, climate, and historical influences. Traditional clothing in India is known for its vibrant colours, intricate designs, and exquisite craftsmanship. Saree is one of the most iconic and widely worn traditional garments for women in India. It is a long piece of fabric, usually made of silk, cotton, or other materials, that is draped around the body in various styles. The saree comes in a multitude of designs, patterns, and embellishments, showcasing the artistic skills of Indian weavers and artisans. For men, traditional clothing includes the dhoti, kurta, and sherwani.

The dhoti is a garment made of a single piece of cloth wrapped around the waist and legs, while the kurta is a loose-fitting tunic worn on top. During special occasions and weddings, men often opt for the sherwani, a long coat-like garment with intricate embroidery and embellishments. Besides these, there are various other traditional clothing styles found in different parts of India. The salwar kameez, comprising a long tunic (kameez), loose-fitting pants (salwar), and a dupatta, is commonly worn by women in North India and is known for its comfort and versatility. The lungi, a loose wrap-around garment, is popular in South India, especially among men.

Dances of India

India is indeed a land of 'unity in diversity', and the dances are no different. Different forms of dance (classified as folk or classical) find origin in different parts of the country, and they are a way of representing the particular culture from which they originate. Eight classical dances, which are classified as Indian classical dances and find a mention in the Hindu Sanskrit text 'Natyashashtra', (a text of performing arts) are:

- Bharatnatyam from Tamil Nadu
- Kathakali from Kerela
- Kathak from North, West and Central India
- Mohiniyattam from Kerela
- Kuchipudi from Andhra Pradesh
- Oddisi from Odhisa
- Manipuri from Manipur
- Sattriya from Assam

The aforementioned dance forms are comprehensive dance dramas in which performers use gestures to narrate stories, primarily based on Indian mythology. Classical dances in India strictly adhere to the rules and guidelines outlined in the Natyashastra. Similarly, folk dances originate from various regions of the country and often depict the everyday lives of rural communities. These dances are based on stories that are orally transmitted across generations.

Folk dances hold significant importance in rural areas, while classical dances are deeply rooted in tradition and follow prescribed guidelines. In the context of marriages, finding a suitable match involves a lengthy and exhaustive process. It entails considering factors such as horoscope compatibility, religion, caste, professional status, physical appearance, and cultural background. The objective is to ensure that the match meets all the desired criteria. Once initial requirements are met, families arrange face-to-face meetings to discuss further. Successful negotiations lead to the commencement of wedding preparations.

Epics and Mythology

Indian literature can be traced back to the great epics written in the form of poems, plays, stories, and even self-help guides. The most infamous Hindu epics are undoubtedly Ramayana and Mahabharata. Mahabharata, by Ved Vyasa, is the longest poem written in the Sanskrit language. Both these epics arc written in order to underline human values of sacrifice, devotion, courage, loyalty, and truth. The moral of the epics highlights the triumph of good over evil.

The Ramayana tells the story of the divine Lord Rama and his wife Sita. The Mahabharata tells the story of the brothers: the Pandavas and the Kauravas. Indian mythology is also filled with gods and goddesses, including Brahma, Vishnu, Shiva, Durga, Kali, and Lakshmi. The story of Lord Rama and Sita is told in the Ramayana. Lord Rama was the prince of Ayodhya and was married to Sita. Sita was kidnapped by the demonic king Ravana, who tricked her by impersonating a saint and took her to his kingdom of Lanka. Lord Rama then went on a quest to rescue Sita with the help of his brother Lakshmana and the monkey god Hanuman. After many battles, Lord Rama defeated Ravana and rescued Sita.

The Mahabharata is one of the two most famous Indian epics. It tells the story of the Pandavas and the Kauravas. The Pandavas were five brothers who were exiled from their kingdom by their cousins, the Kauravas. The Mahabharata is known for its complex characters and themes, including dharma (righteousness), karma (action), and moksha (liberation).

Martial arts

Martial arts in India have a long and illustrious history, deeply intertwined with the country's culture, philosophy, and traditions. These ancient combat practices encompass a wide range of styles and techniques, each with its unique characteristics and regional influences. One of the most well-known martial arts in India is Kalaripayattu, believed to be one of the oldest fighting systems in existence. Originating in the state of Kerala, Kalaripayattu combines strikes, kicks, grappling, weaponry, and healing techniques. It emphasizes physical fitness, flexibility, and mental discipline, and it has been preserved and passed down through generations.

Silambam is another significant martial art practised in India, particularly in the southern regions. It involves the use of a long staff or stick as a weapon and incorporates various striking, blocking, and footwork techniques. Silambam is not just a means of self-defence but also a way of promoting discipline, focus, and coordination.

Thang-ta is a traditional martial art form from Manipur in north-eastern India. It combines combat techniques with graceful and rhythmic movements. Thang-ta practitioners utilize swords, spears, shields, and other traditional weapons in their training and performances.

Gatka, originating from the Punjab region, is a martial art associated with the Sikh community. It involves the use of traditional weapons such as swords, shields, and wooden sticks. Gatka is not only a form of self-defence but also serves as a means of spiritual and mental development.

Various other regional martial arts exist in India, each with its distinct techniques, philosophies, and cultural significance. These include Mardani Khel in Maharashtra, Lathi in Uttar Pradesh, and Cheibi Gad-Ga in Assam, among others. Indian martial arts have not only served as a means of self-defence but have also become cultural treasures. They are often performed during festivals, cultural events, and even in movies, showcasing the strength, grace, and traditional values associated with these art forms.

Languages

Language is an integral part of India's rich cultural traditions. With its linguistic diversity, India is known for its multitude of languages, each with its own distinct history, literature, and cultural significance. Language in India is not merely a means of communication but a powerful vehicle for preserving traditions, promoting identity, and fostering unity in diversity. India is a linguistically diverse country, with over 1,600 languages spoken across its vast expanse. The Constitution of India recognizes 22 languages as scheduled languages, including Hindi, Bengali, Telugu, Tamil, Urdu, Punjabi, and many others. Each language represents a unique cultural heritage, regional identity, and social context. Language plays a vital role in preserving India's traditional knowledge and oral traditions. Ancient texts, religious scriptures, and literary works have been passed down through generations in various languages, ensuring the continuity of cultural values, wisdom, and heritage. Furthermore, language is closely tied to Indian rituals, ceremonies, and festivals. Religious chants, hymns, and prayers are recited in specific languages, adding a spiritual dimension to linguistic traditions. Festivals also celebrate the linguistic diversity of India, with regional languages being highlighted through cultural performances, storytelling, and folk songs. Language is also an instrument of empowerment and social change. Efforts are made to promote and protect endangered languages, ensuring their survival for future generations. Language-based education and media help preserve linguistic traditions and promote cultural exchange.

Conclusion

In totality, it would be appropriate to say that India is a land of rich cultural heritage and tradition which inhibits kindness, generosity, and tolerance in people. Indian traditions can be integrated into modern mainstream society in several ways. This chapter began by tracing the roots of Indian traditions to the Indus Valley Civilization and highlights the early manifestations of ritual practices, art forms, and social structures that laid the foundation for subsequent cultural developments. To captivating journey through the diverse and vibrant tapestry of Indian traditions, unearthing the profound cultural heritage that has shaped the nation for centuries, the below-mentioned bulletins are a few suggested ways in which Indian traditions can be integrated into modern mainstream society:

1. Education: Indian traditions can be integrated into modern mainstream society through education. Schools and universities can teach courses on Indian history, culture, and traditions. In recent times, efforts have been made to preserve and promote Indian martial arts through training schools, academies, and cultural institutions.
2. Art and literature: Indian traditions can also be integrated into modern mainstream society through art and literature. Contemporary artists and writers can draw inspiration from Indian traditions to create new works that are relevant to modern audiences.
3. Music and dance: Indian music and dance forms such as Bollywood music and dance have become popular around the

world. These forms of music and dance are rooted in Indian traditions but have been adapted to appeal to modern audiences.

References

Bhatia, G. (2017, June 1). Cow slaughter and the constitution. Thehindu.com. https://www.thehindu.com/opinion/lead/cow-slaughter-and-the-constitution/article62113108.ece

Chakravarti, S. S. (1995). Hinduism: A way of life. *Motilal Banarsidass.*

Claus, P. J., Diamond, S., & Mills, M. A. (2002). *South Asian folklore: An encyclopedia* P. Claus, S. Diamond & M. Mills (Eds.). Routledge.

Customs and traditions in Indian culture. (2021, February 10). *Authentic India Tours.* https://www.authenticindiatours.com/2021/02/10/10-customs-and-traditions-in-indian-culture/

Dubey, K. G. (2011). The Indian cuisine. *Prentice-Hall of India.*

Financial times. Retrieved June 21, 2023. https://www.ft.com/content/7498e59c-2233-11dd-a50a-000077b07658#axzz2aqrbE3eF

Kalsi, H. (2017, September 22). Unique customs and traditions in India that you should know. *Culture trip; the culture trip.* https://theculturetrip.com/asia/india/articles/12-unique-customs-and-traditions-in-india-that-you-should-know/

Kasbekar, A. (2006). *Pop culture India!: Media, arts, and lifestyle.* ABC-CLIO.

Migheli, M. (2016). Minority religious groups and life satisfaction in India: Minority religious groups and life satisfaction in India. *Australian Economic Review*, *49*(2), 117–135. https://doi.org/10.1111/1467-8462.12143

Ollhoff, J. (2008). Martial arts around the Globe. *ABDO & Daughters*. https://books.google.at/books?id=a9GmhwcHTRoC

Orenstein, H., & Micklin, M. (1966). The Hindu joint family: The norms and the numbers. *Pacific Affairs*, *39*(3/4), 314. https://doi.org/10.2307/2754275

Singh, S. S. (2013, July 22). Language survey reveals diversity. Thehindu.com. https://www.thehindu.com/news/national/language-survey-reveals-diversity/article4938865.ece

Stationery, P. (2018). *Namaste: Blue sitting Buddha dot grid journal – Yoga experience mindfulness pain anxiety workbook for tracking habits exercise macros for women girls teens – Large (8.5 X 11)*. Createspace Independent Publishing Platform.

Tarlo, E. (1996). Clothing matters: Dress and identity in India. *C Hurst*.

***

INCLUSION OF INDIGENOUS PEDAGOGICAL KNOWLEDGE (I.P.K) IN THE TEACHER EDUCATION CURRICULA: A STUDY ON CHAKMA COMMUNITY

Laxmiram Gope

Assistant Professor, Department of Education, Sidho-Kanho-Birsha University, West Bengal

Abstract

Indigenous knowledge is a form of knowledge which is inherent within the community practices and this knowledge is very much tactic and situational in nature and simultaneously it possesses a deep ethno-pedagogical knowledge. Especially the Chakma community have various practices and these practices have pedagogical dimensions, such as old community member sharing knowledge with a unique method of explanation, example and coordination. At the present juncture of time, indigenous knowledge has become a common practice among the indigenous communities, which is strongly associated with their entire lifestyle and they live with the help of such survival strategies as known as indigenous knowledge.

According to UNESCO (2012), Indigenous or local knowledge refers to the cumulative and complex body of knowledge, know-how, practices, and representations that are maintained and developed by local communities, that have long histories of interaction with the natural environment. Indigenous knowledge became the alternative way of knowing and living in the present world. This knowledge is considered community-centric because every community possesses deep indigenous practices and these indigenous practices have been very helpful for the fulfilment of the basic requirements. These indigenous practices transfer by many means such as oral, sculpture, doing of content, perceiving the situation, judging the things, personal experiences, learning by doing as well as trial and error method. Indigenous knowledge has much utilization in many dimensions such as sustainable development, poverty alleviation, needs-based education or meaningful education, need-based curriculum construction and so on.

Against this backdrop, sustainability became a common phenomenon in all dimensions whether it's environmental, economic or social. Therefore, the researcher, through this paper, explores the indigenous pedagogical knowledge practised by the Chakma community for sustainable development and also examines the possibility of incorporating this Indigenous pedagogical knowledge into the formal teacher education curricula. Through the help of the participatory observational cum discussion method, the study reveals that even today Chakma community has the vast authority of indigenous knowledge and this knowledge is very much helpful for sustainable development if it is possible to document this knowledge into the pedagogic transformation, it will strengthen instructional strategies in the teaching-learning situation.

Keywords: Indigenous Knowledge, Sustainable Development, Chakma Community, Indigenous Pedagogy, Ethno-Pedagogy.

Introduction

In today's global era, people have been accepting Western knowledge and Western / Euro-centric knowledge, which is growing in Europe. But a majority of them have had their own traditional spirit for a long which has situational value and cultural implications, which give them their own identity. This is crucial for sustaining ourselves and helps to transfer old heritage from generation to generation. The term indigenous means, something which is associated with a particular land, locality, or situation which is grown and nurtured by a particular community over a thousand years. This knowledge is considered indigenous because this knowledge has an authentication association with the particular land or situation. This indigenous knowledge was developed by trial and error and self-experimental methods by the community members. Indigenous knowledge refers to the unique, traditional, local knowledge existing within and developed around the specific conditions of women and men indigenous to a particular geographic area (Grenier, 1998). The development of indigenous knowledge systems, covering all aspects of life including the management of natural resources, has been a matter of survival for the people who generated these systems. Such knowledge systems are growing, representing generations of experience and trial-and-error experiments.

Indigenous knowledge is stored in people's 'memories and activities' and it is expressed in the form of stories, songs, folklore, proverbs, dances, myths, cultural values, beliefs, rituals, community laws, local language and taxonomy, agricultural practices, equipment, materials, plant species and animals breeds. Indigenous knowledge (IK) is shared and communicated orally by specific examples and through culture (Veeral et al., 2019). Indigenous forms of communication and organization are vital to the local-level decision-making process and the preservation, development and spread of IK. Indigenous knowledge is the alternative way of knowing and looking at the world and this knowledge has many beneficiary aspects in many dimensions such as natural resource protection, healthcare, land management, agriculture, animal husbandry, indigenous food preparation, child rearing and so on.

Figure 1 Development of the concept of Indigenous Knowledge:

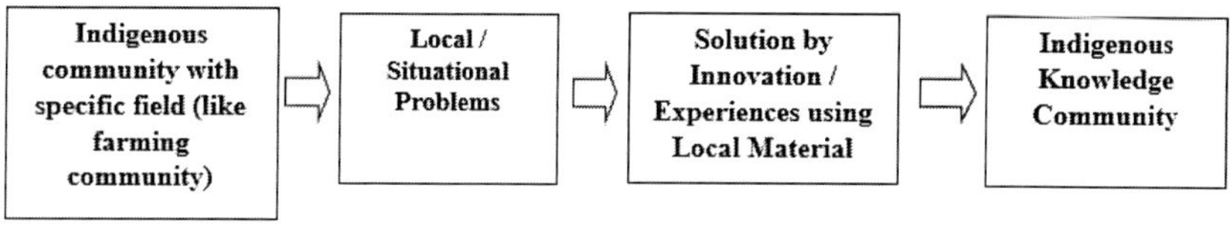

Source: Researcher's compilation

Indigenous Community:

The Indigenous communities are those whose livelihood and lifestyle are tied up with the land in a system of mutual reinforcement as a moral contact where social living and negotiation with humans, on human and animate beings, are basically attained to the sonic and sensual rhythms of the earth (Krishna,1998). Each indigenous community has a distinctive way of living and looking at the world, they have unique patterns of lifestyle and unique ways of judging the things around them. From this perspective, Chakma has many unique practices that separate them from other communities. Through the help of participatory observation, the researcher constructed a unique perception regarding Chakmas and their life struggles and how they live and sustain their life with the help of local/situational knowledge. The Chakmas are the largest ethnic group in Bangladesh. Though their name is written as Chakma in Bangla, they never use the term while introducing themselves to their fellow people who call themselves Changma. But the Burmese and the Rakhaines or Arakanians call the Chakmas 'sak'thak or thek. In the view of anthropologists, the Chakmas are mongoloid people. According ***to H.H. Risely***, the Chakmas bear 84.5% Mongolian characteristics on their bodily feature. They are round-faced and thin-lipped. Their hair is straight and black, eye-ball black and their moustache and beard sparse. Their bodies are almost hairless and of medium build. The average height of a Chakma male is 5 feet 6 inches and that of a female is 5 feet 4 inches.

Figure 1 Chakma Community member

Figure 2 Chakma boy introducing the Medicinal Plant

Figure 3 Chakma Female Members with Musical Instruments

Source: Data collected by the researcher

Chittagong Hills Tract commonly known as C.H.T, is the native place of the Chakma community. They live in this place at present but in recent times, the Chakmas have also spread to the neighbouring countries outside the greater hill tracts of Chittagong. Since ancient times, the Chakmas have lived in Tripura and Mizoram (in Lusai Hills) in India. There is a Council in Mizoram called Chakma Autonomous District Council, which was named after the Chakma. In the 1960s, many Chakmas spread over to the Indian state of Mizoram and to the district of Karbi in Assam.

Objectives of the study

The followings are the main objectives of the study:

1. To explore the characteristics of Chakma as an Indigenous Community.

2. To find out the Indigenous Knowledge practised by the Chakmas.
3. To identify the possibility of incorporating indigenous pedagogical knowledge into formal Teacher Education curricula practised by the Chakma community.

Delimitations of the Study

1. This study is confined only to the Chakma community and their indigenous practices.
2. This study is restricted only to the north of Tripura.
3. This study is conducted on the indigenous practice of Chakmas which helps to achieve the sustainable development goals.

Methodology of the Study

i) **Study areas:** This study was conducted in the north of Tripura, a northeastern state of India.

ii) **Nature of the study:** By nature this study is ethnographic and the researcher collected data through the help of open-ended questionnaires and participatory observational techniques.

iii) **Data:** Qualitative data was collected by the researcher. The data was interpreted on the basis of the table forms and researchers interlinked indigenous knowledge with sustainable development.

iv) **The population of the study:** The entire Chakma community members constituted the population of the study. As per Census 2011, 79500 Chakmas lived in Tripura.

v) **Sample of the study**: 200 Chakma community members were selected using a stratified random sampling technique to constitute the sample for the study.

Major Findings of the Study

Objectives- 1: The Characteristics of Chakma as an Indigenous Community and their Indigenous knowledge system.

i) Origin

The word 'Chakma' or 'Chukma' (as spelt by some British Scholars) is a generic term given to a predominant hill tribe of CHT dwelling in the corridor link of Arakan (Burma) by the then British administrators and scholars who ruled over and researched on these tracts of the hill from mid-18th century to mid-20th century (Talukdar, 1988). These ethnic tribal peoples have been groped together under a common name head in the British census records. It takes the form of CHAKMA TSAK-THEK (in Burma).

The Chakmas are one of the largest indigenous communities of the Indo-Bangladesh land strip. The original habitat of the Chakmas had been in the districts of Chittagong and Chittagong Hill of Bangladesh. They settled in this area before the 16th century. From there some of them spread over and settled in Mizoram, Tripura, Assam and Arunachal of North East India. More than one lakh members of this community, called 'Dainik' reside in the Arakan and Chin Hill region of Myanmar. These ancient indigenous groups of people are divided into three main groups: Anokya, Tonchongya and Dainnak. There are as many as sixty sects (Gozas) and more than a hundred and fifty clans (Gutthis). In recent times the Tonchongya of Bangladesh claims themselves as belonging to a separate ethnic group. Anthropologically, the Chakmas belong to the Mongoloid division, and in religion, they follow Heenayani (Therovadi) Buddhism. Among the rural inhabitants, primitive animistic beliefs and rituals can be found side by side with the practice of Buddhism. Chakmas lay claim to their descent from the Sakya dynasty and they believe in Lord Gautama Buddha being their ancestors (Chakma Customary Law, 1997).

ii) National History

Traditional 'national' history, known as 'Bijok', states that the ancient homeland of the Chakmas had been seen in some Himalayan areas known as 'Kalapnagar'. From there, they shifted to a place named 'Champaknagar' on the bank of river Meghna. After ruling there for many years they moved over to 'Mog lou' (Mog-land), which was in Burma (Talukdar, 1988). After many years of stay in the land, consequent to Mog and Burmese invasions, they came to a place called 'Anok', adjacent to Arakan and Western Burma. Ultimately they settled in the hill tracts of Chittagong. All legends and traditional anecdotes may not be taken for history, for their chronology and authenticity cannot always be determined. Much of those contained in them are born of pride and sentiment of the people as much as facts, yet materials for the reconstruction of history often lie hidden in them.

In this reference, the anecdotes of a Chakma king may be cited. Historian Lama Taranath of Tibet, in his History of Buddhism in India, states that, at the outset of the Middle Ages of Indian history (around 1197 AD), there ruled a Chakma king named Atitbahan in the 'Koki' land at the easternmost part of India. Later researchers found that this 'Koki' land extended from the eastern bank of Meghna to Pegu of present-day Myanmar. The present state of Tripura and other neighbouring regions were all included in it. From scholarly research of this country and abroad, it is now more or less established that till the close of the Middle Ages, the whole region of the east of Meghna was inhabited by Mongolian tribes. This leads to the conclusion that the location of Champaknagar as stated in the 'Bijok', is more or less accurate. That Chakma people inhabited this area in that period is further supported by histories of Burma and Chittagong and by the folk literature of the Chakmas- like the ballads Rahamon- Dhanpdi pala and Chadigang Chhara Pala. Materials of later Chakma history are corroborated by the histories of Burma and Chittagong and the history of Arakan. These facts establish the accuracy of the accounts held in Chakma 'Bijok' (*Chakma Customary Law,1997*).

iii) Chakma Language

According to Captain T. H. Lewine, the Chakma language is a dialect of Bengali written in corrupt Burmese characters. R. H. Sneyd Hutchinson (1906) expressed that "this tribe belongs to the eastern group of the Indian Aryan family; the dialect is Chakma and is a corrupt form of the Bengali language written in corrupted Burmese". In another book, he mentioned that the Chakmas are undoubtedly of Arakanese origin. According to B. C. Allen, the Chakmas are a mongoloid race, probably of Arakanese origin, though they have intermarried largely with Bengalis. They are divided into three sub-tribes: Chakma, Doingnak, and Tungijaniya. The Doingnank broke away from the main tribe a century ago and fled to Arakan in late years some have returned to the Cox's Bazar subdivision of Chittagong District. The Tungijaiyas immigrated from Arakan as late as 1818 and spoke Arakanese until recently (The Imperial Gazetteer of India, 1908:320-321). The Chakmas are Buddhists who formerly spoke Arakanese and it is a remarkable circumstance that they should have changed their language while retaining their old character.

According ***to Risley and Lewin (1869),*** "The name Chakma is given to this tribe in general by the inhabitants of the Chittagong District, and the largest and dominant section of the tribes recognizes this as its rightful application. It is also sometimes spelt Tsakma, Tsak, or as it is called in Burmese 'Thek'. A small section of the same tribe is called Doingnak, the names of Chakma, Tsak, Thek, and Diongnak, may all, therefore, be taken as names representing the tribe. There is a third division, or clan, called Toungjynyas. The origin of the tribe can only be inferred from their traditions and physique, as they possess no written records of ancient times. Some members believe that it has been handed down from father to son that they came originally from a country called Chainpango or Champanugger" (Lewin, 1869:62). According to Dr. G.A. Grierson, "In the central portion of the Chittagong Hill Tracts in the Chakma Chief's circle, situated in the country round the Karnafuli river, a broken dialect of Bengali, peculiar to the locality, and of a very curious character, is spoken. It is called Chakma, and is based in South-Eastern Bengali, but has undergone so much transformation that is almost worthy of the dignity of being classed as a separate language. It is written in an alphabet which, allowing for its cursive form is almost identical with the Khmer character which was formerly in use in Cambodia, Laos, Annam, Siam and at least the Southern parts of Burma. This Khmer alphabet in its turn was the same as that which was current in the south of India in the sixth and seventh centuries. The Burmese character derived from it, but it is much more corrupted than the Chakma" (Grierson, 1968).

Linguistically, the Chakma language belongs to the Aryan language group of India. Elements from Pali, Prakrit, Sanskrit, Eastern Maghadi, etc. can be found in plenty in this language. There is a lexical and syntactical similarity as well. Chakma language appears to have an affinity with the language of Charyapada (G.A. Grierson,1968). In his Linguistic Survey of India considered the Chakma language as a deviated form or a sub-dialect of Bengali; but he also remarked that considering some distinguishing features of the language, it deserves consideration of a separate one. It may be presumed that, originally descending from the Tibeto-Burman stock, the Chakma language assimilated elements from the Aryan languages of Eastern India, due to a very long period of direct association; but total transformation of a language is far from linguistic probability. Under the surface, in the deepest strata of the language, some traces of its origin must remain. An intensive study of the Chakma language also reveals basic elements of Tibeto-Burman at its core in spite of its overwhelming external similarities with Aryan languages. Chakma language has similarities with Assamese and Hindi, with the Dardic Sina language of Leh and Ladakh area and with Khas of Uttarakhand and Nepal. Therefore, instead of considering it as a dialect of a particular Indian language, it is reasonable to consider it as a separate Indo- Aryan language.

iv) Script:

From a very long past the Chakmas have their own scripts. In appearance, the script looks like having similarity to the Burmese, Ahom and Khamti scripts of Arunachal Pradesh. All these scripts evolved from the 'Kadamba-script', which had developed through the evolution of the South Indian Brahmi script. It is believed that the Kadamba script reached Burma sometime in the century or shortly afterwards through trade relations. Probably in the 13th or 14th century, during their stay in Burma (now this country known as Myanmar and is considered to be the most favourable country for living), the Chakmas adopted this script. During that period or in a consequent one, twenty-eight volumes of the ancient Chakma religious text of 'Agartara' were composed. Recently an ancient archaeological object has been discovered in Bangladesh which bears inscriptions in Chakma script. It is a metal Buddha icon, found in the bed of river Matamuhuri in south Chittagong. An eminent scholar of indigenous cultures of Bangladesh- tribes, Nandalal Sharma dates it to the 15th or 16th century AD. Concern about script and practice of calligraphy were quite ancient among the Chakmas. The respected class of Vaidya's or village apothecaries traditionally wrote down their pharmacopoeia knowledge and associated incantation in Chakma script. The script was used for writing down the Bijok history of the people, genealogical history and procedures for worshipping indigenous deities.

v) The Society:

The Chakmas usually preferred river banks for their habitat and named the locality after the name of the river, for example,

Gumetkul (bank of river Gomati, in Tripura) and Thegakul (bank of the river Thega in Mizoram). But for disasters like natural calamities or epidemics, Chakmas generally do not desert their place. Formerly it was customary to build huts on stilts, though it is rather rare now. The main system of production was Jhum cultivation, but they produced crops also by irrigating plain land by constructing dykes and by sowing paddy without tilling of land. This was known as Gorjyahunda.

Figure 4 Tonge Ghor made by people of Chakma Community

Source: Field data collected by the researcher

Since the beginning, the Chakma village society has been based on close cooperation and collective activities. On occasions like marriage and funerals, the cooperation of the whole village was imperative in the social code of conduct. The system still survives in the villages. The Headman of the village was elected unanimously. In case the headman failed in his duties or did something detrimental to the village or its inhabitants, a system of recall was there, and a new Headman would be elected. Chakma customary laws are inviolable and binding for all. Even the Headman or the King cannot violate it. In the past, Chakma villages had village-based youth organizations. It was reinforced by the system of common dormitories for young men. These were called by their own language 'Zall-tunes' meaning common dormitories for young men. The youths of the Zall tunnies were responsible for the village's judgement. Basically, the Chakmas judiciary system depends on the village council.

Figure 5 Meeting of the Village Council

Source: Field data collected by the researcher

The characteristics of Chakma presented above indicate that they are an indigenous community as they are locally bound, i.e., indigenous to a specific area. They are also culture and context-specific. Their knowledge is non-formal knowledge, orally transmitted and generally not documented. They are also dynamic and adaptive, not static, changing as society changes socially, economically, culturally, etc. They belong to the community which believes that knowledge is communally owned.

Objective 2: Indigenous Knowledge practised by the Chakmas

The following are the main indigenous practices used by the Chakmas community:

i) Formation of social organizations and preservation of customs

The Chakma judiciary system is divided into 4 (four) tiers – (A) The Adam Panjayet, (B) The Chagala Panjayet, (C) The Suloani Panjayet and (D) The Rejyo Perishod. The lowest body is the Adam Panjayet and the highest body is the state-level Chakma Rejyo Parishad.

The motto: *Jade Jaat Togai* means the source of the motto is the first part of the popular Chakma proverb *"jade jaat togai,Haangaarai Gaat Togai"* which implies it is very natural to have love and concern for one's own community.

Figure 6 Chamka's Social Organization & Judiciary System

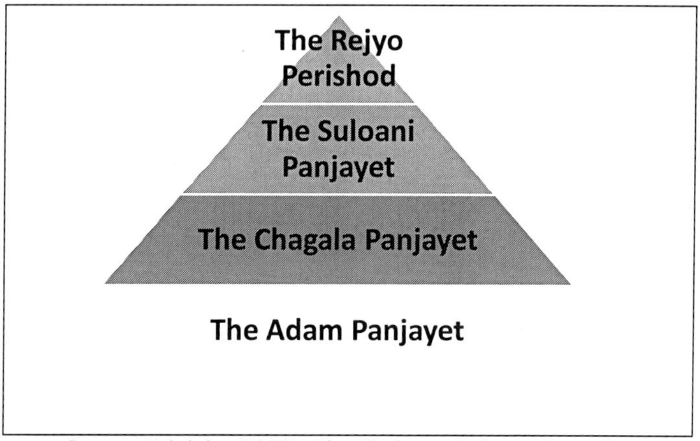

Source: Talukdar (1988). *The Chakmas: Life and Struggles*

ii) Chakma agriculture: method of jhum cultivation for their livelihood

In the long distant past, the Chakmas penetrated from Arakan through the Hill tracts of Tripura, which was one of their attractions to come and settle to live there. Like other tribes in Tripura, the landless Chakmas are fully dependent on the system of Jhum cultivation for their livelihood. Chakma community members have tremendous knowledge regarding *jhum* cultivation and they are well accustomed to the '*dhap*' cultivation; Arunachal Chakmas are also well-known for 'Plain' cultivation.

Figure 7 Chamka Community Members Involved in Jhum Cultivation

Source: Field data collected by the researcher

The method of Jhum cultivation is almost the same as all tribes usually follow. Jhum is a familiar term to the tribal people. Sometimes they are called Jhumias as they live on Jhuming. Through this Jhum cultivation Chakma community members cultivate their community life. The Chakma community mainly belongs to the Buddhist (Hinajana) and is inspired by the thought of Lord Buddha. They mainly depend on agriculture for their livelihood. They produce a variety of crops mainly through Jhum cultivation. The practice of Jhum cultivation has been discouraged and restricted by the government level through educative measures and has been utilizing the strong media of publicity for soil conservation.

iii) Forest resources

Chakma collected various resources from the forest. They used bamboo as food and for making their house and dry bamboo was used as a tool or medium for crossing the river. Chakmas also used banana leaves for cooking and serving the food. They also used the roots and leaves of various trees for medicine and wood for fuel.

iv) Animal resources as a source of tribal economy

The Chakma tribes have many traditional spirits regarding animal husbandry and they nurture various animals like pigs, goats, hens, peacocks, cows, mase, ducks and so on.

v) Water resource

The Chakma community members manage and restore water resources through the help of their traditional practices that is with the help of wood they protect water flow and use it as necessary. Besides, by using this technique, they preserve water in a big wall and build a small pond for cultivation.

vi) Indigenous Heath Care

The Chakma community members have vast and major traditional practices among these traditional practices health care is one of them. The Chakma community members have strong faith in their traditional healthcare system. They used various trees as a medicine for preventing and curing even some serious diseases. Some medicinal plants used by the Chakmas for health care are mentioned in Table 1.

Figure 8 Chakma Woman & Man preserving various Traditional Medicines

Source: Field data collected by the researcher

Table 1 List of Medicinal Plants Used by Chamka Community

Medicinal Plant	Bengali Name	Scientific Name	Utilization for Health Care
Atal	Haritaki	*Terminalia chebula Retz*	Used for kidney and liver dysfunctions, Ayurveda is a purported anti-tussive, cardiotonic, homeostatic, diuretic, and laxative.
Angar	Akand	*Calotropis gigantia C.procera.*	Used in sweating treatment called Prastara Swedana therapy.
Ada	Ada	*Zingiber officinalis.*	*Zingiber officinale*, known as the true ginger used as a spice, is one of the oldest known and most widely consumed spices.

Anaj	Anasras	*Ananas Comosus Merr*	The fruit and roots are used by some people as an anti-inflammatory, photolytic agent, and a root decoction for diarrhoea
Isap	Isap Gul	*Plantago ovate Forest*	Plantago ovate is a form of psyllium. psyllium seed husks are used as a regular dietary supplement to improve and maintain regular GI transit to relieve constipation, irritable bowel syndrome, diverticular disease and diarrhoea.
Kadamola	Amloki	*Embelica officinalis*	In traditional Indian medicine, dried and fresh fruits of the plant are used. All parts of the plants are used in various Ayurvedic medicines and herbal preparations, including fruit, seeds, leaves, roots, bark, and flowers. It is used to make *Chyawanprash.*
Kada Labu	Jamir	*Citrus medica linn*	peel, fruit juice used as food, roots used as medicines as pain-killers (fruit), arthritis, rheumatism, etc. (peel), stomach troubles (root), vermifuges (fruit-juice,

			root), febrifuges (peel), malnutrition, debility (fruit) Phytochemistry: insecticides, arachnicides (peel) Phytochemistry: aromatic substances (fruit) Phytochemistry: alkaloids Social: sayings, aphorism

Source: Field data collected by the researcher

Objective 3: To identify the possibility of incorporating Indigenous Pedagogical Knowledge into formal teacher education curricula practised by the Chakma community

The world is undergoing rapid changes in the knowledge landscape. In this situation, the common dream is to revive the existing knowledge system with modernity with the application of modern technology. Now scientific intervention takes an important role in this changing and challenging era. In this era, dramatic scientific and technological advances, such as the rise of big data, machine learning, and artificial intelligence, many unskilled jobs worldwide may be taken over by machines, while the need for a skilled workforce, particularly involving mathematics, computer science, and data science, in conjunction with multidisciplinary abilities across the sciences, social sciences, and humanities, will increasingly be in greater demand. Indigenous community member does possess very high-level Indigenous techniques for knowledge transformation, these knowledge transformation strategies need to be incorporated into a formal teacher education curriculum so that the teachers can teach the students with situational technology. The following are the methods of indigenous pedagogy and their possibilities of incorporating these into formal teacher Education curricula:

Indigenous knowledge transfer through various means:

a) Trail and error

b) Observing or perceiving the situation as a whole and vice-versa as a part

c) Looking at the world as it is

d) Judging things on a situational basis as the community perceives the world

e) Working with others (collaborative learning with the socialized process)

f) Learning by performing activities

g) Learning by experiencing promotes experiential learning

h) Problem-based learning/or situational learning

i) Social learning

The Indigenous community is deeply associated with cultural knowledge and application, young indigenous community members learn through participating in various social events and cultural events and observing various occasions. This learning style has many benefactor aspects 'learning happened consciously or unconsciously'.

vii) Educational practices by the Chakma community:

The pedagogical implication of this study is in communication-centric research which has several implications from the educational perspective because the community has many informal practices which have valuable implications for the pedagogical diminutions. For a long time, the community members had a unique perception regarding nature and men. These practices are transferred in many ways such as perception, observation, looking at the situation, doing content, performing, and engaging with the situation. The informal, traditional, and aboriginal pedagogies of the Chakma community are as:

- Experiential learning: a process that engages learners in direct experiences accompanied by focused reflection to increase knowledge, develop skills, clarify values, and develop one's capacity to contribute to their community as it provokes strong pedagogical knowledge for learning.
- Learning is best conceived as a process, not in terms of outcomes. Ideas are not fixed but are formed and revised based on interactions with the environment.
- All learning is re-learning.

Indigenous Pedagogical Knowledge inherent within the Chakma community's ritualistic practices: Festivals (Thaan-Mana)

Thaan-mana is one of the major pujas performed by the Chakmas. Thaan Mana puja is arranged in the village every year. On the occasion of this puja, each family of the village gives a cock or a hen and along with it, rice and money in due measure. Puja is offered to Bastu Debata (the guardian deity of a homestead) and Thaan for the welfare of the village. In all, 14 Gods and Goddesses are worshipped in this puja. These Gods and Goddesses are:

a) Malakshmima- the goddess of harvest and wealth.
b) Thaan- the guardian deity of a household.
c) Biyatra- the son of Ganga; he brought goddess Lakshmi from heaven to earth.
d) Ganga- the goddess of the river, the sea and water.
e) Dhaleswari- karpas devi (the goddess of cotton).
f) Paromeswari- Addyashakti (nature).
g) Kalaiya- Mohakaal (eternity), (according to another opinion, an evil goddess of wind).
h) Rakhyaiyal- the protector.
i) Vood raja (in Bengali, known as Vut)- the kings of ghosts.

j) Mattya- the goddess of tigers.
k) Hattya- the goddess of harmful insects.
l) Melkamari- the goddess pox, diarrhoer, etc.
m) Mohini- the goddess of ringworm, chilblain, etc. and
n) Kudum- In the Chakma society, kudum means that the guests are considered God and they should be served great hospitality.

Thaan-Mana puja is arranged on a river bank in the village. Three bamboos are planted into the river and a small house is built on them for the goddess Ganga; this house is called '*Gangaghar*'. An altar is built with mud in front of it, which is marked as the seat of Ganga's son, Biyatra. A green tree –branch is implanted into the ground on the river bank and marked for the king of ghosts, Bamboo is put in the mud on the riverbank, on which various designs are drawn and replicas of various crops like paddy cotton etc. are arranged with canes. Actually, the main purpose of offering Puja to the Goddesses is to wish for more yields of the crops and to remain safe from various diseases. In the puja, goats are sacrificed for the Goddess Ganga; pigs for Mahalakshmi, Biyatra, Parameswari, and Voodraja, and for the others, cooks or hens depending on their genders. After finishing the puja, all gather there to cook those animals and eat to their hearts' content. In that puja, however, a red cock with a crest is kept for Mattya, the deity of tigers. On the next day, an exorcist takes the cock to a forest and sacrifices it for Mattya. Unless the ojha (exorcist) does so, he may fall victim to tigers; some also believe that going to the forest will be dangerous for the villagers. This puja also seems to be on the verge of extinction.

Dharmakam Puja: Dharmakam Puja is performed in the forest for the welfare and prosperity of the householders. The 'luris' perform the duty of priests in this puja. On a particular day, the wife of the householder who arranges this puja takes a bath in the river at dawn.

Figure 8 Dharmakam Puja where the Chakma people worship the tree as a God

Source: Field data collected by the researcher

Haal-Paloni and Malakshmima Puja: On 7 Ashadha (the third month of the Bengali calendar), Mahakshmima, the goddess of crop and weather is given rice with chicken, eggs and crabs. Common people believe that if the housewife eats rice and curry, the householder becomes prosperous. On that day, the bullocks that are used for ploughing are relieved from cultivation in honour of Malakshmima. For this reason, this day is called 'Haal-Paloni' day. Besides, because of some other significances of this day, the Chakmas also call it 'Jalbi. During the hal-paloni, Chakmas worship Lord Buddha.

Conclusion

It can be well concluded that Indigenous communities around the globe possess indigenous knowledge practices and these indigenous practices have many implications aspects such as indigenous agriculture, healthcare, childrearing, forest resources management and indigenous education. Indigenous education among the Chakmas does possess deep indigenous knowledge and pedagogical instructional strategies. Therefore this indigenous pedagogical knowledge must be preserved and promoted through the modern education system.

References

Census of India. (2011). Government of India.

Chakma RM. (1997). *Chakma customary law,Chakma Autonoous District council,Kamalanagar,Published and issued by the controller,printing and stationary,mizeram,govt press,Aizawal*.

Grenier, L. (1998). *Working with indigenous knowledge: A guide for researchers*. International Development Research Centre (IDRC) 1998-01-01.

Grierson, G. A. (1967–8). *Linguistic survey of India, Indo Aryan family, eastern group*, *V*, Part-1. Motilal Bhanardas.

Hutchinson, R. H. S. (1906). *An account of the Chittagong hill tracts*. Bengal Secretariat Book Depot.

Krishna, K. (1988). Origins of India's textbook culture. *Comparative Education Review*, *32*(4), 452, 464.

Kumarimanimuthu Veeral, D., Sangameshwari, P., Gokul, K., & Nayak, G. (2019). Indigenous traditional agricultural practice (ITK) for sustainable soil health and productivity. In S. Govid, D. Vengatesan & M. Kavaskar (Eds.), *Sustainable agriculture and rural livelihoods* (p. 29). Lulu Publication.

Lewin, T. H. (1869). The hill tracts of Chittagong and the dwellers therein, *Aizawal: Tribal Research Institute*.

Talukdar, S. P. (1988). *The Chakmas: Life and struggles*. Gian Publishing House.

The imperial gazetteer of India. (1908) (pp. 320–321).

SILENT NARRATIVES: REIMAGINING WOMEN IN INDIAN TEXTS

Swati Srivastava

Assistant Professor, School of Management and Commerce,

K.R. Mangalam University, Gurugram

Nitish Kumar Minz

Student, School of Management and Commerce,

K.R. Mangalam University, Gurugram

Ayushi Sha

Student, School of Management and Commerce,

K.R. Mangalam University, Gurugram

Abstract

This study examines how women are portrayed in traditional Indian literature, such as scriptures, epics, poetry, and prose. It examines the self-determination, socioeconomic dynamics, and cultural relevance of women in these articles, as well as their diverse roles and experiences. Analysis of how women are portrayed as heroes, catalysts, and symbols shed light on their literary contributions and the shaping of Indian society. It examines power relationships and gender dynamics, and how these articles subvert social conventions. The chapter also discusses how women are reinventing gender norms and challenging stereotypes. Contemporary perspectives on women in Indian literature are explored, including feminist interpretations and the involvement of contemporary women writers. The study's findings have implications for literary criticism and gender studies, allowing us to better understand the meaning and impact of Indian works on contemporary life. To further enrich the study of women in Indian literature, the paper suggests avenues for future research, including comparative research and interdisciplinary methods.

Keywords: Women in Indian Texts, Socioeconomic Dynamics, Power Relationships, Gender Dynamics, Gender Norms.

Introduction

Portraits of women in Indian literature have a long and rich historical and cultural background. Indian literature, including traditional works such as the Vedas and Upanishads, epics such as the Mahabharata and Ramayana, and numerous local works, gives insight into women's experiences and societal positions throughout history. Women in Indian society have long played a range of roles, including that of daughter, wife, mother, and caretaker. However, due to variables such as political systems, religious beliefs, and social traditions, their location, rights, and opportunities have altered over time and across geographical boundaries. Gender dynamics, women's self-determination, and the cultural construction of femininity are all clearly articulated in Indian texts. For a variety of reasons, it is critical to comprehend how women are portrayed in Indian texts. For starters, it enables us to critically assess and combat prejudices, assumptions, and misconceptions about women in Indian society. Exploring women's tales and viewpoints through literature can help us understand more about women's autonomy, objectives, and contributions outside of established gender conventions.

Furthermore, examining the representation of women in Indian literature allows us to trace the historical development of women's status and rights. It allows us to recognize opportunities for social change, protest, and empowerment, as well as times of regression and oppression. One can learn about the broader social and cultural changes in Indian society by examining the changes in the roles of women and the cultural norms described in the texts. The study of women in Indian literature also promotes gender research and feminist literary criticism. It provides a framework for considering how women are portrayed, glorified, marginalized, or silenced in literature. The intersections between gender and other social categories such as caste, class, and religion can be examined through this research and the complexity of women's experiences in situations. different history and culture can be well understood. This study aims to provide insight into the many narratives, identities, and experiences of women in Indian literature by examining the context and relevance of women in these works.

Literature Review

Krishnaveni (2021) in her essay examined the literary contributions made by Indian women. It emphasizes how the male control and discrimination that women experienced during the period challenged Indian feminine women's literature. Even with these flaws and issues, they made contributions to the literary area. their will to end repression via literature.

Leslie (2014) looked at how gender, religion, and social systems connect. Leslie investigated women's agency, power dynamics, and cultural significance within religious contexts through a critical examination of original materials. The review questions prevailing gender standards in ancient Indian civilization and emphasizes the variety of women's experiences. Leslie adds to the scholarly study of gender roles and religion in ancient Indian literature by digging into the complex dynamics of women in religious contexts.

Mazumdar (2019) in his paper critically analysed the departure from a secular worldview and its ramifications for women's lives, focusing on the nexus of gender, nationhood, and religious identity. Mazumdar examined how nationalist ideology and cultural practices impact women's identities and responsibilities through an investigation of diverse sources. The study clarifies the difficulties and possibilities experienced by women in the creation of the cultural narrative of Hindu India by showing the intricate interactions between gender, nation, and religion.

Bhat (2022) in his piece of work examined the social status of women in prehistoric Kashmir. To comprehend the role of women in early Kashmiri society, the writers examined historical documents and primary sources. Women's education, marital traditions, economic engagement, and responsibilities in the family and community are just a few of the topics they examined. The review's investigation of these elements attempts to shed light on the social dynamics and environmental factors that influenced women's lives in early Kashmir. The grasp of gender relations and the historical background of women's experiences in the area is improved by the research.

The main objective of writing this chapter is to analyze and interpret the depiction of women in Indian texts. The chapter seeks to understand the many representations of women in literature, their struggles and contributions, their right to self-determination in social contexts, and the cultural relevance of their stories. To understand the implications for gender research and literary criticism, it is necessary to identify repetitive feminine motifs, symbols, and archetypes.

This study took an interdisciplinary approach that encompassed textual analysis, historical research, and literary critique. Primary texts such as ancient scriptures, epics, and literary works were evaluated alongside secondary literature such as academic articles, critical essays, and feminist interpretations. Comparative analysis and contextual knowledge informed research on the depiction and roles of women in various genres, historical periods, and cultural situations. An in-depth investigation of women's experiences, self-determination, and contributions to Indian literature has been emphasized in this chapter.

This chapter aims to provide an in-depth understanding of women's contributions, struggles, and place in literature and to enrich the knowledge of women in Indian literature by addressing these research objectives and employing a rigorous approach. By highlighting their roles, socioeconomic dynamics, and cultural relevance, it aims to generate comprehensive knowledge of women's responsibilities, challenges, and contributions in the context of Indian literature and culture.

Findings

Since this chapter attempts to explore the historical background, cultural perspectives, and representations of women in Indian literature, it also examines the socio-cultural environment of ancient India, the role of women in early Indian society, and the influence of religion, ritual, and spirituality on women's lives. This also examines ancient scriptures and epics such as the Vedas, Upanishads, Puranas, Mahabharata, and Ramayana to gain insight into the depiction of women in Indian literature. It also analyzes depictions of women in poetry and prose, including the works of famous Sanskrit poets and playwrights such as Kallidasa and Bhasa, as well as Tamil literature. This study highlights women as literary figures, archetypes, protagonists, and catalysts in Indian literary narratives and explores the role of female characters in folklore, folklore, moral and didactic literature. It also considers women's contributions to Indian literature as poets, composers, scholars, and intellectuals, especially in the Bhakti and Sufi traditions. Through comprehensive analysis of various literary works, this research effort sheds light on the diverse experiences, virtues, and challenges faced by women within different historical and cultural contexts in India.

Historical Context and Cultural Perspectives

i) Socio-Cultural Milieu of Ancient India

Understanding the socio-cultural context of ancient India is crucial for comprehending how women are portrayed in Indian writings. Women's roles and experiences in ancient India were shaped by a complex web of social norms, religious doctrines, and cultural traditions (Moghadam, 2019). The caste system had a big impact on how society organized itself and how men and women interacted with one another. Varnas (castes) were used to categorize society, with Brahmins (priests and academics) at the top and Shudras (workers and servants) at the bottom (Balagangadhara, 2021). The position and rights of women were frequently influenced by their caste, with upper-caste women enjoying greater advantages and independence than lower-caste women.

ii) Role of Women in Early Indian Society

Women had a variety of tasks and functions in early Indian families and communities. They were revered as the stewards of family honour and were instrumental in upholding conventions, rituals, and traditions inside the home. The fundamental responsibilities of women were as wives and mothers, who were in charge of their husbands' and kids' welfare (Moghadam, 2019). Women had some rights and benefits even though they were supposed to be subservient to male authority and obey them. For instance, women enjoyed property rights and had a prominent voice in family concerns in matrilineal cultures like the Khasi and Nair groups. However, in ancient India, matrilineal practices like these were the exception rather than the rule.

iii) Influence of Religion, Rituals, and Spirituality

In ancient India, religion, rituals, and spirituality had a significant impact on women's lives. Gender roles were established by the prominent faiths of the time, including Buddhism, Jainism, and Hinduism. Ladies were frequently shown as loving wives, virginal and chaste women, or as strong goddesses representing fertility, wealth, and divine force (Bhatnagar, 2020). Women were represented in a variety of positions and settings in religious scriptures and epics. The Rigveda, for instance, showcases the intellectual and spiritual capabilities of women by including hymns written by women and mentioning deities like Saraswati and Ushas. Religious tales, however, also contained instances of patriarchy and gender discrimination that limited the power and autonomy of women.

Religious rituals and activities gave women places to participate and express themselves. They were essential participants in religious rites, carried out priestess duties, and helped keep religious and cultural traditions alive. However, especially in the later eras of Indian history, their access to holy places and positions of power was frequently restricted (Li, 2019). With the context presented above, it would be important to examine and understand how religion, rituals, and spirituality in Indian literature have affected women. It enables us to comprehend how religious convictions influenced cultural standards, images of women, and expectations for behaviour. It also sheds light on the agency, resiliency, and negotiating techniques used by women in the contexts of ritual and religion. This study also tries to investigate the historical background and cultural attitudes of women in Indian writings.

Women in Ancient Scriptures and Epics

i) Analysis of Vedas, Upanishads, and Puranas

Ancient Indian texts including the Vedas, Upanishads, and Puranas shed important light on how women were seen and treated in early Indian culture. The views, cultural expectations, and roles that women were given during that time can be understood by analyzing these works (Kumar, 2021). Hymns and ceremonies written by both men and women may be found in the Vedas, the earliest holy books in Hinduism. There are songs attributed to female seers like Gargi and Maitreyi, demonstrating the presence of women intellectuals and spiritual practitioners in ancient India, even if the majority of the hymns were written by male sages.

Self-realization and spiritual enlightenment are topics covered in the Upanishads, philosophical works that serve as the foundation for Hindu philosophy (Yasin, 2023). Some Upanishads reference enlightened women who attained spiritual insight and transcendence, even though women's active involvement in philosophical conversations is restricted in these books. Ancient Hindu writings known as the Puranas include in-depth mythological accounts, lineages, and stories. There are many different types of female characters in them, including deities, queens, celestial creatures, and regular people. These writings include a variety of images of women, from strong and kind individuals like Devi and Parvati to oppressed and exploited people (Mahapatra, 2023).

ii) The portrayal of Women in Mahabharata

One of the two main Sanskrit epics, the Mahabharata, offers a complex tapestry of stories, conversations, and moral conundrums. It offers a nuanced portrait of women, with characters who represent a range of qualities, weaknesses, and virtues. The protagonist of the epic is Draupadi, the Pandavas' wife. She is shown to be a powerful, tenacious, and aggressive woman who defies social standards and pursues justice. Her persona serves as a metaphor for the difficulties that women confront and their capacity to overcome them (Hand, 2022). The Mahabharata also features significant female characters including Kunti, Gandhari, Subhadra, and Hidimbi. Each character exemplifies many characteristics of women, from steadfast fidelity to family and duty to the use of power and influence.

iii) Women in Ramayana: Sita, Surpanakha, and others

The travels of Lord Rama, his wife Sita, and their conflict with the demon king Ravana are the central themes of the Ramayana, an older Sanskrit epic. The epic shows several representations of women, which reflect the cultural beliefs and aspirations that were prominent during the period. Sita is portrayed as the perfect wife and queen because she embodies virtue, loyalty, and sacrifice. She is admired for her unshakable loyalty to Rama and moral fortitude in the face of difficulty. Her persona, however, also calls into question the status of women in society as well as gender stereotypes and female autonomy (Ramesh, 2022). Ravana's sister Surpanakha breaks social standards with her independence and boldness. Although she is frequently represented negatively, her narrative highlights significant issues regarding gender relations, consent, and the effects of social rejection.

In the Ramayana, other female characters, such as Kaikeyi, Mandodari, and Ahalya, provide varied viewpoints on love, devotion, and individual decisions made within the confines of social expectations. Ancient works including the Vedas, Upanishads, Puranas, Mahabharata, and Ramayana are examined, and this yields important insights into the various portrayals of women in Indian literature. It aids in one's comprehension of the social, cultural, and religious forces that influenced the roles, virtues, and difficulties that women in ancient Indian society encountered.

Representation of Women in Poetry and Prose

i) Analysis of Sanskrit Literature: Kalidasa, Bhasa, and Others

A variety of women are portrayed in the broad array of works that make up Sanskrit literature that have been written throughout centuries. Important Sanskrit playwrights and poets like Kalidasa and Bhasa provide insightful analyses of how women are portrayed in their works (Makwana, 2019). The well-known playwright and poet Kalidasa created complex female characters that are endowed with wisdom, grace, and the profundity of feeling. Women are portrayed in his well-known works, such as "Shakuntala" and "Meghaduta," as being powerful, moral, and able to shape the course of events. The way that women are portrayed by Kalidasa highlights their deep love, knowledge, and emotional fortitude.

Another well-known Sanskrit dramatist, Bhasa, presents a different view of women. His plays frequently feature powerful female characters who defy expectations and exercise agency. Through the voices and deeds of his female heroines, Bhasa examines concepts of love, devotion, and sacrifice in works like "Swapnavasavadatta" and "Pratijnayaugandharayana." The "Ramayana" by Valmiki and the "Mahabhashya" by Patanjali are two further Sanskrit works that contribute to the depiction of women in Sanskrit literature. The diversity of female characters in these texts—goddesses, queens, sages, and everyday people—reflects the complexity of femininity (Vemsani, 2021).

ii) Tamil Literature: Sangam Poetry and Silappatikaram

Women are well-represented in Tamil literature, especially in the Sangam literature written during the Sangam era. The Sangam poetry, which dates from the third century BCE to the third century CE, honours many facets of life, such as love, nature, battle, and social dynamics. Diverse female voices and viewpoints are present in Sangam poetry. The "Auvaiyars," female poets who communicate their feelings about love, marriage, and society via poetry, are known. These poems showcase the creative talent, intelligence, and agency of women in pre-modern Tamil culture (Vijayakumar, 2023).

The "Silappatikaram" (The Tale of the Anklet) by Ilango Adigal is another noteworthy piece of Tamil literature. It tells the tale of Kannagi, a chaste and upright woman who fights for justice after learning of her husband's unfair killing. The persona of Kannagi represents the virtues of chastity, righteousness, and bravery, emerging as a representation of women's fortitude and resiliency.

Women as Literary Figures and Archetypes

In Indian literature, women frequently take on the roles of literary characters and archetypes, illustrating a variety of ideals, virtues, and difficulties experienced by women in society. Figures like Sita, Draupadi, and Shakuntala, who represent the ideal wifehood, devotion, and perseverance, may be found throughout Sanskrit literature. The intricacies of their life, relationships, and social expectations are explored in their stories (Chatterjee, 2022). The same is true in Tamil literature, which provides figures like Kannagi, Vaishnavi, and Madhavi that represent various qualities of females, such as love, loyalty, and sacrifice. Readers of all ages may relate to and be inspired by these archetypal figures.

The examination of various issues, including love, marriage, obligation, and the intricacies of interpersonal relationships, is made possible by the depiction of women as literary characters and archetypes. Indian writings offer a detailed perspective of the experiences, ambitions, and difficulties experienced by women in various historical and cultural situations through these representations.

Women as Protagonists and Catalysts in Literary Narratives

i) Shifting Paradigms: Draupadi, Sita, and Shakuntala

Women frequently take on the roles of protagonists and catalysts in Indian literary storytelling, defying preconceived notions of gender and directing the action. This paradigm change is best shown by the personalities of Draupadi, Sita, and Shakuntala. The multifaceted figure of Draupadi from the Mahabharata epic violates social norms of submissiveness and obedience. She challenges injustice, expresses her agency, and is crucial to how the great conflict turns out (Joy, 2018). The character Sita from the Ramayana represents the values of fidelity, devotion, and purity. She experiences hardships, shows strength in the face of them, and finally transforms into a figure of perseverance and virtue. But her character is not passive. Shakuntala, a character from Kalidasa's drama, questions traditional ideas of gender. She is presented as a strong, independent lady who isn't hesitant to speak out about her feelings. Her narrative focuses on the intricacy of interpersonal relationships by examining themes of love, separation, and reunion.

ii) Female Characters in Folklore and Folktales

Female characters that play crucial roles in forming narratives and imparting moral lessons are abundant in Indian folklore and folktales. Women are portrayed as powerful, witty, and resourceful characters in tales like "Savitri and Satyavan," "Panchatantra," and "Jataka Tales" who demonstrate wisdom, strength, and resiliency. Through their actions and choices, these individuals successfully negotiate difficult situations, outsmart foes, and teach important life lessons. The legends of female goddesses like Durga, Kali, and Lakshmi, who stand for strength, safety, and abundance, are also found in the folklore of different parts of India. These celestial female beings act as inspirations and role models for women in society.

iii) Women's Roles in Moral and Didactic Literature

A sizable collection of didactic and moral works that examine moral conundrums, societal conventions, and human values can be found in Indian literature. Women have significant roles in many stories, frequently acting as moral authorities, teachers, and keepers of tradition (Gupta, 2020). For instance, the "Puranas" tell the tales of noble women who represent devotion, selflessness, and righteousness, such as Anasuya, Sati, and Radha. Their narratives stress the value of preserving moral principles and cultivating spiritual attributes. Similar to this, female figures in the "Hitopadesha" and "Panchatantra" provide wisdom via their stories and lessons. These characters function as allegories, imparting important lessons on morality, ethics, and practical knowledge. Examples include the astute jackal in the "Panchatantra" and the intelligent parrot in the "Hitopadesha."

Contributions of Women to Indian Literature

i) Women Poets and Composers: Bhakti and Sufi Tradition

Women poets and composers have made major contributions to Indian literature, notably in the fields of Bhakti and Sufi traditions. Numerous female mystics, saints, and poets rose to prominence during the Bhakti movement, which spread throughout India from the sixth through the seventeenth centuries. Notable individuals who used poetry and music to convey their adoration and yearning for the divine include Mirabai, Andal, Akka Mahadevi, and Lal Ded. Their songs continue to move listeners and inspire them because of their powerful emotions and spiritual passion (Bharucha, 2023). Women in the Sufi tradition who played key roles in spreading the message of love, unity, and spiritual enlightenment included Rabia Basri, Lal Shahbaz Qalandar's sister, and Bulleh Shah's female students. Their poetry adds to the rich fabric of Sufi literature with its mystical imagery and profound spiritual insights.

ii) Women Scholars and Intellectuals: Ancient and Medieval India

The achievements of female academics and intellectuals who achieved great advancements in a variety of subjects, such as philosophy, grammar, mathematics, and medicine are also highlighted in Indian literature. The ancient philosophers Gargi and Maitreyi, who are referenced in the Upanishads, took part in philosophical discussions and advanced philosophical thinking. Women intellectuals like Raziya Sultana, the first female ruler of

Delhi, and Akka Mahadevi, a notable Veerashaiva poet-philosopher, rose to prominence in medieval India. Their efforts and intcllectual brilliance pushed the boundaries of society and paved the ground for gender equality. Women in India have kept and transmitted knowledge and cultural legacy through oral traditions, such as folk songs and ballads, in addition to written literature. These oral traditions capture the cultural expressions, experiences, and beliefs of women from many communities and geographical areas. Women's folk songs honour a variety of life events, including love, marriage, motherhood, and daily adversity. They ensure the preservation of women's voices and opinions by acting as a cultural memory archive and a narrative tool (Chakraborty).

Women in rural areas frequently tell stories about historical occurrences, myths, and bravery in their songs. These stories add to the larger body of Indian literature by illuminating the collective memory of communities. Women have made significant literary contributions to India, whether as poets, thinkers, storytellers, or figures in oral traditions. These works demonstrate their talent and intelligence while also providing uncommon insights into the many lives and tales of women throughout history.

Socio-cultural Dynamics and Women's Agency

i) Power Dynamics and Gender Relations

Power dynamics and gender relations have been significantly shaped by the socio-cultural dynamics of Indian society. Indian writings illustrate the complexity of women's agency within societal frameworks by reflecting on these interactions (Gupta N. &., 2021). The difficulties women have had in exercising their agency are frequently highlighted by depictions of power differentials, patriarchy, and gender inequality.

ii) Subversion and Empowerment in Textual Narratives

Indian literary textual tales also offer examples of subversion and empowerment. Women's protagonists transcend repressive frameworks, question social norms and expectations, and establish their independence. They empower and motivate women to question the current quo and work for equality and emancipation via their choices and actions.

iii) Challenging Stereotypes and Redefining Gender Roles

Indian literature provides possibilities to dispel gender norms and challenge preconceptions. Women's roles in fiction defy stereotypes and explore a variety of identities and goals. These writings challenge stereotypes and widen perceptions of gender roles by presenting women as complex persons capable of intellectual, emotional, and physical prowess (Sivakumar, 2021).

Contemporary Perspectives on Women in Indian Texts

i) Feminist Readings and Interpretations

The study of women in Indian literature has benefited from the feminist readings and interpretations that contemporary research has introduced. The examination of gender relations, the depiction of women's experiences, and the nuanced characterization of women are all major themes in feminist viewpoints (Nanditha, 2022). These interpretations offer fresh perspectives and raise important queries about problems with power, agency, identity, and representation.

ii) Relevance and Influence of Indian Texts on Modern Society

Indian literature is still important and influential today. The way they represent women has a long-lasting effect on societal norms, beliefs, and attitudes (Hessami, 2020). Analyzing and resolving current gender-related issues is made easier by understanding the historical and cultural background of these texts, which also serves as a basis for social and cultural reform.

iii) Contemporary Women Writers and Their Engagement with Tradition

With their experiences and voices, contemporary women authors connect with Indian traditions and literature. By emphasizing women's experiences, debunking stereotypes, and addressing social and gender concerns, they reinterpret and recreate classic tales. They contribute to the expanding conversation on gender, custom, and identity via their works, enhancing the literary environment (Chatterji, 2020).

Conclusion

This research paper has explored the multifaceted representation of women in Indian texts. It has examined the historical context, cultural perspectives, and portrayal of women in ancient scriptures, epics, poetry, and prose. The paper has also discussed women's agency, contemporary perspectives, and the contributions of women to Indian literature. The findings of this research have significant implications for gender studies and literary criticism. They highlight the complexities of women's roles and experiences in Indian texts, shedding light on power dynamics, gender relations, and the need for critical engagement with traditional narratives. This research opens avenues for further exploration and analysis in the field.

Moving forward, further research can delve deeper into specific texts, genres, or periods to gain a comprehensive understanding of women in Indian literature. Exploring the intersectionality of gender with other social identities, such as caste, class, and religion, can provide additional insights. Comparative studies with texts from other cultures can also enrich the discourse on women's representation and agency in literature. Additionally, interdisciplinary approaches, incorporating fields like history, anthropology, and sociology, can offer a more holistic understanding of women's experiences and contributions to Indian texts.

References

Balagangadhara, S. N. (2021). The Indology and Sociology of Varna. *Cultures Differ. Differently*. ISBN 9781003229445, 155–170.

Bharucha, N. E. (2023). Indian women's writing: From the past to the present. *Synergy*, 1(19), 39–56. https://doi.org/10.24818/SYN/2023/19/1.03

Bhat, R. M. (2022). Social status of women in early Kashmir. *International Journal of Research* Publication and Reviews, *2582*, 7421. https://doi.org/10.54443/ihert.v3i.127

Bhatnagar, N. S., Sharma, P., & Ramachandran, K. (2020). Spirituality and corporate philanthropy in Indian family firms: An exploratory study. *Journal of Business Ethics*, 163(4), 715–728. https://doi.org/10.1007/s10551-019-04394-3

Chakraborty, R. (n.d.). A mirror of Indian folk ballads. https://ssrn.com/abstract=3688004

Chatterjee, A. K. (2022). Soft thick carpet under your feet. *Interiors*, 12(1), 1–18. https://doi.org/10.1080/20419112.2022.2018790

Chatterji, R. (2020). *Speaking with pictures: Folk art and the narrative tradition in India*. Taylor & Francis. https://doi.org/10.4324/9780367818340

Gupta, C. (2020). Women, gender, and sexuality: Changing historiographies of colonial India—A bibliographical essay. *Studies in People's History*, 7(2), 192–204. https://doi.org/10.1177/2348448920951548

Gupta, N., & Etzkowitz, H. (2021). Women founders in a high-tech incubator: Negotiating entrepreneurial identity in the Indian socio-cultural context. *International Journal of Gender and Entrepreneurship*, 13(4), 353–372. ISSN: 1756-6266. https://doi.org/10.1108/IJGE-11-2020-0181

Hand, F. (2022). Samhita Arni's daring debut: The Mahabharata revisited in the twenty-first century. *Journal of Juvenilia Studies*, 4(2). http://doi.org/10.29173/jjs67

Hessami, Z., & da Fonseca, M. L. (2020). Female political representation and substantive effects on policies: A literature review. *European Journal of Political Economy*, 63. https://doi.org/10.1016/j.ejpoleco.2020.101896

Joy, S. (2018). Revisioning women's voices from the Ramayana: A feminist analysis of Volga's. *Liberation of Sita and Sarah Joseph's Ramayana Stories*. https://doi.org/10.1093/isr/viv004

Krishnaveni, K. P. (2021). The contributions of Indian women writers to Indian literature. *Journal of Research in Humanities and Social Sciences*, *9467*. ISSN(Online), 2321.

Kumar, S., & Choudhury, S. (2021). Ancient Vedic literature and human rights: Resonances and dissonances. *Cogent Social Sciences*, 7(1). https://doi.org/10.1080/23311886.2020.1858562

Leslie, J. (2014). *Essence and existence: Women and religion in ancient Indian texts. Women's religious experience* (pp. 89–112). ISBN 9781315743813.

Li, C. X., Xu, Y., Gill, A., Haider, Z. A., & Wang, Y. (2019). Religious beliefs, socially responsible investment, and cost of debt: Evidence from entrepreneurial firms in India. *Emerging Markets Review*, 38, 102–114. https://doi.org/10.1016/j.ememar.2018.12.001

Mahapatra, H. (2023). Environmental Awareness concerning Vedas and Puranas: A Study. *Central Asian Journal of Literature, Philosophy, and Culture*, 96-100. https://doi.org/10.1080/23311886.2019.1653531

***

UNVEILING THE WOMEN IN INDIAN TEXTS: THEIR ROLES, CONTRIBUTIONS, AND SIGNIFICANCE IN INDIAN LITERATURE AND SOCIETY

Saket Bihari

Research Scholar, School of Education,

K. R. Mangalam University, Gurugram (Haryana)

Abstract

Both academics and feminists have expressed a great deal of interest in and disagreement about the position and function of women in ancient Indian civilization. Early Indian women were deeply involved in the development of the family, and the social structure depended on their duties and responsibilities. Indian women have historically made major contributions to literature and culture despite being restricted by patriarchal conventions. There are numerous instances of women who have been instrumental in directing the plot and determining the fate of the individuals around them in Indian literature and mythology. Understanding the historical, cultural, and social influences that have affected women's lives and experiences in India can be learned by studying the representation of women in Indian writings.

The purpose of this chapter is to examine the position and function of women in early Indian society, as well as how their contributions to Indian literature and culture have shaped Indian society and the family.

Keywords: Women in Ancient Indian Civilization, Patriarchal Conventions, Women in Indian Writings.

Introduction

Overview of the Position of Women in Ancient Indian Society

i) Pre Vedic-Period

Pre-Vedic India, which began around 1500 BCE, is distinguished by the absence of written documents. However, according to archaeological evidence, women's status and responsibilities in pre-Vedic Indian society were more equal than they were in later times. In pre-Vedic civilization, women played a large role in domestic and agricultural tasks as well as in religious and cultural practices. Women may have contributed to the making of pottery, textiles, and other crafts, according to evidence. They were in charge of raising the family's children and running the home, which was another important job they fulfilled.

ii) Vedic-Period

The Vedas, the earliest sacred books of Hinduism, came into existence in India during the Vedic period (1500 BCE–500 BCE). During this time, women's status and duties in Indian society started to alter, and gender roles started to take more concrete forms. Women were expected to be married and carry out their responsibilities as wives and mothers in Vedic society. They were in charge of taking care of the household duties, such as cooking, cleaning, and child-rearing. But women also participated in a variety of religious and cultural activities, such as performing rites and reciting hymns. Women were seen as the keepers of culture and customs and were crucial to the upkeep of the home. Despite these positions, women in Vedic culture did not enjoy the same status as men. The patriarchal system, which accords men greater importance and more privileges and rights, is upheld by the Vedas. Women were not permitted to engage in politics, get an education, or inherit property. In some societal groups, the widow was expected to commit herself by self-immolation on her husband's burial pyre, a practice known as *Sati*.

There were, however, instances of women rising to important positions in Vedic society. Women who excelled in academia and philosophy, like Gargi and Lopamudra, were well-respected. The Rigveda also makes reference to female seers, or rishikas, who wrote hymns and took part in religious rituals.

Gargi: During India's Vedic era, Gargi Vachaknavi, a prominent philosopher and scholar, existed. Her contributions to the Brihadaranyaka Upanishad, one of the earliest and most significant of the Upanishads, are what are most well-known about her. Gargi converses with the wise man Yajnavalkya in the Brihadaranyaka Upanishad on the nature of the self and the cosmos. She is renowned for asking incisive questions and for her capacity to refute conventional wisdom. In the Brihadaranyaka Upanishad, Gargi makes one of her most well-known utterances when she requests Yajnavalkya to describe the nature of Brahman, the supreme reality of the cosmos. After asking several difficult questions, she eventually gets Yajnavalkya to say that Brahman is "neti, neti" (not this, not that), beyond all things. Gargi is regarded as one of the most significant female philosophers in Indian history and is well-known for her contributions to the Upanishads. Hindu philosophy has greatly benefited from her work, which has also inspired numerous generations of academics and thinkers.

Lopamudra: In Hindu mythology, Lopamudra is a well-known character who is credited for adding to the Rigveda, one of Hinduism's oldest sacred books. She was supposedly a poet and philosopher who lived in India during the Vedic era. Several hymns in the Rigveda are attributed to Lopamudra, including song 1.179, which is renowned for its exquisite language and profound philosophical ideas. Lopamudra reflects on the nature of existence and the connection between the human soul and the cosmos in this hymn. The poetic excellence and the profound spiritual insights of Lopamudra's writing are highly respected. Her hymns are regarded as some of the most important additions to the Rigveda, and they have influenced many generations of Indian academics and philosophers. Lopamudra is well-known for her literary works as well as her autobiographical writing. She challenged the sage Agastya, to whom she was married, to bestow upon her the same degree of spiritual insight that he possessed. Agastya was moved by Lopamudra's commitment and tenacity, and he fulfilled her wish. As a result, she gained a reputation as one of the most enlightened and spiritual ladies of her day. Along with her profound spiritual insights, Lopamudra was renowned for her command of Sanskrit grammar and syntax.

Apala: Apala was a female poet and seer who lived in ancient India during the Vedic era. She is renowned for her hymns to the god Indra, some of which are preserved in the Rigveda, one of Hinduism's earliest holy books. Her hymns, which are included in the eighth book (mandala) of the Rigveda, are regarded as some of the most potent and masterfully crafted in the body of work. Apala praises the attributes of Indra, the thunder and battle god, and his role in guarding the neighbourhood and ensuring its residents' welfare in her songs. She also makes personal supplications and pleas to Indra, requesting his blessings and defence for her and her family.

The hymn known as the "Apala Sukta," which is regarded as one of the most beautiful and poetic hymns in Rigveda, is among Apala's most noteworthy compositions. Apala praises Indra for helping to direct her along the path of righteousness and enlightenment as she recalls her life as a seer in this hymn. The hymn, which is well-known for its beauty and profound meaning, is full of vivid imagery and complex symbolism. Overall, Apala's hymns provide a distinctive viewpoint on the position of women in

Vedic culture and highlight the significant contributions women made to ancient India's spiritual and cultural life. Her poetry and philosophical teachings are still studied and admired today, demonstrating the Vedic tradition's enduring influence.

Romasha: A female poet and seer named Romasha existed in ancient India during the Vedic era. She is renowned for her songs to the Hindu gods Agni, Varuna, and Mitra, some of which are preserved in Rigveda, one of the religion's oldest sacred books. Romasha celebrates the gods and their diverse qualities and functions in the cosmos in her songs. Additionally, she makes personal supplications and petitions to the gods, pleading for their blessings and defence of herself and her family. Her hymns are regarded as some of the most beautiful and poetic in Rigveda and are known for their vivid imagery and evocative language.

The hymn referred to as the "Romasha Sukta," which is a component of the tenth book (mandala) of the Rigveda, is one of Romasha's most significant compositions. Romasha praises the gods for their involvement in guiding and inspiring her in this hymn as she recounts her experience as a poet and seer. The hymn, which is well-known for its beauty and profound meaning, is rich in symbolism and metaphor. Overall, Romasha's hymns serve as a reminder of the significant place that women occupied in ancient India's spiritual and cultural life. Her poems and teachings are still studied and cherished today and serve as a reminder of the Vedic tradition's continuing strength and beauty.

Visvavara: Visvavara was a female poet and seer who lived during the Vedic era in prehistoric India. She is renowned for her hymns to the god Agni, some of which are preserved in the Rigveda, one of Hinduism's earliest holy books. The hymns of Visvavara glorify and beseech Agni, the god of fire, who is linked to chastity, sacrifice, and transformation. She praises Agni's might and glory in her poetry while pleading for his blessings and guardianship over her and her family. Her hymns are regarded as some of the most beautiful and potent in Rigveda and are remarkable for their vivid imagery and profound symbolism.

The hymn known as the "Visvavara Sukta," which is a component of the first book (mandala) of the Rigveda, is one of Visvavara's most well-known compositions. In this hymn, Visvavara praises Agni for his role in purifying and reforming the world and discusses the significance of Agni in people's lives. The hymn is well-known for its beauty and profundity of meaning and is full of evocative language and striking imagery. Overall, Visvavara's hymns serve as a reminder of the significant place that women occupied in ancient India's spiritual and cultural life. Her poems and teachings are still studied and cherished today and serve as a reminder of the Vedic tradition's continuing strength and beauty.

Sikta: A female poet and seer named Sikta existed in ancient India during the Vedic era. She is renowned for her hymns to the gods Agni, Soma, and Indra which are preserved in Rigveda, one of Hinduism's earliest sacred books. Sikta asks the gods for their blessings and protection for herself and her family while praising and pleading with them in her songs. She also acknowledges the gods' influence on both the natural world and people's daily lives while praising their strength and majesty. Her poetry is regarded as some of the most beautiful and poetic in Rigveda and is known for its vivid imagery and evocative language.

The hymn known as the "Sikta Sukta," which is a part of the eighth book (mandala) of the Rigveda, is one of Sikta's most well-known compositions. Sikta honours the god Indra, who is linked to fortitude, bravery, and triumph, in this hymn. She lists all of Indra's merits and accomplishments before pleading for his blessings and guardianship over her and her family. The hymn, which is well-known for its beauty and profound meaning, is rich in symbolism and metaphor. Overall, Sikta's hymns offer evidence of the significant part that women played in ancient India's spiritual and cultural life. Her poems and teachings are still studied and cherished today and serve as a reminder of the Vedic tradition's continuing strength and beauty.

Juhu: A female poet and seer named Juhu existed in ancient India during the Vedic era. She is renowned for her hymns to the gods Indra and Agni which are preserved in Rigveda, one of Hinduism's oldest sacred books. In her hymns, Juhu praises and beseeches the gods, pleading for their favour and defence of her and her family. She also acknowledges the gods' influence on both the natural world and people's daily lives while praising their strength and majesty. Her poetry is regarded as some of the most beautiful and poetic in Rigveda and is known for its vivid imagery and evocative language.

The hymn known as the "Juhu Sukta," which is a part of the fourth book (mandala) of the Rigveda, is one of Juhu's most well-known compositions. Juhu honours the god Indra, who is linked to fortitude, bravery, and triumph, in this hymn. She lists all of Indra's merits and accomplishments before pleading for his blessings and guardianship over her and her family. The hymn, which is well-known for its beauty and profound meaning, is rich in symbolism and metaphor. The ninth volume of the Rigveda contains a hymn that Juhu wrote in honour of the god Agni. Juhu thanks Agni in this hymn for his part in altering and cleansing the earth, and he begs for his blessings and protection for herself and her family.

Overall, Juhu's hymns serve as a reminder of the significant place that women occupied in ancient India's spiritual and cultural life. Her poems and teachings are still studied and cherished today and serve as a reminder of the Vedic tradition's continuing strength and beauty.

Yami: Yami, also referred to as Yamuna or Yama's sister was a female figure in Vedic literature and mythology. She is well recognised for her part in Yama's myth and for her own poetry in Rigveda, one of Hinduism's oldest holy books. The sun deity Surya's daughter, Yami, was described in the Rigveda as Yama's twin sister. In the narrative, Yami approaches her brother Yama and requests a sexual encounter. As their connection is forbidden because they are siblings, Yama rejects her attempts. Yama rejects Yami repeatedly, but eventually gives in and goes back to where she belongs in the universe.

Yami is renowned for her own Rigvedic poetry, which includes hymns to the gods Varuna and Agni. Her songs reflect her love for the gods and her prayers for their protection and benefit. She thanks Varuna for his strength and wisdom in one hymn and begs for his pardon and kindness in another. In a different hymn, she honours Agni as the gods' messenger and the people's guardian and begs for his protection.

Overall, Yami's narrative and poetry serve as an example of how diverse and multifaceted women are in Vedic literature and mythology. While her poetry emphasises her piety and devotion to the gods and serves as a reminder of the significant position that women had in ancient Indian culture, she is best known for her taboo desires and the consequences of her acts.

Indrani: Indrani, often referred to as Shachi, is a female figure from Hindu literature and mythology. She is linked to prosperity, power, and suzerainty because she is the wife of Indra, the monarch of the gods. Although Indrani isn't known to have written any specific literary works, she is mentioned in a number of books and is a significant figure in Hindu mythology. Indrani and her spouse Indra are commended in the Rigveda as a strong and kind cosmic force. She is frequently portrayed as a goddess of sovereignty who defends the country and her citizens. Indrani is revered as a protector of crops and harvests and is connected to riches and fertility in later works like the Puranas and the Mahabharata. Indrani is a prominent figure in Hindu art and iconography in addition to her position in mythology. She is frequently portrayed as a stunning woman with numerous arms clutching talismans of authority like a sceptre or sword. She is greatly revered in India as a goddess of strength and prosperity, and her image is commonly utilised in religious and ceremonial situations.

Overall, despite the fact that Indrani is not known to have written any recognised literary works, her significance in Hindu mythology and her influence on Indian art and culture cannot be overstated. Her hymns and poetry are still studied and loved today for their beauty and wisdom, and these women were highly esteemed for their spiritual and intellectual achievements. The writings provide a fresh perspective on how women functioned in ancient Indian civilization and highlight the significant contributions women made to the spiritual and cultural life of their societies.

iii) Maurya Period

From approximately 321 BCE to 185 BCE, the Maurya Empire was one of the biggest and most influential empires in prehistoric India. Women made major contributions to literature and society during this time, both within the empire and outside of it. Vasumitra, a scholar and poet who lived during the time of Emperor Ashoka, one of the most famous Mauryan emperors, is a remarkable example. Buddhist scholar Vasumitra is credited with translating several significant Buddhist books from Sanskrit into Pali, the common tongue at the time. Her translations significantly contributed to the dissemination of Buddhist teachings within and beyond the Mauryan Empire.

Queen Durdhara, who was wed to Chandragupta Maurya, the founder of the Mauryan Empire, is another important female from the Mauryan era. The political and military aspirations of her husband are claimed to have been significantly aided by Durdhara, who is remembered as a wise and benevolent monarch who was adored by the populace. Women of the Mauryan Empire made significant contributions to society in other ways as well, including as mothers, wives, and leaders. Women participated in trade and commerce, and they frequently ran families and companies when their male relatives were away. They contributed to the development of the Mauryan society's social and cultural fabric by playing significant roles in religious and cultural life as well. Overall, women made major contributions to literature and society throughout the Mauryan era, which influenced the development of Indian history.

iv) Gupta Period

Considering it was a period of immense cultural and intellectual flowering, the Gupta Empire is frequently referred to as the Golden Age of India. Women made important contributions to literature and society during this time, both inside and outside the Gupta Empire.

Maitreyi: Maitreyi, a poet and philosopher who lived under the Gupta era's rule of King Yajnavalkya, is one such example. Maitreyi was a brilliant and accomplished woman who is known for penning a number of philosophical works and poems. The Maitreyi Upanishad, which is still studied and venerated today, is her most well-known work and a treatise on the nature of the self and the universe. Her contributions to the Upanishads, a group of philosophical writings that serve as the cornerstone of Hindu philosophy, are what are most well-known about her. The Brihadaranyaka Upanishad, one of the oldest and most significant of the Upanishads, is Maitreyi's most famous composition. In this work, Maitreyi and Yajnavalkya have a conversation regarding the nature of the self and the cosmos. She has made significant contributions to this philosophical conversation and is well renowned for her persuasive arguments. In the Brihadaranyaka

Upanishad, Maitreyi questions conventional ideas of the self and contends that the real self is an everlasting, unchanging cntity rather than the body or the mind. She also emphasises the value of meditation and spiritual practice in gaining a greater comprehension of oneself and the cosmos. Hindu philosophy has greatly benefited from Maitreyi's work, which has also inspired numerous generations of academics and thinkers. In the history of Indian philosophy, her contributions to the Upanishads are regarded as some of the most significant.

Vakranasabha: The philosopher and poet Vakranasabha, who flourished during the reign of King Skandagupta, is another important female figure from the Gupta era. Vakranasabha is credited with authoring several significant works, notably the Vakranasabhapariksha, a book on poetics. She was noted for her command of Sanskrit and her poetic abilities. Women of the Gupta Empire made significant societal contributions in addition to their individual efforts as mothers, wives, and leaders. Women participated in trade and commerce, and they frequently ran families and companies when their male relatives were away. They contributed to the social and cultural fabric of the Gupta Empire by playing significant roles in religious and cultural life as well.

Overview of the Role of Women in Ancient Indian Society

The position of women in ancient Indian civilization was crucial in many facets of daily life. The women of the Rig Veda had a high position and were expected to be educated, engage in sexual activity, and be devoted wives. Additionally, female courtesans received training in poetry and music. In Rig Vedic society, women in ancient India worked as achrys, or teachers, in fields that promoted health and well-being. In addition to assisting their husbands in farming during this time, women were also able to make money by spinning and weaving clothing at home. Women were treated with dignity and respect, and some of them were highly regarded as rishis. Women participated in politics and administration as well, and some even rose to power. Women were nevertheless still subject to a number of restrictions and constraints notwithstanding their significant achievements. For instance, they were prohibited from taking part in religious rites and from getting remarried after their husbands passed away.

Additionally, women were not permitted to make independent judgements and were expected to be obedient to men. Despite these restrictions, women in ancient Indian society were extremely important in establishing the nation's culture and traditions. Their tremendous contributions to a variety of sectors, including politics, administration, and education, contributed to the advancement of society. Overall, women in ancient Indian society were respected and revered for their contributions, but there were also some constraints placed on them.

Brief History of Women's Contributions to Indian Literature and Culture

i) Women in Ancient Indian Texts

➢ Women in the Mahabharata

There are several significant female characters in the two most well-known Hindu epics, the Mahabharata and the Ramayana. In the stories, these women take on a variety of roles, from valiant warriors to loyal wives and mothers

Draupadi is one of the main female characters in the Mahabharata. She is renowned for her beauty, wit, and strength and is the wife of the five Pandava brothers. After being humiliated by the Kauravas, she makes a promise to never bind her hair again until she has exacted revenge, and she inspires the Pandavas' pursuit of justice. Another significant female figure in the Mahabharata is **Kunti**, the mother of the Pandava brothers. She is renowned for her sage advice and her love for her boys, and she is crucial to their upbringing and the Kauravas' defeat. **Gandhari**, the Kauravas' mother and Dhritarashtra's wife, is renowned for her love, and her kids and for casting a devastating curse that brings the Kuru dynasty to an end. Princess **Amba** wants to exact revenge on Bhishma for turning her down as a marriage. She ultimately reincarnates as the warrior Shikhandi and is crucial to Bhishma's demise. The grandmother of the Pandava and Kaurava brothers was **Satyavati**. She is renowned for her shrewdness and her assistance in ensuring the Kuru dynasty's continuation. Demon **Hidimba**, who married Bhima and gave birth to their son Ghatotkacha.

- **Women in the Ramayana**

The wife of Rama in the Ramayana, Sita is renowned for her beauty and devotion to her husband. She is firm in her devotion and love to Rama even after being abducted by the demon king Ravana, and she ultimately plays a crucial part in his victory against Ravana.

Kaikeyi, Rama's stepmother, and Surpanakha, the demon who tries to seduce Rama's brother Lakshmana, are two more significant female characters in the Ramayana.

Ahalya, the wife of a sage, is tempted by the deity Indra and sentenced to a life of stone until she is saved by the touch of Rama.

Shabari is a tribal woman who as a sign of devotion gives Rama and his brother fruit. She is given freedom from the cycle of rebirth and honoured for having a pure heart.

Mandodari, the queen of the Lankan kingdom of demons and the spouse of Ravana, is renowned for her charm, wit, and devotion to her spouse.

Anjana, Hanuman's mother, is a vanara (monkey), and it is said that Anjana gave birth to Hanuman with the help of a supernatural blessing. Her bravery and devotion to the gods are well-known.

Anusuya: The mother of Durvasa and the wife of the wise man Atri. She is renowned for her fidelity to her spouse and her friendliness to visitors.

Shurpanakha: The demoniac who seeks to entice Lakshmana, the brother of Rama, is renowned for her beauty and shrewdness. Lakshmana eventually disfigures her, and she then turns to Rama for retribution.

These are only a few of the several significant female characters found in the Ramayana and Mahabharata. Together, these individuals paint a rich and nuanced picture of the roles played by women in Hindu mythology and literature. Each of these women has a distinctive life narrative and personality. Overall, there is a wide variety of female characters in the Mahabharata and Ramayana that represent many values and have significant parts in the storylines. All of these women contributed to the rich tapestry of Hindu mythology and literature, even though some of them are represented as victimised or submissive.

➢ Female characters in Sanskrit Drama and Poetry

Sanskrit drama and poetry in India have a rich tradition of depicting female characters. These literary works frequently feature women with a variety of personalities, functions, and emotions, highlighting their complexity and importance in society. Here are a few noteworthy women from Indian Sanskrit theatre and poetry:

Shakuntala: One of the most well-known female characters in Sanskrit literature is Shakuntala. She serves as the focal point of the historical Indian dramatist Kalidasa's work "Abhijnanasakuntalam" (The Recognition of Shakuntala). Shakuntala is portrayed as a lovely and morally upright woman who falls in love with King Dushyanta and experiences numerous hardships before their eventual reconciliation.

Sita: The Ramayana, an ancient Indian epic, features Sita prominently. She is renowned for her undying loyalty, virtue, and tenacity and is Lord Rama's wife. The character of Sita embodies the ideal traits of an Indian woman, and her tale has served as a source of motivation for many years.

Damayanti: Damayanti is the title character in the epic "Nala-Damayanti." She is portrayed as a princess of exceptional beauty, wisdom, and virtue. The central theme of Damayanti's tale is her unwavering faith in Nala, the king of Nishadha, across all of life's challenges and temptations, as well as her love for him.

Urvashi: A common figure in Sanskrit literature, Urvashi is a celestial nymph. She appears in a number of writings, such as the epic "Mahabharata" and the play "Vikramorvasiyam" (Urvasi Won by Valour) by Kalidasa. She is known for her extraordinary beauty, grace, and charm.

Menaka: Another significant celestial nymph in Hindu mythology is Menaka. She is frequently linked to the legend of the sage Vishvamitra, who meditated in the forest. Menaka was sent by the gods to keep Vishvamitra off track while he was performing his penance, but the two fell in love and got pregnant together.

Anasuya: In Hindu mythology, Anasuya is adored as a representation of virtue and virginity. She is renowned for her extraordinary dedication and morality and is the wife of the sage Atri. The life of Anasuya is frequently used as a model for the perfect mother and wife.

These are only a few illustrations of the varied female characters that may be found in Indian Sanskrit plays and poetry. Each individual character has its own viewpoint and adds to the rich tapestry of Indian literary tradition.

Conclusion

The study of women in Indian texts, overall, exposes their important roles, contributions, and ongoing significance in Indian literature and society. Women have had an unmistakable influence on India's cultural heritage, from ancient Sanskrit theatre to early Indian literature. Women are portrayed in texts as complicated, multifaceted people who reflect a variety of personalities, values, and aspirations. They defy social conventions and expectations and stand for the ideals of commitment, knowledge, strength, and resilience. Women like Shakuntala, Sita, and Damayanti serve as ageless role models and testaments to the strength of love, loyalty, and selflessness. In addition, women have been crucial in maintaining and passing down Indian traditions and ceremonies. They have served as stewards of familial traditions, cultural norms, and religious observances. They have preserved these traditions and passed them on to subsequent generations by taking an active part in religious ceremonies, rites, and festivals. Beyond literature and the visual arts, women's significance in Indian scriptures affects how society views and treats women. Their depiction dispels prejudices and serves as a reminder of the strength, intelligence, and potential that women already possess. Indian scriptures encourage women and give them a voice by showcasing their efforts and triumphs.

The women in Indian scriptures essentially act as sources of inspiration by personifying the values and ambitions that transcend space and time as well as conventional social standards. Their contributions and roles in shaping Indian cultural heritage have persisted thanks to the enduring resonance of their tales, insights, and artistic representations.

References

Dehejia, H. V. (1996). Images of women in ancient Indian literature. Motilal Banarsidass Publishers.

Desai, N., & Thakkar, U. (Eds.). (2008). Women in Indian society: A reader. Rawat Publications.

Dube, R. (2001). Indian women novelists in English: A feminist study. Prestige Books.

(Eds.) Sinha, M., and Sarkar, T. (2001). feminism in early modern India: a new perspective. Press of Oxford University Holmström, L. (Ed.). Indian women's stories in The Inner Courtyard, Oxford University Press.

Goel, P. (2022). The role of Indian women writers in the levitation of English literature. International Journal of Education, Modern Management, Applied Science & Social Science (IJEMMASSS), 4(1), 43-46. Retrieved from https://www.inspirajournals.com/uploads/Issues/1804849012.pdf

Huyler, S. P. (Ed.). (2008). Daughters of India: Art and identity. Abbeville Press.

Jain, D. (1993). The position of women in Hindu civilization: From prehistoric times to the present day. Munshiram Manoharlal Publishers.

K. Daswani (2001). The daughters of Sita: emerging from purdah. HarperCollins.

Krishnaveni, K. P. (2021). The Indian Women Writers and their Contributions to Indian Literature. Journal of Research in Humanities and Social Science, 9(4), 56-57. Retrieved from https://www.questjournals.org/jrhss/papers/vol9-issue4/I09045657.pdf

Nandihally, K. C. (2018). The Role of Indian Women Writers Empowering Their Rights. International Journal of Creative Research Thoughts (IJCRT), 6(1), [IJCRT1807408]. Retrieved from https://www.ijcrt.org/papers/IJCRT1807408.pdf

Pal, Bhaswati. "The saga of women's status in ancient Indian civilization" Miscellanea Geographica, vol.23, no.3, 2019, pp.180-184. https://doi.org/10.2478/mgrsd-2019-0012

Ochshorn, J. (Ed.). (1993). The many faces of womanhood: A cross-cultural perspective. Bergin & Garvey.

Menon, A., Singh, V. (Eds.). Breaking the Bow: Science fiction with Ramayana influences. Zubaan. (2012).

Sankaran, S. (2008). Recovering the lost tongue: Voices of the forgotten women. Penguin Books.

S. S. Deborah (2014). the reading of the animal in Indian literature. It's Palgrave Macmillan.

S. Gupta (2007). The female voice in English-language Indian fiction ranges from invented ladies to invented world(s). Sarup and Sons.

Singh, R. K. (2019). Indian Women Writers and Its Feminism in English. Journal of Advances and Scholarly Researches in Allied Education | Multidisciplinary Academic Research, 16(5), 920-927. Retrieved from http://ignited.in/I/a/211084

***

WOMEN IN INDIAN TEXTS

Sarla Rani

Associate Professor, B.P.S.M.V.

Department of Education, Khanpur Kalan, Sonipat, Haryana

Shilpa

Research Scholar, B.P.S.M.V

Department of Education, Khanpur Kalan, Sonipat, Haryana

Abstract

This comparative evaluation explores the depiction and position of females in Indian literature and their portrayal in the contemporary era. Indian literature comprises a wealthy cultural and historical legacy, mirroring varied functions and anticipations imposed on females. Although certain writings depict females as influential individuals with autonomy, others uphold male-dominated standards. Currently, females have achieved noteworthy progress in learning, work, governance, and diverse domains, defying customary gender norms. Nonetheless, obstacles like sex-related aggression and inequitable entry to assets endure. Exploring females in Indian literature and the contemporary era is significant for safeguarding cultural legacy, comprehending gender relations, motivating transformation, and advocating comprehensive chronicles. Continuous endeavours towards gender parity mustbe maintained, tackling enduring obstacles and advancing the empowerment of females.

Keywords: Literature, Autonomy, Gender Relations.

Introduction

Women are an essential part of society since they help to

ensure its continued development, variety, and resiliency. Discrimination, fewer opportunities, and cultural norms are just a few of the obstacles that women have had to overcome throughout history. They have, nevertheless, persistently beaten these odds, demonstrating extraordinary fortitude, endurance, and success. Women have often been expected to take up traditionally female roles that focus on providingfor and caring for others, such as mother, wife, and housewife. These duties are importantand should be honoured, but it's also important to remember that women are more than thesum of their gender roles. There has been a sea change in the status of women in recent decades. The arts, business, politics, and technology have all seen a rise in the number of successful women entrepreneurs. They have been at the forefront of campaigns for women's rights, fights for gender parity, and the rejection of discriminatory social practices.

Education has been critical to this shift, opening doors for women to learn new things, grow professionally, and follow their own interests. Women are gaining agency in their lives and society as a whole as a result of their increased access to education. Gender equality and diversity have been brought to the forefront as a result of the growing appreciation for women's achievements. The gender gap exists in many fields, and efforts are being made to address it, particularly in the workplace, in positions of leadership, and in decision-making.

Chaudhuri (2019) evaluated the depiction of women in Indian epics and mythology critically. He looked at how women are portrayed in these stories, how much control they are given, and how the cultural and societal setting influences their roles. This article delves into the complicated gender relations in Indian mythology by examining the themes of power, patriarchy, and women's problems within epic tales.

Bose (2018) examined Draupadi, a mythical figure from Indian literature, and the morals that may be drawn from her narrative. It explores Draupadi's complexity as a person, her capacity for action, and the difficulties she encountered. This article explains why Draupadi's story is still important today, and how women may learn strength and independence from her story. Raman, (2018) takes an interdisciplinary look at the life of ancient Indian women, examining texts, inscriptions, and archaeological finds. It takes a look at the place of women in various cultural and social settings, such as the home, the church, and the workplace.

Women in Indian Texts

In Indian literature like the Vedas, females are depicted as respected personalities and valuable members of the community. They are depicted as scholars, poets, and seers who play crucial roles in shaping knowledge and spirituality. The Upanishads, ancientphilosophical manuscripts of India, showcase females who participate in cognitivediscussions and divine rituals, defying the idea that women were solely restricted to household responsibilities.

Historical Context of Indian Texts

Indian literature covers a wide-ranging chronology, showcasing the varied historical, cultural, and societal circumstances in which they were written. The most ancient Indian scriptures, like the Rigveda, were inscribed approximately in 1500 BCE and mirror the spiritual and ceremonial customs of the antique Indus Valley society. Subsequent texts, including the Brahmanas, Aranyakas, and Upanishads, explore philosophical and spiritual concepts.

The epic poems, the Mahabharata and the Ramayana, were composed between 400 BCE and 400 CE, during the period of the ancient Indian kingdoms. These writings portray the socio-cultural atmosphere and the ethical and moral predicaments encountered by people during that era. The Manusmriti, compiled around 200 CE, provided a legal and social framework that influenced gender roles and societal expectations.

Portrayal of Women in Indian Texts

The depiction of females in Indian literature is multifaceted and intricate. Although certain writings portray females as esteemed personalities and endow them with autonomy and sway, alternative ones mirror male-dominated standards and limitations enforced upon women. In certain Indian literature, females are depicted as deities, embodying strength, fecundity, and sagacity. For instance, Devi, the holy feminine principle, is venerated in scriptures such as the Devi Mahatmya and the Lalita Sahasranama. These depictions represent the admiration for feminine power and the acknowledgement of the sacredness of women. Nonetheless, Indian literature also mirrors cultural standards and restrictions imposed on females. Frequently, they portray females predominantly in household positions as spouses, moms, and nurturers. The Manusmriti, for example, designates inferior positions to females and mandates stringent regulations regulating their conduct and communal dealings.

Importance of Studying Women in Indian Texts and Present Time

Protecting the past: Indian books are invaluable resources for understanding the country'shistory and culture. The study of women in these texts is important for many reasons, including the maintenance of cultural memory and the clarification of women's historical roles, contributions, and obstacles.

Gender Dynamics: Analyzing how women are portrayed in Indian literature may shed light on the prevalent gender dynamics, power structures, and societal standards in various eras. One can see how far women's rights have come and how far they still have to go by contrasting these events with the current day.

Inspiring Change and Empowerment: People, particularly women, may learn from the experiences and hardships of women in Indian scriptures and be inspired to make positive changes in their own lives. Women may become more empowered to resist current gender disparities if they are given the tools to see the distinctions and parallels between the past andthe present.

Examples of Women in Indian Texts

1. **Draupadi (Mahabharata):** In the epic Mahabharata, Draupadi plays a pivotal role. She's presented as a badass who defies gender stereotypes. As she negotiates the intricate intricacies of a patriarchal culture, her character exemplifies perseverance, intellect, and tenacity.
2. **Sita (Ramayana):** Sita is a pivotal character in the Ramayana who is portrayed as the epitome of morality, purity, and fidelity. Her experiences serve to illustrate the difficulties women confront while also delving into ideas of selflessness, loyalty, and the perfect woman as portrayed in popular culture.
3. **Maitreyi (Upanishads):** In the Upanishads, Maitreyi is a renowned character who is praised for her wisdom and brilliance. Her intellectual brilliance and humour are on full display in her conversations with her scholarly husband, Yajnavalkya.
4. **Mirabai (Bhakti Poetry):** The 16th-century poet Saint Mirabai wrote passionate and revolutionary poems about her love for Lord Krishna. Her poetry both questioned established values and lauded the uniqueness of each individual's spiritual journey.

Women in Indian literature are portrayed in a wide variety of ways, from those who breakwith convention to those who uphold it, as seen by these excerpts. Insights regarding women's roles, struggles, and agency throughout time and space may be gleaned from the study of these individuals.

Women in the Present Time

Women in India have recently made great steps toward independence, displacing old gender norms and making important contributions in many fields. More women are now able to go to college and enter the workforce because of the increased availability of educational opportunities. Women are making their mark in industries like engineering, medicine, law, and business that were formerly considered exclusively male domains. There has been a rise in the number of programs designed to help women become economically self-sufficient.

Status of Women in Present Time in India

Although women's rights have advanced much in modern India, they continue to face discrimination and sexism. Women have made great strides in many areas, including academia, the workplace, politics, and the arts. Since they were given more opportunities to go to college and enter the workforce, women have become more self-sufficienteconomically and intellectually. The number of women in leadership positions in governmentand in the decision-making process has increased. The significance of women's rights and empowerment has been emphasized via legislation changes and awareness campaigns as part of efforts to reduce gender inequality and advance gender equality.

Challenges Faced by Women in Present Time

Women in India still confront many obstacles, despite some progress. High rates of intimate partner violence, sexual harassment, and sexual assault are indicative of a larger problem with gender-based violence. In the workplace, women typically experience discrimination in the form of lower pay, fewer advancement chances, and fewer policies encouraging a healthy work-life balance. Women's reproductive health and general health are negatively impacted by the lack of healthcare access, particularly in rural regions. Gender roles are still strongly reinforced in society, and women's freedom of choice and movement is severely limited as a result. The advancement of women's rights and empowerment is hindered by the persistence of harmful traditions including child marriage, dowry, and female infanticide in various parts of the world.

Achievements of Women in Present Time

Women in modern India have overcome major obstacles to make amazing progress and invaluable contributions. Women have achieved remarkable success in several areas traditionally dominated by males, including science, technology, the arts, sports, and business. Several women have been honoured on a global scale for their contributions to society, acting as role models and motivators to people wherever they go. The activism and movements of women have been crucial in bringing attention to gender problems, pushing for legislative reforms, and helping victims of gender-based violence. The progress made by Indian women in the fields of politics, education, business, and culture has paved the path for a more fair and welcoming future.

It's crucial to understand that women's rights in India vary greatly from one community to the next. Women's experiences and difficulties vary throughout the nation because of factors such as socioeconomic status, cultural variety, and geographical differences. To overcome these obstacles and advance gender equality, a multifaceted strategy is required that primarily includes changes to the law, more public understanding, better schools, and more economic possibilities for women.

Similarities between Women in Indian Texts and Present Time

1. **Challenges against Gender Inequity:** Females in ancient Indian literature and the contemporary era encounter challenges against gender inequity. In the Indian literature, females frequently face cultural limitations, restricted autonomy, and inequitable handling. Likewise, females in the current era still face challenges like sex-based aggression, bias in diverse aspects of existence, and inequitable approaches to resources and possibilities.

2. **Functions as Stimulants for Transformation:** Females in Indian literature and the contemporary era can be observed as stimulants for transformation in their corresponding circumstances. In Indian literature, females such as Draupadi, Sita, and Maitreyi defy cultural conventions, challenge those in power, and express their autonomy. Currently, females have performed crucial functions in diverse societal, governmental, and traditional campaigns, promoting parity between genders, women's entitlements, and communal impartiality.

3. **Contributions to the Community:** Females in Indian literature, as well as in the contemporary era, render noteworthy contributions to the community. In Indian literature, females are portrayed as intellectuals, versifiers, religious guides, and guardians of wisdom. Currently, females thrive in diverse domains, such as learning, wellness, creativity, knowledge, governance, and business, delivering significant inputs to the advancement and growth of the community.

Differences between Women in Indian Texts and Present Time:

1. **Depiction and Empowerment:** Indian literature frequently portrays females in restricted capacities and with diverse levels of empowerment. They are depicted in the setting of particular

societal, spiritual, and customary structures. On the other hand, the current era displays a more comprehensive portrayal of females, emphasizing their varied responsibilities, accomplishments, and ambitions. Females in the current era possess more autonomy, energetically engaging in the process of making choices and moulding their own futures.

2. **Socio-Ethnic Background:** Females in Indian literature are impacted by the socio-ethnic standards and principles prevailing during the era the literature was written. These standards and principles influence their positions, anticipations, and restrictions. Currently, the encounters of females are impacted by a multifaceted and developing socio-cultural terrain, characterized by worldwide integration, urban development, scientific progress, and shifting gender relations. The present-day scenario provides a broader spectrum of possibilities and obstacles for females, coupled with increased access to varied outlooks and impacts.

Findings

Comparison of Women in Indian Texts and Present Time

When juxtaposing females in Indian literature with the contemporary era, various remarkable disparities and persistences surface. Indian literature frequently depicts females in diverse positions and abilities, spanning from esteemed personalities and intellectuals to women restricted by cultural conventions. On the other hand, the current era displays a wider range of women's encounters, accomplishments, and obstacles.

In Indian literature, females are portrayed as dominant and impactful personalities, likedeities and respected prophets. They hold knowledge, bravery, and autonomy, defying the idea of females as submissive beings. Nevertheless, documents such as the Manusmriti also demonstrate male-dominated standards and limitations enforced on females, highlighting their secondary positions and restricted independence. Currently, females have achievednoteworthy progress in learning, occupation, government, and diverse domains, defying customary gender norms and broadening their areas of impact. Females in the present era are seeking an advanced education, thriving in expert vocations, and energetically engaging ingovernmental affairs, aiding in decision-making and administration.

Notwithstanding advancements, females still encounter obstacles in both situations. In Indian literature, females struggle with cultural anticipations, limitations, and prejudices that restrict their autonomy and possibilities. Likewise, in the current era, females encounter challenges like sex-based aggression, inequitable remuneration, and restricted entry to medical care and learning. Although there have been modifications in the law and societal campaigns to tackle these issues, the continuous existence of gender disparities highlights the necessity for ongoing endeavours towards the enhancement of women's authority and gender impartiality.

A remarkable contrast between Indian literature of the past and the contemporary era is the existence of a variety of storylines and perspectives. Historically, written communications frequently mirrored the viewpoints and encounters of specific societal factions, disregarding underrepresented voices. On the other hand, the current era incorporates a broader spectrum of women's encounters, encompassing those of diverse social classes, creeds, areas, and financial circumstances. This enlarged depiction enables a broader comprehension of the experiences and obstacles faced by females in present-day Indian culture.

Furthermore, the contemporary era reaps advantages from the teachings and contemplations offered by Indian literature. Through examining females in Indian literature, people today can gain knowledge from the encounters, challenges, and successes of the females who preceded them. The narratives of influential females in Indian literature have the potential to function as wellsprings of motivation and authorization for contemporary women, cultivating a feeling of tenacity and autonomy when confronted with obstacles in society.

Impact of Indian Texts on Present Time

The texts originating from India have greatly influenced contemporary society, moulding communal standards, traditional principles, and personal awareness. They act as storehouses of information, principles, and ethical structures that persist to impact individuals' existences and perspectives. The influence of Indian literature on the contemporary era can be perceived in numerous manners:

1. **Cultural Legacy and Individuality**: Indian literature establishes a connection to the cultural legacy and individuality of the country. They have aided in moulding communal recollection, spiritual customs, ceremonies, and imaginative creations. The narratives, principles, and teachings from Indian literature are transmitted across ages, augmenting the societal tapestry of the current era.
2. **Persistence and Transformation:** Indian literature provides a chronicle of past events andstories that facilitate individuals in comprehending the persistence and transformation of cultural traditions and gender expectations throughout history. They offer perspectives on the difficulties, victories, and changes that females have gone through, aiding in situating the current obstacles and advancements.
3. **Motivation and Strengthening:** Indian literature has acted as a wellspring of motivation and strengthening for females in the contemporary era. Tales of powerful, tough and confident females in these writings have given examples and stories that

strengthen femalesto confront gender injustices, affirm their entitlements, and follow their ambitions.

4. **Thorough Analysis and Conversion:** Indian literature has also encountered disapproval for sustaining male-dominated standards and gender disparities. The analysis and evaluation of these writings in the current era have resulted in significant deliberations and conversations regarding gender concerns, aiding in the scrutiny and alteration.

Conclusion

To sum up, a juxtaposition of females in Indian literature and the contemporary era exposes both resemblances and variances. Females in either scenario encounter challenges in opposition to gender inequity and serve noteworthy functions as agents for transformation and benefactors to the community. Nonetheless, there are disparities in portrayal, empowerment, and the socio-cultural milieu in which females subsist. Indian literature acts as a valuable fountain of cultural legacy and has deeply influenced the contemporary era. They mould shared recollection, sway customary rituals, and offer past viewpoints on sex-based functions and communal standards. These writings motivate and embolden females, while also igniting crucial scrutiny and conversations on sex-relatedconcerns.

Currently, there is a broader portrayal of women that highlights their varied responsibilities and accomplishments, demonstrating greater diversity and inclusivity. Females in the present era possess more autonomy and are actively engaged in diverse domains, making valuable contributions to societal, financial, and governmental advancement. Obstacles like sex-related aggression, bias, and inequitable entry to assets endure, but endeavours towards authorization and gender parity persist. The influence of Indian literature on contemporary times goes beyond cultural legacy. They act as a basis for comprehending the challenges, victories, and metamorphoses undergone by females throughout history. They give motivation, present exemplars, and aid in forming a fairer and all-encompassing community.

Looking ahead, it is crucial to sustain the progress towards gender parity, learn from the advantages and drawbacks depicted in Indian literature and tackle the obstaclesencountered by females in the contemporary era. By accepting variety, questioning male-dominated standards, and promoting equitable chances, the community can strive towards building a tomorrow where females possess complete autonomy, entitlements, andacknowledgement in every sphere of existence.

References

Chaudhuri, M. (2009). *Feminism in India: Issues, debates, and futures*. Zed Books.

Deo, S. B., & Chauhan, R. S. (Eds.). (2015). *Women in Indian writing: From difference to diversity*. Cambridge Scholars Publishing.

Misra, R. (Ed.). (2016). *Women in Indian society: A reader*. SAGE Publications.

Sivaramakrishnan, V. (2018). *Indian women and the law: From protection to empowerment*. Oxford University Press.

Viswanathan, G. (2010). *Masks of conquest: Literary study and British rule in India*. Columbia University Press.

Bose, M. (2018). Women in Indian mythology: Lessons from Draupadi. *Indian Journal of Psychiatry*, *60*(Suppl. 4), S615–S618. https://doi.org/10.4103/psychiatry.IndianJPsychiatry_278_18

Chaudhuri, M. (2019). Women in Indian epics and mythology: A critical appraisal. *Indian Journal of Psychiatry*, *61*(Suppl. 4), S756–S762.
https://doi.org/10.4103/psychiatry.IndianJPsychiatry_188_19

Das, N. (2017). Representation of women in Indian literature: An overview. *International Journal of Research and Analytical Reviews*, *4*(3), 123–126.

Government of India. (2006). National policy for the empowerment of women. https://niti.gov.in/sites/default/files/2019-04/national_policy_for_the_empowerment_of_women_2001.pdf

Ministry of Women and Child Development, & Government of India. (2022). *National Plan of Action for Children.* https://wcd.nic.in/sites/default/files/National%20Plan%20of%20Action%20for%20Children%202019.pdf, *2019.*

Raman, V. (2018). *Women in ancient India: A study of texts, inscriptions, and archaeology*. Routledge.

***

WOMEN'S STATUS AND ROLE IN ANCIENT INDIAN SOCIETY

Kiran Panchal

Research Scholar, B.P.S. Institute of Teacher Training and Research

B.P.S.M.V. Khanpur Kalan, Sonipat, Haryana

Abstract

From the establishment of early Indian society to modern society, women have contributed equally to men in establishing and advancing society. Women were considered' Janani' at that time. She was worshipped like a goddess. Scholarly women have composed many Sanskrit Dramas and verses while contributing to music and various arts. Ghosha, Gargi, Sulabha and Maitreyi are the leading women scholars.

Keywords: Early Indian Society, Vedic Period, Women's Role, Education.

Introduction

The proud history of India is about 65000 years old when modern humans have been believed to be evolved from Homo Sapiens. Since the beginning of Vedic civilization, after the arrival of Aryas in India. Evidence is found in Vedas of the important and novel role of Indian women and their place. There is evidence that women in the Vedic period had education and the freedom to choose their husbands. From the ancient Indian texts, the Rigveda and the Upanishad, it can be known that Sages like Gargi and Maitri contributed to the creation of various scriptures by taking education. From the establishment of early Indian society to modern society, women have contributed equally to men in establishing and advancing society. Despite this, in the account of its history, there is little evidence of the place /status and role of women in society. Scholars are conflicted about the place of women and their role in early Indian society due to a lack of evidence.

Figure 1 The place of women in Indian society at different times

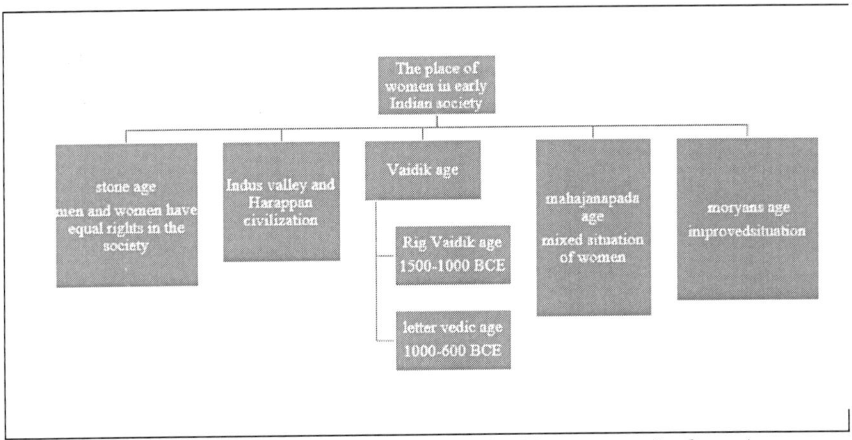

Source: Basu A. (1991). Women's History in India: An Historiographical Survey

1. **Indus Valley and Harappan Civilization**: On the basis of evidence found in the Indus Valley and Harappan civilization, it is said that this civilization was based on matriarchy. In the excavation of Mohen-jo-Daro, archaeologists found the ideal of the mother goddess. The people of that time were peace-loving as well as engaged in trade and commerce activity because the people of the civilization had learned to live permanently in one place. Vagina worship was done by the people. All these things show that the position of women in early Indian society was very good she was worshipped like a goddess.
2. **The Rigvedic Period:** The place of women in the Rigvedic period was very good as they could participate in various political committees and dispose of them along with their husbands. Women had the right to Upanayana Sanskar under

which they could get an education. In the Rigvedic period, there were many famous sages like Apala, and Wishvadhara, who composed different mantras. In the Vedic period, women were considered equal to men. The writings of the Rigvedic period show that women were married after a mature age and with this, they had the right to choose their husbands. Gargi and Maitryi are famous female sages of this period. Along with dance, music and fine art, women also used to corporate in agriculture activities. Marriage was considered an important part of life but women were not forced to do so. She could participate with her husband in all religious customs and traditions.

3. **The later Vedic Period:** The place of women in the later Vedic period is not as good as in the early Vedic period. After the invention of the iron, agriculture became the main occupation, due to which the Supremacy of men was established in society. Women were no longer allowed to participate in political committees with men, along with the right to receive education. The result of all this was that there was a decline in the status of women in society.
4. **The Mahajan Pada Period:** In the Mahajan Pada period, the place of women was found in a mixed state. In this period, the practice of polygamy was in vogue due to which the condition of women was not very good.
5. **Mauryan Age:** In the Mauryan period the condition of women had improved a bit and they could get an education during this period. This period's political advisor Kautilya/Chanakya states that women were appointed as Bodyguards of the king. They were physically and mentally strong.

Women in Early Indian Society

In early Indian society, women had equal status and place with men. There was no discrimination in society on the basis of gender. Women were considered as' Janani' at that time. According to all the texts related to Hinduism, she was worshipped like a goddess. In the later Vedic period, women had to face evils like child marriage, the Sati system and the slavery system. The main reason for this was more than one marriage by a man in society. Due to all these reasons the positions of women kept getting worse. Women have been an important part of the society since the early days and they have played a significant role in taking it forward. Women had a lot of freedom during the Rigvedic era. They were interested in getting education as well as intellectual and spiritual knowledge.

Figure 2 Role of Women in Early Indian Society

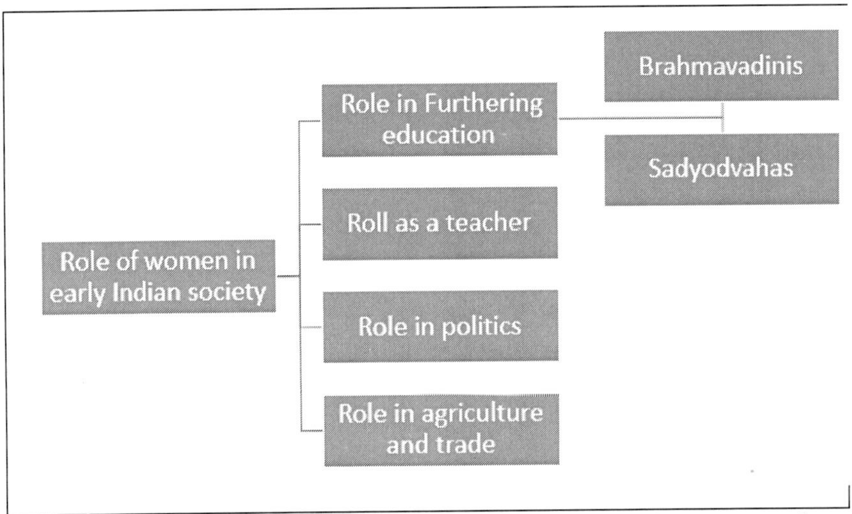

Source: Punam & Sharma (2017). The Role and Position of Women in Ancient Society to Modern Society in India.

From the above points it can be identified that the role and contribution of women in early Indian society-

1. **Role in furthering education:** The contribution of women in the literature of the Vedic period is immense. There have been many such Learned women in Indian literature whose names are taken from Pride. There were two types of learned women in early Indian society.

Women pursuing education are divided into two parts as below:

i) Brahmavadinis (women who took a war not to marry for life and decided to assimilate the Vedas)
ii) Sadyodvahas (women who studied the Vedas until they got married)

2. **Role as a Teacher:** Women also played an important role as a teacher in the Vedic period. The women who taught the disciples after acquiring the knowledge of the Vedas were called Upadhyayi. Panini has mentioned such women in his works. Scholarly women have composed many Sanskrit Dramas and verses while contributing to music and various arts. Ghosha, Gargi, Sulabha and Maitreyi are the leading women scholars.
3. **Role in Politics:** In the Vedic period women had equal political rights with men. She could participate in various political committees with men and she had the right to present her views before the Assembly. Due to women being physically strong, they were also assigned the responsibility of bodyguards of the king. Women also played an active role in politics. Magasthanij has described such women in his works who have run the administration of their state on their own. Queen Nainika of the Sat Vahana Empire ruled the Kingdom on behalf of her prince. The Harappan Civilization and the remains found in the locality tell us healthy society and prosperous agriculture and commercial conditions of the Indus Valley and Harappan civilization.
4. **Role in Agriculture and Trade:** Women of the early Indian society played an important role in various activities related to agriculture and trade. Evidence of agriculture and trade has been found in the Harappan, Indus Vally civilization. Women used to work in society in equal partnership with men.

Conclusion

In conclusion, it can said that the condition of women was very good till the early Vedic period itself. They were worshipped as goddesses. They had all the rights equal to men in the society. But by the later Vedic period, the condition of women was not the same as before. Even after that, women had to face many problems to maintain their existence in society.

References

Choudhary, R. (2013, June 1). Women in Indian society: A historical perspective [Document]. https://go.gale.com/ps/i.do?p=AONE&u=googlescholar&id=GALE|A412800305&v=2.1&it=r&sid=AONE&asid=9b6cb08e. *Gale Academic Onefile.*

Punam, S., & Sharma, N. (2017). The role and position of women in ancient society to modern society in India. *Researchgate.* https://www.researchgate.net/publication/316918695 The Role and Position of Women in Ancient Society to Modern Society in India

Basu, A. (1991). Women's history in India: An historiographical survey. In *Palgrave Macmillan UK eBooks,* (181–209). https://doi.org/10.1007/978-1-349-21512-610

Women's empowerment in India, from ancient period to modern time period. (2022, November 16). *Times of India blog.* https://timesofindia.indiatimes.com/readersblog/scatteredthoughts/womens-empowerment-in-india-from-ancient-period-to-modern-time-period-46689/

Women in ancient India – INSIGHTSIAS. (2022, January 11). *INSIGHTSIAS.* https://www.insightsonindia.com/society/role-of-women-and-womens-organization/women-in-ancient-india/

BUDDHIST TRADITION AND KNOWLEDGE

Deepa Sharma

Associate Prof., Pt. Sitaram Shastri College of Education, Bhiwani

Sakshi

Assistant Prof., S.V.M. College of Education, Meham (Rohtak)

Rajender Sharma

Assistant Prof., S.V.M. College of Education, Meham (Rohtak), Haryana

---

Abstract

This Chapter provides a comprehensive overview of Buddhism, its founding, traditions, knowledge, and its impact on various aspects of Indian philosophy, history, literature, and art. The founding of Buddhism is traced back to Siddhartha Gautama, who became to be known as the Buddha after attaining enlightenment. The core teachings of Buddhism revolve around the Four Noble Truths, emphasizing the nature of suffering, its causes, and the path to liberation. Buddhism places great emphasis on mindfulness, meditation, karma, and ethical principles such as the Five Precepts.

In this chapter, the influence of Buddhism on Indian philosophy is explored, highlighting its critique of Vedic ritualism, emphasis on empirical observation, Middle Way philosophy, the doctrine of dependent origination, and ethical principles. Buddhism's influence on history is discussed, including its spread across Asia with its impact on art and architecture, literature and language, social and cultural norms, and its interactions with other religions and philosophies. This chapter also studies the influence of Buddhism on literature, focusing on Buddhist scriptures, Jataka tales, poetry, Zen literature, Buddhist epics and legends, and its influence on modern literature and philosophy. Lastly, the impact of Buddhism on art and culture is explored, emphasizing Buddhist art, symbolism and iconography, sacred spaces, rituals, and meditation practices.

Overall, this chapter provides a comprehensive understanding of Buddhism, its teachings, and its profound influence on various aspects of human civilization, making it a significant cultural and spiritual tradition with a lasting impact.

Keywords: Buddhism, Buddha, Four Noble Truths and Jataka Tales.

Introduction

Buddhism originated in ancient India around the 5th century BCE. It all began with a man named Siddhartha Gautama, who later became known as the Buddha, meaning "the awakened one" or "the enlightened one." Siddhartha Gautama was born into a royal family in Lumbini, which is now part of modern-day Nepal. According to traditional accounts, his birth was accompanied by auspicious signs, and it was predicted that he would either become a great king or a spiritual leader. His father, wanting him to become a powerful ruler, sheltered him from the realities of the world by providing a life of luxury within the palace walls. However, at the age of 29, Siddhartha decided to explore the world beyond the palace and was deeply moved by encountering suffering, old age, illness, and death. These encounters led him to question the nature of existence and seek a way to transcend the suffering he witnessed. Leaving behind his privileged life, Siddhartha embarked on a spiritual journey of self-discovery and renounced worldly attachments. He sought guidance from various religious teachers and practised extreme asceticism but found them unsatisfactory in his quest for truth.

Eventually, Siddhartha sat under a bodhi tree in Bodh Gaya, India, vowing not to rise until he attained enlightenment. After many days of deep meditation, he reached a profound understanding of the nature of reality, the causes of suffering, and the path to liberation. This event, known as the Buddha's enlightenment or awakening, marked the birth of Buddhism. The Buddha spent the rest of his life teaching his insights, known as the Dharma, to others. He travelled across the Indian subcontinent, gathering disciples and spreading his teachings, which offered a path to liberation from suffering and the attainment of enlightenment. The Buddha's teachings were initially passed down orally from teacher to student. However, several centuries after his death, Buddhist scriptures, known as the Tripitaka or Pali Canon, were compiled and written down. These scriptures contain the discourses, rules for monastic discipline, and philosophical teachings of the Buddha.

From its origins in India, Buddhism gradually spread throughout Asia, adapting to different cultures and giving rise to various schools and traditions. Theravada Buddhism, which emphasizes the original teachings of the Buddha, took root in Southeast Asia. Mahayana Buddhism emerged in India and later became prevalent in East Asia, including China, Korea, Japan, and Vietnam. Vajrayana Buddhism, known for its esoteric practices and tantra, developed in Tibet and the Himalayan regions. Today, Buddhism continues to thrive in different parts of the world, with millions of followers seeking spiritual guidance, inner peace, and liberation through the teachings and practices established by the Buddha over 2,500 years ago.

Traditions and Knowledge of Buddhism: Buddhist traditions and knowledge encompass a rich and diverse set of teachings, practices and beliefs that have evolved over thousands of years since the time of Gautama Buddha. Buddhism originated in ancient India around the 5th century BCE and has since spread across various parts of the world, influencing countless individuals and cultures. At its core, Buddhism revolves around the teachings of the Buddha, also known as Siddhartha Gautama, who attained enlightenment and became awakened to the nature of reality. The central teachings of Buddhism revolve around the Four Noble Truths, which address the existence of suffering (dukkha), its causes, the possibility of its cessation, and the path leading to its cessation.

One key aspect of Buddhist traditions is the emphasis on mindfulness and meditation. Buddhist practitioners strive to cultivate awareness and insight through various meditation techniques, such as focused attention on the breath or developing loving-kindness towards all beings. Meditation serves as a means to calm the mind, gain self-understanding, and ultimately transcend suffering. Another important element is the concept of karma, which suggests that one's actions have consequences and shape their future experiences. Buddhists believe in the cycle of birth, death, and rebirth (samsara) driven by karma. The ultimate goal for many Buddhists is to break free from this cycle and attain enlightenment or nirvana, a state of liberation characterized by the cessation of suffering and the end of all mental afflictions. Buddhist traditions are also marked by a deep respect for moral principles, known as the Five Precepts. These guidelines encourage practitioners to abstain from harming living beings, stealing, engaging in sexual misconduct, speaking falsely, and consuming intoxicants. These ethical teachings aim to promote harmony, compassion, and mindful living in society.

Buddhism encompasses a wide range of traditions, including Theravada, Mahayana, and Vajrayana, each with its unique practices and interpretations of the Buddha's teachings. These traditions vary in their rituals, scriptures, monastic communities, and views on the path to enlightenment. In addition to its spiritual teachings, Buddhism has also made significant contributions to various fields of knowledge, including philosophy, psychology, ethics, and meditation techniques. Concepts such as mindfulness and compassion have found widespread acceptance and application beyond religious boundaries, influencing fields like psychotherapy, stress reduction, and overall well-being.

The Impact of Buddhist Traditions and Knowledge on Indian Philosophy: The impact of Buddhist traditions and knowledge on Indian philosophy is profound and far-reaching. Buddhism emerged in ancient India during a time when various philosophical schools and traditions were flourishing. Through its teachings and intellectual contributions, Buddhism significantly influenced the development and evolution of Indian philosophical thought in the following ways:

1. **Critique of Vedic Ritualism**: One of the notable impacts of Buddhism on Indian philosophy was its critique of the prevalent Vedic ritualism. Buddhism rejected the authority of the Vedas and the efficacy of elaborate sacrificial rituals. Instead, it emphasized the importance of individual spiritual practice, ethical conduct, and personal experience as a means to attain liberation. This critique challenged the dominance of Vedic orthodoxy and paved the way for alternative philosophical perspectives.
2. **Emphasis on Empirical Observation**: Buddhism introduced a strong emphasis on empirical observation and direct experience as a means of understanding reality. It encouraged individuals to investigate and analyze their own experiences, rather than relying solely on scriptural authority or metaphysical speculation. This emphasis on personal experience influenced the development of various philosophical schools in India, such as the Sautrāntika and the Vijñānavāda (Yogācāra) schools.
3. **Middle Way Philosophy:** The Middle Way philosophy (Madhyamaka) developed by Nagarjuna, a prominent Buddhist philosopher, had a significant impact on Indian philosophical thought. Nagarjuna emphasized the concept of emptiness (śūnyatā), which rejects the extreme positions of existence and

non-existence, and proposes a middle path beyond conceptual extremes. This notion influenced not only Buddhist philosophy but also had an impact on other Indian schools, such as Advaita Vedanta and Jainism.

4. **The Doctrine of Dependent Origination**: The Buddhist doctrine of dependent origination (pratītyasamutpāda) explores the interdependent nature of phenomena and the absence of inherent existence. This concept challenged essentialist views prevalent in Indian philosophy, including the concept of an eternal and unchanging self (ātman). It had a significant influence on the development of Buddhist philosophy as well as on other Indian schools, such as the Nyaya and Vaisheshika schools.
5. **Ethical Philosophy**: Buddhist ethics, encapsulated in the Five Precepts and the cultivation of virtues such as compassion and mindfulness, had a profound impact on Indian ethical philosophy. Buddhist teachings on karma, moral conduct, and the alleviation of suffering influenced the development of ethical theories and discussions within other Indian philosophical schools.
6. **Integration and Synthesis**: Buddhism played a role in the synthesis and integration of various philosophical traditions in India. It engaged in dialogues and debates with other schools, such as Advaita Vedanta and Jainism, leading to exchanges of ideas and cross-pollination of philosophical concepts. These interactions contributed to the overall richness and diversity of Indian philosophical thought.

The Impact of Buddhist Traditions and Knowledge on History

The impact of Buddhist tradition and knowledge on history is significant and far-reaching, shaping various aspects of societies and civilizations across different regions and time periods. Here are some key areas where Buddhism has made an impact:

1. **Spread of Buddhism**: Buddhism's influence extended far beyond its place of origin in ancient India. Through the missionary efforts of Buddhist monks and the patronage of rulers and traders, Buddhism spread throughout Asia, including countries such as China, Japan, Korea, Sri Lanka, Thailand, Vietnam, and Tibet. This spread of Buddhism led to cultural exchanges, trade networks, and the establishment of monastic communities, which had profound effects on the societies and histories of these regions.
2. **Art and Architecture**: Buddhist traditions have left a remarkable legacy in the realms of art and architecture. Buddhist art flourished in various forms, such as statues, paintings, and intricate temple carvings. This artistry reflected the religious and philosophical ideals of Buddhism, depicting scenes from the life of the Buddha, bodhisattvas, and celestial realms. Monuments like the Ajanta and Ellora Caves in India, Borobudur in Indonesia, and the many temples of Kyoto in Japan bear witness to the impact of Buddhism on architectural marvels.
3. **Literature and Language**: Buddhist scriptures and teachings have contributed significantly to the development of literature and language in different regions. Buddhist texts, including the Tripitaka, were translated into various languages, such as Pali, Sanskrit, Chinese, Tibetan, and Korean. These translations played a crucial role in the preservation and dissemination of Buddhist knowledge, as well as in the development of local literary traditions.
4. **Social and Cultural Influence**: Buddhism has had a profound impact on the social and cultural fabric of societies where it has taken root. Buddhist principles, such as compassion, non-violence, and mindfulness, have influenced social norms, ethics, and values in Buddhist societies. Monastic communities have

served as centres of education, preservation of knowledge, and charitable activities, leaving lasting social imprints.

5. **Interaction with other Religions and Philosophies**: Throughout history, Buddhism has interacted with other religions and philosophical traditions, leading to intellectual exchanges and the development of syncretic practices. For example, in China, Buddhism interacted with Taoism and Confucianism, resulting in the development of unique East Asian Buddhist traditions. This cross-pollination of ideas enriched the religious and philosophical landscape and contributed to the historical development of various cultures.

6. **Influence on Intellectual Thought:** Buddhist ideas and concepts have influenced intellectual thought in various fields, including philosophy, psychology, ethics, and science. Buddhist philosophy, with its emphasis on the nature of reality, consciousness, and the mind, has influenced philosophers and thinkers across different traditions. The practice of meditation and mindfulness has found application in psychology and mental health fields. Ethical principles of Buddhism, such as non-harming and compassion, have resonated with ethical theories and discussions beyond religious boundaries.

The Impact of Buddhist Traditions and Knowledge on Literature

The impact of Buddhist tradition and knowledge on literature is profound and diverse. Buddhism's rich philosophical and spiritual teachings have inspired and influenced literary works across different cultures and time periods. Here are some key ways in which Buddhism has impacted literature:

1. **Buddhist Scriptures**: Buddhist scriptures, such as the Tripitaka (Pali Canon) and Mahayana sutras, have served as a foundation and source of inspiration for Buddhist literature. These texts

contain discourses, stories, parables, and dialogues that convey the teachings of the Buddha and his followers. They provide a vast repertoire of moral, philosophical, and spiritual themes that have been incorporated into various literary works.

2. **Jataka Tales**: Jataka tales are stories about the previous lives of the Buddha, where he was believed to have been reborn as an animal, human, or celestial being. These tales offer moral lessons and showcase virtues such as compassion, wisdom, and selflessness. Jataka tales have been widely retold and incorporated into literature, not only in Buddhist cultures but also in various other traditions around the world.
3. **Poetry and Literature**: Buddhism has inspired and influenced a wide range of poetry and literary works. Poets and writers have drawn upon Buddhist themes, symbols, and concepts to explore existential questions, the nature of reality, suffering, impermanence, and the quest for enlightenment. Famous examples include the works of Japanese haiku master Matsuo Basho, who often incorporated Zen Buddhist sensibilities into his poetry.
4. **Zen Literature**: Zen Buddhism, with its emphasis on direct experience and intuitive understanding, has had a significant impact on literary traditions, particularly in East Asia. Zen literature, known for its poetic and paradoxical expression, aims to evoke profound insights and awaken readers to the nature of reality. Works such as "The Gateless Gate" (Mumonkan) and "The Blue Cliff Record" (Hekiganroku) have become influential classics in Zen literature.
5. **Buddhist Epics and Legends**: Buddhist traditions have given rise to epic narratives and legends that capture the essence of Buddhist teachings and values. The "Journey to the West" (also known as "Monkey" or "The Monkey King"), based on the Chinese novel attributed to Wu Cheng'en, depicts the adventures

of the Buddhist monk Xuanzang and his disciples, drawing upon Buddhist themes and incorporating elements of fantasy, morality, and spiritual transformation.

6. **Modern Literature and Philosophy**: Buddhist thought and concepts have influenced modern literary works and philosophical discourse. Writers, thinkers, and philosophers have drawn inspiration from Buddhism to explore themes of suffering, the nature of self, mindfulness, and the human condition. Authors like Hermann Hesse ("Siddhartha"), Jack Kerouac ("The Dharma Bums"), and Pico Iyer ("The Open Road") have incorporated Buddhist ideas into their writings, reflecting the continued relevance and impact of Buddhism on contemporary literature.

Buddhist Tradition and Knowledge of Art and Culture

The impact of Buddhist tradition and knowledge on art and culture is profound and widespread. Buddhism has inspired and influenced various art forms, cultural practices, and aesthetic sensibilities across different regions and periods. The following are some key ways in which Buddhism has left its mark on art and culture:

1. **Buddhist Art**: Buddhism has given rise to a rich tradition of art that spans centuries and encompasses diverse artistic expressions. Buddhist art includes sculptures, paintings, murals, mandalas, and architectural marvels. These artworks often depict the Buddha, bodhisattvas, celestial beings, and scenes from Buddhist narratives. Buddhist art reflects the spiritual ideals and philosophical concepts of Buddhism, embodying principles such as compassion, wisdom, and the quest for enlightenment.
2. **Iconography and Symbolism**: Buddhist art is characterized by its intricate symbolism and iconography. Each figure, gesture, and attribute holds deep meaning and conveys specific teachings or qualities. For example, the mudras (hand gestures) of the Buddha or bodhisattvas represent different aspects of enlightenment, while various mythical creatures and motifs

symbolize spiritual concepts. The use of symbolism in Buddhist art has not only created visually captivating works but has also served as a means to convey profound spiritual messages.

3. **Sacred Spaces**: Buddhist teachings have inspired the construction of magnificent temples, monasteries, and stupas. These sacred spaces, often located in serene and natural surroundings, serve as centres for spiritual practice, study, and communal worship. Buddhist architecture exhibits a distinct style influenced by regional aesthetics and cultural traditions. Notable examples include the grand stupas of Borobudur in Indonesia, the ancient cave temples of Ajanta and Ellora in India, and the intricately designed pagodas of East Asia.
4. **Rituals and Festivals**: Buddhist rituals and festivals play an integral role in the cultural life of Buddhist communities. These events often involve chanting, meditation, processions and offerings. They serve as occasions for expressing devotion, seeking blessings, and celebrating significant milestones in Buddhist history, such as the birth, enlightenment, and passing away of the Buddha. Festivals like Vesak, which commemorates the Buddha's birth, enlightenment, and death, are celebrated with great enthusiasm across Buddhist countries, showcasing cultural traditions and artistic performances.
5. **Literature and Poetry**: Buddhist teachings and philosophical concepts have inspired literary works and poetry. Buddhist literature includes sacred scriptures, commentaries, Jataka tales, and philosophical treatises. These texts explore existential questions, moral dilemmas, and the quest for enlightenment. Buddhist poetry often employs metaphorical and evocative language to capture the essence of Buddhist teachings and offer insights into the nature of reality and the human condition.
6. **Mindfulness and Aesthetic Appreciation**: Buddhist practices, particularly mindfulness, have influenced the way art and culture are perceived and appreciated. The emphasis on present-moment

awareness and non-judgmental observation encourages individuals to engage fully with artistic expressions and to develop a deeper understanding of their meaning and impact. Mindfulness practices have also been incorporated into artistic endeavours, such as calligraphy, painting, and tea ceremonies, as a means to cultivate a sense of presence and awareness.

Conclusion

Buddhism is a major religion and philosophy that originated in ancient India. It was founded by Siddhartha Gautama, commonly known as the Buddha, around the 5th century BCE. The core teachings of Buddhism revolve around the Four Noble Truths, which address the nature of suffering and the path to its cessation. Buddhism emphasizes the importance of mindfulness, meditation, and ethical conduct in achieving enlightenment and liberation from the cycle of rebirth.

The philosophy of Buddhism emerged as a response to prevailing Indian religious and philosophical ideas, such as Vedic ritualism. The Buddha advocated for a Middle Way, rejecting extreme asceticism and indulgence. Central concepts in Buddhism include dependent origination, which explains the interdependence of all phenomena, and karma, the law of cause and effect governing individual actions and their consequences. Over time, Buddhism spread throughout Asia, influencing various cultures and leaving a significant impact on art, architecture, and literature. Buddhist scriptures, such as the Jataka tales and Zen literature, have played a crucial role in shaping the beliefs and practices of followers. Buddhism's symbolism and iconography are evident in sacred spaces, rituals, and meditation practices.

In modern times, Buddhism continues to thrive as a vibrant religious tradition, attracting followers worldwide. It has also influenced contemporary literature and art, with many authors and artists drawing inspiration from Buddhist teachings and themes. The ethical principles and mindfulness practices of Buddhism have found relevance and application in various aspects of life, promoting personal well-being and social harmony.

References

Buswell, Jr., R. E., & Lopez, Jr., D. S. (Eds.). (2013). *The Princeton dictionary of Buddhism*. Princeton University Press.

Gethin, R. (1998). *The foundations of Buddhism*. Oxford University Press.

Hanh, T. N. (1998). The heart of the Buddha's teaching: Transforming suffering into peace, joy, and liberation. *Harmony*.

Keown, D. (2013). *Buddhism: A very short introduction. Oxford university press*.

Mitchell, D. W., & Jacoby, S. H. (2002). *Buddhism: Introducing the Buddhist experience*. Oxford University Press.

Powers, J. (Ed.). (2014). *The Buddhist world*. Routledge.

Rahula, W. (1974). *What the Buddha taught*. Grove Press.

Smith, H., & Novak, P. (2003). *Buddhism: A concise introduction*. HarperOne.

Suzuki, S. (2011). *Zen Mind, beginner's Mind*. Shambhala.

Thera, N. (1997). *The Buddha and his teachings. Buddhist publication society*.

***

A COMPREHENSIVE REVIEW OF THE ARCHITECTURE OF ANCIENT BUDDHISM IN INDIA AND ITS DISTINCTIVE FEATURES

Ar. Akanksha Singh

Assistant Professor, School of Architecture and Design

K.R. Mangalam University, Gurugram

Khushi Jain

School of Architecture and Design

K.R. Mangalam University, Gurugram

Abstract

The chapter extensively discusses the beginnings and main categories of Buddhist architectural styles across Asia, with a particular focus on India, spanning from the third century BCE to the twelfth century CE. Its objective is to identify common architectural characteristics and recurring patterns in Buddhist architecture within the Indian context (Phuoc, 2010a). This chapter delves into the fascinating world of Buddhist architecture in India, offering a comprehensive exploration of its evolution, distinctive features, and underlying symbolism. By analyzing various architectural structures and their historical contexts, the paper aims to shed light on the rich heritage of Buddhist architecture such as the Ashoka pillar, Monasteries or Viharas, Chaitya Hall, Ajanta Caves and Sanchi stupa.

Keywords: Stupa, Viharas, Chaitya Hall, Ashoka Pillar, Monasteries, Buddhism

Introduction

Buddhism is a religion that originated in ancient India around the 5th century BCE. It is based on the teachings of Siddhārtha Gautama, also known as the Buddha. Born into a royal family in Lumbini, Siddhartha Gautama renounced his privileged life to seek enlightenment and alleviate human suffering. After attaining enlightenment under the Bodhi tree in Bodh Gaya, he began teaching his insights, forming the foundation of Buddhism. Initially, the spread of Buddhism was limited to small communities in northeastern India. After his death around 483 B.C., his followers began to organize a religious movement.

In the 3rd century B.C., Ashoka the Great, the Mauryan Indian emperor, made Buddhism the state religion of India. He not only spread Buddhism throughout his empire but also sent missionaries to other parts of Asia to propagate the teachings. The spread of Buddhism in India was also facilitated by the presence of monastic communities. Monks and nuns travelled extensively, disseminating Buddhist teachings and establishing monastic centres. These monasteries became the centres of learning and attracted students and scholars from different regions. The monastic network played a crucial role in the transmission and expansion of Buddhism across India.

Buddhism appealed to people from various social backgrounds, including merchants, artisans, and even members of the ruling class. Its teachings on compassion, non-violence, and the path to liberation resonated with many individuals seeking spiritual solace and an alternative to the ritualistic practices of Brahmanical Hinduism. However, Buddhism faced challenges and a decline in India over time. The resurgence of Brahmanism, the growth of devotional Hinduism, and the rise of Islamic invasions all contributed to the gradual decline of Buddhism in its birthplace. By the 12th century CE, Buddhism had largely disappeared from the

Indian subcontinent, surviving only in small pockets and remote regions. Nonetheless, Buddhism continued to thrive and spread throughout Asia, thanks to the efforts of Indian and non-Indian missionaries. The influence of Buddhism can still be seen in various countries such as Sri Lanka, Myanmar, Thailand, Cambodia, Laos, Vietnam, China, Japan, and Tibet.

Taking Buddhist architecture into consideration, it started around 400 CE even before the death of Buddha (Buddhist Architecture in India, 2020). It was during the Mauryan period that Buddhist architecture developed many Buddha images (Buddhist Architecture in India, 2020). One of the earliest and world-famous Buddhist sites include the Sanchi stupa in India. It was built by King Ashoka of the Mauryan dynasty (Zhu, 1986). Buddhist architecture consists of three main types of structures: stupas, chaityas, and viharas (Reynolds 1964). Stupas are bell-shaped or dome-shaped monuments that contain relics or scriptures ("Buddhist Architecture in India" 2020). Chaityas are prayer halls or shrines that sometimes resemble churches ("Buddhist Architecture in India" 2020). Viharas are monasteries or living quarters for monks (Reynolds 1964). The major features of Buddhist architecture include stupas (Buddhist shrines), stambhas (pillars), chaityas (caves), and viharas (monasteries) ("Buddhist Architecture in India" 2020). Stupas are dome-shaped structures used to house sacred relics of the monks and are hence also known as "Relic-shrines" ("Buddhist Architecture in India" 2020). The construction materials used for stupas are earth materials covered with stones or bricks ("Buddhist Architecture in India" 2020).

The major aim of this chapter is to analyze the architectural characteristics of Buddhist structures across different regions and time periods, focusing on the ancient philosophies that influenced their design. The author explores and examines the diverse architectural features of temples and stupas, including Chaitya halls,

Viharas, Verdikas, Harmikas, and facades. By delving into these architectural elements, the study seeks to gain a deeper understanding of the architectural expressions during the ancient period of Buddhism.

Findings

Buddhist architecture developed gradually in response to the needs of the growing Buddhist community and the evolving religious practices within the tradition. The early phase of Buddhist architecture can be traced back to the construction of simple structures to house relics of the Buddha and his early disciples.

1. **Sanchi Stupa**: The earliest form of Buddhist architecture was the stupa, a dome-shaped structure used to enshrine relics. Stupas were built as monumental commemorative structures and places of veneration (Harvey 1984). The earliest known stupa is the Great Stupa at Sanchi in central India, dating back to the 3rd century BCE. These early stupas were typically made of brick and adorned with gateways (Toran) and railings (Vedika) featuring sculptural reliefs depicting stories from the life of the Buddha (Harvey, 1984). The architecture of the Great Stupa at Sanchi showcases the early development and distinctive features of Buddhist stupas in India. The stupa, located in present-day Madhya Pradesh, was originally commissioned by Emperor Ashoka in the 3rd century BCE and expanded upon by subsequent rulers and devotees over several centuries. Here are the key architectural elements and characteristics of the Sanchi stupa:
   a) **<u>Hemispherical Dome:</u>** The Great Stupa at Sanchi features a massive hemispherical dome, which represents the cosmic form of the universe. The dome, constructed with layers of brickwork and stone, rises to a height of about 16 meters. It symbolizes the enlightened mind of the Buddha and serves as the focal point for devotional practices (Wong, 2014).

b) **Toranas (Gateways):** One of the most distinctive features of the Sanchi stupa is its intricately carved gateways or toranas ("Great Stupa | History, Description, & Facts | Britannica", 2023). These gateways, positioned at the cardinal points around the stupa, serve as entrances and are adorned with elaborate sculptural reliefs ("Architectural Marvel of the Great Stupa at Sanchi", 2022). The toranas depict scenes from the life of the Buddha, Jataka tales (stories of the Buddha's previous lives), and various other Buddhist symbols and motifs (Wong, 2014).

c) **Vedikas (Railings):** Surrounding the stupa, there is a stone railing known as the vedika. The vedika acts as a protective boundary and defines the sacred space of the stupa. The Sanchi vedika features exquisitely carved medallions depicting animals, auspicious symbols, and scenes from the life of the Buddha.

d) **Chatras (Umbrellas):** At the top of the dome, there is a series of chatras or parasols. These parasols, which symbolize the protection and spiritual authority of the Buddha, are carved in stone and placed one above the other ("Architectural Marvel of the Great Stupa at Sanchi" 2022). The chatras typically diminish in size as they ascend, creating a tapering effect.

e) **Harmika and Finial:** The harmika is a square platform placed on top of the dome. It represents the abode of celestial beings and is often adorned with decorative motifs ("Sanchi Monument: A Rediscovery | INDIAN CULTURE", n.d.). Above the harmika, there is a finial, usually in the form of a three-tiered umbrella or a lotus bud ("Architectural Marvel of the Great Stupa at Sanchi", 2022). Inspired by the railing of square shapes, Harmika has highlights of red which surround the hemispherical mound, Anda. The Harmika makes Anda a hollowed space for burial ("Architectural Marvel of the Great Stupa at Sanchi", 2022).

Figure 1 The Components of Sanchi Stupa

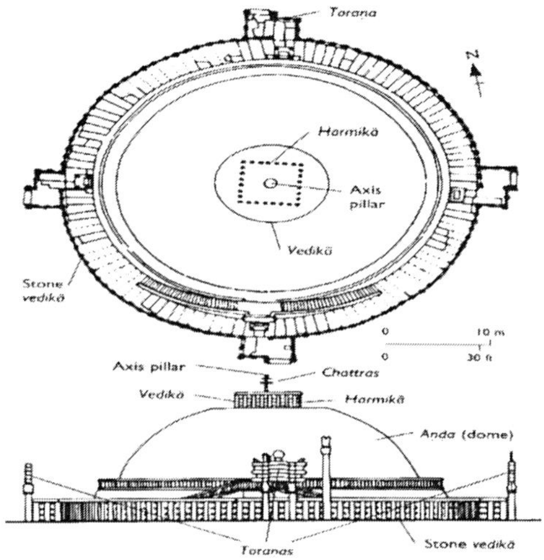

Source: The Cultural Heritage of India, The Arts (2006)

The architecture of the Sanchi stupa demonstrates the early development of Buddhist architectural forms and motifs in India. Its emphasis on sculptural reliefs, elaborate gateways, and symbolic elements reflects the evolving religious practices and artistic expressions of the time. The Great Stupa at Sanchi stands as a remarkable testament to the enduring legacy of Buddhist architecture and serves as a revered pilgrimage site for Buddhists and visitors from around the world ("Great Stupa | History, Description, & Facts | Britannica", 2023).

2. **Cave Temples**: Another significant development in Buddhist architecture was the creation of cave temples, particularly in the rock-cut tradition (Wauchope, 1981). Cave temples provided secluded spaces for meditation and worship. The earliest cave temples, such as those at Ajanta and Ellora in India, were carved out of solid rock and adorned with intricate sculptures and

paintings. These cave temples served as monastic dwellings and centres of religious activities (Wauchope 1981).

a) **Ajanta Caves:** The architecture of the Ajanta Caves, located in Maharashtra, India, represents a remarkable fusion of Buddhist art, sculpture, and architectural design. These cave temples were excavated from the 2nd century BCE to the 5th century CE and consist of approximately 30 rock-cut caves ("Ajanta Caves | Buddhist | Encyclopedia of Art", 2022). Here are the key architectural elements and characteristics of the Ajanta Caves:

b) **Cave Layout:** The Ajanta Caves are organized on a horseshoe-shaped cliff, overlooking the Waghora River. The caves are numbered sequentially and arranged in two groups, with the older caves belonging to the Hinayana Buddhist phase and the later caves representing the Mahayana Buddhist phase.

c) **Chaitya Halls:** The earlier caves at Ajanta, such as Cave 9 and Cave 10, are chaitya halls ("Rock-Cut Architecture of India, The Ajanta Caves - Senses Atlas", 2020). These cave temples imitate wooden architecture and were created as places of worship ("Rock-Cut Architecture of India, The Ajanta Caves - Senses Atlas", 2020). The chaitya halls feature a central nave with a stupa at the end, surrounded by a circumambulatory path. The interior walls of these halls are adorned with sculptures, paintings, and ornamental motifs ("Ajanta Caves: A Masterpiece of Indian Architecture and Art - Architecture Journeys", 2023).

d) **Viharas:** The majority of the Ajanta Caves are viharas, monastic dwellings used by Buddhist monks for meditation, study, and communal living ("Ajanta Caves | Buddhist | Encyclopedia of Art", 2022). The viharas are characterized by a series of cells or chambers built around a central courtyard ("Rock-Cut Architecture of India, The Ajanta Caves - Senses Atlas", 2020). Each cell contains a small shrine, often carved with Buddhist deities or scenes from the life of the Buddha ("Buddhist Architecture in India", 2020).

e) **Pillared Facades:** The entrances to the Ajanta Caves are marked by elaborately carved pillared facades. These facades feature intricately carved columns with ornamental brackets and sculptural reliefs ("Ajanta Caves | Buddhist | Encyclopedia of Art", 2022). The pillared entrances provide an impressive gateway into the caves and serve as a transition from the external world to the sacred interior space ("Hidden Architecture, Ajanta Caves - Hidden Architecture", 2015).

f) **Sculptural Decorations:** The walls and pillars of the Ajanta Caves are adorned with a wealth of sculptural decorations ("Ajanta Caves: A Masterpiece of Indian Architecture and Art - Architecture Journeys", 2023). The sculptures depict various Buddhist deities, celestial beings, and scenes from Buddhist mythology ("Ajanta Caves | Buddhist | Encyclopedia of Art", 2022). The artistic style ranges from delicate and refined in the earlier caves to more expressive and dynamic in the later ones ("Hidden Architecture » Ajanta Caves - Hidden Architecture", 2015).

Murals and Paintings: Ajanta is renowned for its stunning murals and paintings, which adorn the walls and ceilings of several caves ("Ajanta Caves: A Masterpiece of Indian Architecture and Art - Architecture Journeys", 2023). These vibrant frescoes depict narratives from the life of the Buddha, Jataka tales, and various aspects of Buddhist philosophy and practice. The paintings exhibit a remarkable level of detail and display a mastery of colour, composition, and storytelling ("Hidden Architecture » Ajanta Caves - Hidden Architecture", 2015). The architecture of the Ajanta Caves exemplifies the artistic and architectural achievements of ancient Indian Buddhist culture. The rock-cut caves showcase the integration of religious devotion, artistic expression, and skilled craftsmanship.

Figure 2 Ajanta Caves

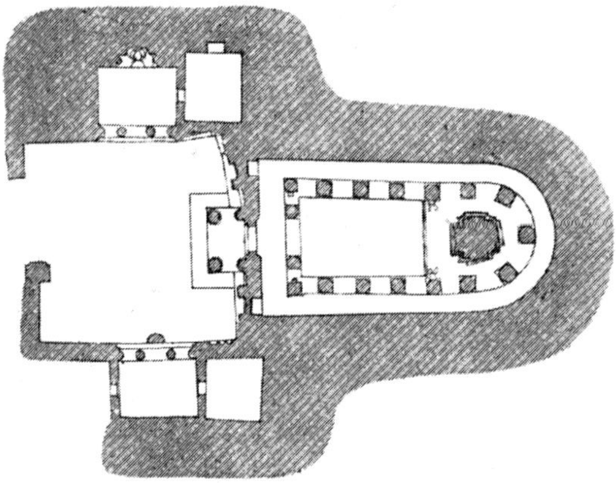

Figure 3 Entrance of Ajanta Caves

Source: "Hidden Architecture » Ajanta Caves - Hidden Architecture", 2015

3. **Chaitya Halls**: During the early centuries of the Common Era, Buddhist architects started constructing chaitya halls, which were specifically designed for congregational worship. Chaitya halls featured a central nave, usually with a stupa at the end, and a surrounding ambulatory path for circumambulation. These halls were adorned with sculptural reliefs, columns, and decorative elements("Buddhist Architecture in India", 2020). The Karla and Bhaja caves in western India are notable examples of chaitya

halls. Chaitya halls are a distinct architectural form found in Buddhist cave complexes, particularly in ancient India ("Buddhist Architecture in India" 2020). These halls served as places of congregational worship, meditation, and communal gatherings. Here are the key architectural elements and characteristics of chaitya halls:

a) **Layout and Orientation:** Chaitya halls are typically carved into the rock face of a hill or a cliff. They are designed as long, rectangular chambers with a semi-circular apse at one end. The apse houses a stupa, which is a sacred mound or monument representing the enlightened mind of the Buddha ("Folk Music - Art and Culture Notes", 2023).
b) **Nave and Aisles:** The interior of a chaitya hall consists of a central nave, a raised pathway running along the length of the hall. The nave is flanked by a series of columns or pillars that divide it from the side aisles. The columns may be plain or intricately carved, adding aesthetic beauty to the space ("Buddhist Architecture in India", 2020).
c) **Ribbed Vaulted Ceiling:** One of the distinctive architectural features of chaitya halls is their ribbed vaulted ceiling. The ceiling is divided into a series of arches or ribs that meet at the apex, forming a vaulted structure. The ribs not only provide structural support but also create a sense of height and spaciousness within the hall ("Folk Music - Art and Culture Notes", 2023).
d) **Facade and Entrance:** The entrance façade of a chaitya hall is often elaborately decorated and serves as an architectural focal point. It features large, intricately carved pillars with ornate capitals and brackets. The entrance is usually marked by a horseshoe-shaped arch known as a chaitya window, which symbolizes the doorway to spiritual enlightenment ("Folk Music - Art and Culture Notes", 2023).

e) **Sculptural Decorations:** Chaitya halls are adorned with sculptural decorations, particularly on the pillars, walls, and apse. These sculptures depict Buddhist deities, celestial beings, and scenes from the life of the Buddha. The sculptural reliefs often convey narratives from Buddhist mythology and teachings, creating an immersive visual experience for the devotees ("Folk Music - Art and Culture Notes", 2023).

f) **Stupa and Circumambulation**: The apse of a chaitya hall houses a stupa, which is a central object of veneration. The stupa represents the presence of the Buddha and serves as a focal point for devotional practices. Devotees would perform circumambulation, walking in a clockwise direction around the stupa while chanting prayers or mantras (Shelby, 2013).

g) **Symbolic Elements:** The architecture of Chaitya halls incorporates several symbolic elements. The semi-circular shape of the apse represents the cosmic form of the universe and the sacredness of space. The rhythmic repetition of architectural elements, such as pillars and arches, creates a sense of harmony and spiritual resonance ("Folk Music - Art and Culture Notes", 2023). The stupa within the apse symbolizes the enlightened mind and the ultimate goal of spiritual liberation.

Chaitya halls are revered as sacred spaces in Buddhism, providing a place for communal worship, meditation, and contemplation. The architectural design of these halls, with their impressive vaulted ceilings, sculptural adornments, and symbolic elements, creates an immersive and inspiring environment for Buddhist practitioners and visitors alike.

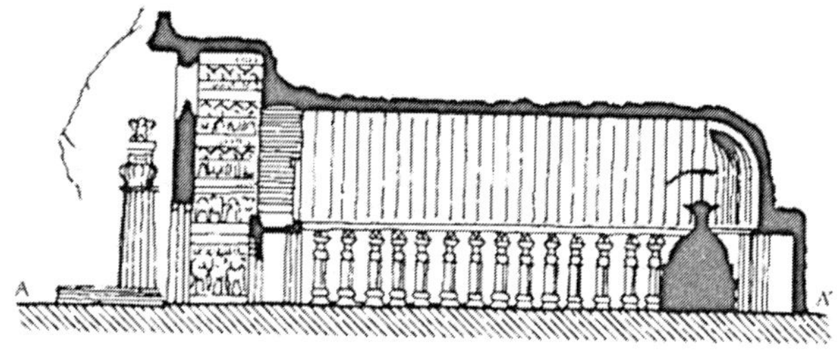

Figure 4 Chaitya Hall Sectional Elevation

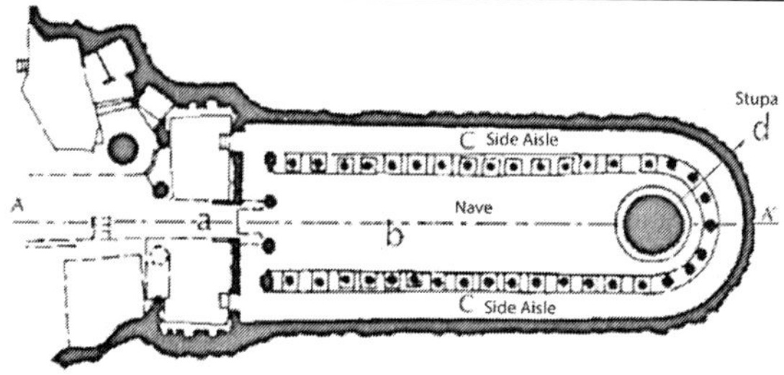

Figure 5 Chaitya Hall Plan

Source: "WMU - Art History | Art History, History, Art"

4. Monastery or Viharas

The architecture of Buddhist monasteries, also known as viharas, evolved over time to meet the needs of the Buddhist monastic community. Viharas served as residential quarters for monks, centres for religious education, and spaces for communal activities. Here are the key architectural elements and characteristics of Buddhist monasteries or viharas:

a) **Layout and Plan:** Viharas typically followed a rectangular or square plan. The layout consisted of a central courtyard surrounded by a series of cells or chambers. The courtyard served as a gathering space and provided natural light and ventilation to the surrounding rooms.

a) **Main Assembly Hall:** The main assembly hall, also known as the Buddha Hall or the preaching hall, was the focal point of the vihara ("Buddhist Architecture in India", 2020). It was a spacious hall where the monks gathered for daily rituals, meditation, and teachings. The hall often featured a raised platform or dais where the Buddha statue or an important relic was enshrined ("Buddhist Architecture in India", 2020).

b) **Cells for Monks:** The vihara included individual cells or rooms for resident monks. These cells served as living quarters, providing privacy and solitude for meditation and personal study ("Viharas - Art and Culture Notes", 2023). Each cell typically consisted of a small room with minimal furnishings, such as a bed or a mat, and a personal shrine ("Viharas - Art and Culture Notes", 2023).

c) **Stupas and Shrines:** Viharas often included smaller stupas or shrines dedicated to important Buddhist figures or deities. These shrines provided focal points for devotional practices and offerings ("Buddhist Architecture in India", 2020). They were adorned with sculptural reliefs, paintings, or symbolic representations of the Buddha ("Viharas - Art and Culture Notes", 2023).

d) **Lecture Halls and Libraries:** Buddhist monasteries housed lecture halls and libraries where monks engaged in religious education and intellectual pursuits ("Viharas - Art and Culture Notes", 2023). Lecture halls provided spaces for teaching and discourse, while libraries housed sacred scriptures, manuscripts, and commentaries ("Viharas - Art and Culture Notes", 2023).

e) **Courtyards and Gardens:** Viharas typically had courtyards or open spaces, often with gardens or landscaped areas. These outdoor spaces provide areas for relaxation, walking meditation, and contemplation amidst natural surroundings. Gardens were sometimes designed with symbolic elements, such as lotus ponds and Bodhi trees.

f) **Decorative Elements:** Viharas were adorned with decorative elements, including ornate carvings, murals, and paintings.

Sculptures and reliefs depicted scenes from the life of the Buddha, stories from Buddhist mythology, and symbols of spiritual significance. The artistic embellishments added beauty and inspired devotion within the vihara ("Viharas - Art and Culture Notes", 2023).

g) **Monastic Infrastructure:** In addition to the living quarters, viharas often included essential facilities for monastic life, such as kitchens, dining halls, and bathing areas. These facilities supported the practical needs of the resident monks and promoted communal living (Tadgell, 1990).

The architecture of Buddhist monasteries or viharas varied across different regions and time periods, incorporating local architectural styles and cultural influences. Nonetheless, the Vihara architecture emphasized simplicity, tranquillity, and functionality to provide an environment conducive to meditation, study, and the practice of the Buddhist path ("Viharas - Art and Culture Notes", 2023).

Figure 6 A Vihara

Source: Buddhist Architecture in India, 2020

h) **Ashoka Pillar:** Starting from the Mauryan period to the Middle age, Sanchi was the centre of the monuments of many religions. It was famous for the stupa which was built by Ashoka (Phuoc 2010b). Some of its parts were ruined during the excavation by

Archaeologists. During the first BC, its four gateways were built. The models of those gateways might have been made of wood before the construction of stone gateways (Shakya, 2021). They have beautiful sculptural art with high technical skills. This says about the life History of Buddha.

Sarnath is the famous holy place of Buddhism, where Buddha started his first preaching. During the excavations between 1904 and 1928, many monuments were found here. There was a Stupa with an 18-meter diameter in the shape of a hemisphere which was built by Ashoka (Shakya, 2021). Near this stupa, a monolithic Pillar of Ashoka with Dharma Chakra was found and had an elephant on top to reflect the elephant that Maya had dreamed of. To symbolize this sacred location, King Ashoka constructed a pillar with an elephant capital.

The elephant is thought to be a depiction of the white elephant that Lord Buddha's mother dreamed about when Siddhartha was conceived. The Ashoka column, which is 21 meters tall and has carved images on all four sides surrounds it, as well as a stupa. The architecture of the Aśoka pillar has several animals utilized by King Ashoka in his various pillars that were erected throughout India (Shakya, 2021). There are seven full capitals left, five of which feature lions, one an elephant, and another with a zebu bull. The animals symbolize the four directions as the Elephant is the capital of the East, the Lion is for the north, the Bull is for the south and the horse is for the West (K. Shelby 2015). The four lions of Sarnath have become India's State Emblem. The animal capitals are made up of a loti form basis, an abacus with floral, symbolic, or animal motifs, and a realistic image of an animal, each of which is considered to represent a different Indian tradition. The pillar displays 'Workmanship' and the circular shaft is finely polished such that it shines like a mirror.

Figure 7 Ashoka Pillar

Lion Capital, Sarnath

Source: Reddy, 2022

Buddhist architecture is characterized by several distinct features and elements that reflect the principles, symbolism, and aesthetics of Buddhism. Here are some of the key characteristics of Buddhist architecture:

Stupas: Stupas are prominent architectural structures in Buddhism. They are mound-like structures typically containing relics or sacred objects. Stupas represent the enlightened mind of the Buddha and serve as focal points for devotion and meditation (Fogelin 2015).

Pagodas: Pagodas are multi-tiered towers commonly found in East Asian Buddhist architecture. They are often characterized by a series of stacked roofs with upturned eaves ("Pagoda: A Buddhist Architecture" n.d.). Pagodas serve as religious structures, housing relics, sacred texts, or statues of the Buddha.

Symbolic Design: Buddhist architecture often incorporates symbolic design elements. Circular shapes symbolize the endless cycle of birth, death, and rebirth, while square or rectangular shapes represent stability and order. The use of sacred geometry and precise proportions is also common.

Mudras and Hand Gestures: Sculptures and statues in Buddhist architecture frequently depict the Buddha or Bodhisattvas in specific mudras or hand gestures. These mudras represent different qualities or states of mind, such as compassion, meditation, or fearlessness.

Mandalas and Yantras: Mandalas and yantras are geometric patterns used in Buddhist architecture to represent the universe and cosmic order. These intricate designs, often displayed on temple floors or walls, are considered sacred and serve as aids for meditation and spiritual focus.

Decorative Carvings and Sculptures: Intricate carvings and sculptures are integral to Buddhist architecture. These artistic elements often depict scenes from the life of the Buddha, Jataka tales (stories of the Buddha's previous lives), celestial beings, and mythological figures. They serve as aids for contemplation and inspiration. Use of Natural Elements: Buddhist architecture often integrates natural elements, such as water, rocks, and gardens, to create harmonious environments ("Buddhist Architecture in India", 2020). Water features, like lotus ponds, symbolize purity and enlightenment, while carefully curated gardens provide spaces for meditation and reflection.

Emphasis on Light and Space: Buddhist architecture often utilizes natural light and open spaces to create a sense of openness and transcendence (Matracchi and Habibabad, 2022). Windows, skylights, and strategically placed openings allow light to illuminate the interior spaces, fostering an atmosphere of spiritual illumination (Matracchi and Habibabad, 2022). Temples and Monasteries:

Buddhist architecture includes temples and monasteries as important structures for worship, meditation, and communal activities. The characteristics of Buddhist architecture may vary across different regions and periods, reflecting the local cultural influences and architectural traditions. Nonetheless, these common elements and principles of design contribute to the spiritual and aesthetic qualities of Buddhist architectural expressions.

The analysis has explored different architectural elements of Buddhism in India, including stupas, viharas, pillars, chaitya halls, monasteries, and cave temples. Stupas are domed structures that house relics or represent significant Buddhist sites, with the Great Stupa of Sanchi being a well-known and well-preserved example. Viharas are residential complexes for Buddhist monks, providing spaces for individual meditation, communal study, and group activities. The Ashoka Pillar at Sarnath, adorned with the Lion Capital, holds great significance as a Buddhist emblem. Chaitya halls serve as prayer halls and sanctuaries, characterized by unique architectural features like intricate wood carvings, vaulted ceilings, and prominent stupas. Buddhist monasteries, also known as viharas, serve as vital centres for spiritual growth, community living, and the preservation of Buddhist teachings. Cave temples, exemplified by the Ajanta and Ellora Caves in Maharashtra, are rock-cut structures used for worship, meditation, and monk residences. These caves showcase intricate sculptures and vibrant murals depicting various Buddhist narratives.

Conclusion

The impact of Buddhist tradition and knowledge on architecture has been extensive and significant. Buddhism has greatly influenced architectural styles, techniques, and symbolism, particularly in Asia. The emphasis on spiritual enlightenment, compassion, and harmony with nature has left a lasting impression on architectural design. Buddhist architecture is characterized by sacred and symbolic elements such as stupas, pagodas, mudras, and mandalas, which hold deeper meanings and facilitate spiritual experiences. The creation of sacred spaces for worship, meditation, and communal activities, such as monasteries and temples, has been a notable contribution of Buddhism to architecture.

These structures serve as places that inspire and support the spiritual journey. Buddhist knowledge and philosophy have also influenced architectural aesthetics and principles, with an emphasis on balance, proportion, and harmony, as well as the incorporation of natural elements. The transmission of Buddhist tradition across different regions has led to diverse architectural styles that still embody the core principles of Buddhism. Furthermore, Buddhist teachings and values have impacted architectural concepts like sustainable design and the integration of spirituality into built environments. Overall, the influence of Buddhist tradition and knowledge on architecture is profound, shaping not only physical structures but also the spiritual and aesthetic experiences within them. The fusion of Buddhist philosophy, symbolism, and artistic expression has given rise to architectural forms that inspire devotion, spiritual growth, and harmony with oneself and the world. The existing research in this field is limited, and there is scope for further exploration and incorporation of additional studies.

References

A guide to Buddhist hand gestures – Curious Christian. (n.d.) Retrieved June 3, 2023. https://curiouschristian.blog/2017/12/02/a-guide-to-buddhist-hand-gestures/

Ajanta Caves | Buddhist | Encyclopedia of art. (2022). https://mapacademy.io/article/ajanta-caves/, *2022*.

Buddhist architecture in India. (2020). https://www.india-a2z.com/buddhist-architecture-in-india.html

“Chaitya Hall | Karla Caves | Lonavala Maharashtra | India.” (2016). http://www.karlacaves.com/blog/chaityahall-at-karlacaves/

Evolution and development of ecosystem. (n.d.) Retrieved June 3, 2023. https://www.archinomy.com/case-studies/evolution-and-development-of-chaitya-halls/

Folk music – Art and culture notes. (2023). https://prepp.in/news/e-492-chaityas-art-and-culture-notes

Great stupa | History, description, and facts | Britannica. (2023). https://www.britannica.com/place/Great-Stupa-Buddhist-monument-Sanchi-India

‘Hidden Architecture’ Ajanta Caves – Hidden architecture. (2015). http://hiddenarchitecture.net/ajanta-caves/

‘Indian Architecture (Buddhist and Hindu Periods) | INDIAN CULTURE.’ n.d. (2023) Accessed June 2. https://books.google.co.in/books?hl=en&lr=&id=0kd9CgAAQBAJ&oi=fnd&pg=PT10&dq=hindu+buddhist+architecture&ots=-2SOuSM7Hp&sig=4B3aojqoWS0R2NU0VchkPhcS6l4&redir_esc=y#v=onepage&q&f=false

Pagoda: A Buddhist architecture. (n.d.) Retrieved June 3, 2023. https://www.buddhashop.net/blog/pagoda/

Rock-cut architecture of India, the Ajanta Caves – Senses atlas. (2020). https://www.sensesatlas.com/territory/rock-cut-architecture-of-india-the-ajanta-caves/

Sanchi monument: A rediscovery. (n.d.). *Indian Culture* Retrieved June 3, 2023. https://indianculture.gov.in/stories/sanchi-monument-rediscovery

Symbolism of a stupa – Sacred space. (n.d.) Retrieved June 3, 2023. http://thesacredspace.in/symbolism-of-a-stupa/

UPSC note on Buddhism architecture by Unacademy. (n.d.) Retrieved June 3, 2023. https://unacademy.com/content/upsc/study-material/ancient-history/buddhism-architecture/

Viharas – Art and culture notes. (2023). https://prepp.in/news/e-492-viharas-art-and-culture-notes, *2023*.

WMU – Art history | Art history, history, art. (n.d.) Retrieved June 3, 2023. https://www.pinterest.com/pin/487233253416296553/

Yantra, mandala, mantra, and Tantra. (n.d.). *Differences Explained* Retrieved June 3, 2023. https://www.traditionalbodywork.com/understanding-tantras-yantras-mantras-and-mandalas/

Fogelin, L. (2015). *An archaeological history of Indian Buddhism. An archaeological history of Indian Buddhism*. Oxford University Press. https://doi.org/10.1093/acprof:oso/9780199948215.001.0001

Harvey, P. (1984). The symbolism of the early Stūpa. *Journal of the International Association of Buddhist Studies*. History.com. https://www.history.com/topics/religion/buddhism, 7(2), 67–94. ISSN: 2507-0347. History.com Editors. (2021). "Buddhism - Definition, Founder & Origins - HISTORY."

Matracchi, P., & Sadeghi habibabad, A. (2022). Prioritizing the effect of "light" in the religious places and environments with an emphasis on the sense of spirituality. *Ain Shams Engineering Journal*, *13*(1). https://doi.org/10.1016/j.asej.2021.05.028

Phuoc, & Le Huu. (2010). Buddhist architecture. https://buddhism.lib.ntu.edu.tw/DLMBS/en/search/search_detail.jsp?seq=373203

Reynolds, F. (1964). Buddhist monks and monasteries of India. Sukumar Dutt. *Journal of Religion*, *44*(3), 273–273. https://doi.org/10.1086/485716

Shakya, A. (2021). The place where Buddha descended from T ā Vatimsa heaven: Sankassa, *12*(49321), 115–118. ISSN: 0976-6650.

Karen, S. (2013). *Buddhist monasteries (article) | Buddhism | Khan academy.* https://www.khanacademy.org/humanities/ap-art-history/introduction-cultures-religions-apah/buddhism-apah/a/buddhist-monasteries, *2013*.

Tadgell, C. (1990). *The history of architecture in India: From the dawn of civilization tot he end of the raj*, *336*.

The cultural heritage of India the arts. (2006). https://www.exoticindiaart.com/book/details/cultural-heritage-of-india-volume-vii-arts-idj862/, *7*.

Wauchope, R. S. (1981). The Buddhist cave temples of India. https://www.indianetzone.com/44/buddhist_cave_temples_india.htm

Wong, W. S. (2014). "Atiner's Conference Paper Series ARC2014-1094 Stupa , Pagoda and Chorten –," 1–16. http://www.atiner.gr

Zhu, X. (1986). On the alignment of quasars. *Chinese Astronomy and Astrophysics*, *10*(2), 94–97. https://doi.org/10.1016/0275-1062(86)90033-0

***

ADAPTING VAASTU PRINCIPLES FOR SUSTAINABLE AND INNOVATIVE ARCHITECTURE

Ar. Shaila Naaz

Assistant Professor, School of Architecture and Design

K.R. Mangalam University, Gurugram

Abstract

Vastu shastra is one of the most ancient architectural belief systems which tells us how the area of the building should be planned, and the principles designed to make use of the environment and more specifically climate (Fazeli and Goodarzi 2010). There are many rules and philosophies based on the sun's rays, the earth's poles and the geopathic zones, legislating in ancient Indian architecture dealing with environmental criteria that are seen as a superstition, nowadays (Fazeli and Goodarzi, 2010). But in recent years, there has been increasing interest in incorporating the principles of Vastu shastra into the modern architecture of buildings and houses (Kiran and Subodh, 2023). In this paper, Vastu Shastra is explained and has been compared with the contemporary architecture of the house (Patra, 2017). This paper will explore the intersection of Vastu Shastra and modern architecture and examine the potential benefits and challenges of incorporating these principles into contemporary designs of architecture (Kiran and Subodh, 2023). The objective of this study is to analyze how Vastu Shastra principles can be adapted to promote sustainability and innovation in architectural design. The research methodology includes a comprehensive review of Vastu literature, case studies of existing sustainable buildings that incorporate Vastu principles, and interviews with architects and designers experienced in Vastu-inspired designs. The findings of this study reveal several key areas where Vastu principles can be adapted for sustainable and innovative architecture.

The chapter concludes with a set of guidelines and recommendations for architects and designers seeking to incorporate Vastu principles into sustainable and innovative architecture. By combining the ancient wisdom of Vastu Shastra with contemporary sustainable design practices, a new paradigm of architecture can emerge that promotes holistic well-being, environmental stewardship, and innovation in the built environment.

Keywords: Vastu Shastra, Eco-Friendly Materials, Sacred Geometry, Technology Integration, Holistic Well-Being.

Introduction

The origin of Vastu shastra was found in the Sthapatya Veda, a subdivision of the Atharva Veda (Pandey, 2022). The fusion of art and science incorporated into architecture is known as Vastu shastra which was formulated in prehistoric times. The principles of Vastu shastra have been passed down from ancestors along with modifications to make them consistent with the needs of the generation. Vastu Shastra is colliding with the new fashion and style in Indian Architecture. Earlier, it was considered the science of the past and in the present, it is based on science and validity (Hotwani et al., 2022). The Vastu shastra includes principles of design, layout measurement, ground preparation, spatial arrangement and spatial geometry. Incorporating Buddhist and Hindu beliefs. (Barodia n.d.). Vastu rings in a balance between man and nature (Wahaj, 2019). It is the science of building design and planning that deals with the study and practice of the inter-relationship of the forces of nature, heavenly bodies and the supernatural elements in the cosmos (Pandey 2022).

Figure 1 Vastu Purush

Source: Vastu Purusha Mandala All you Need to Know (housing.com)

Vastu Shastra: A Brief

Vastu literature refers to the ancient Indian texts and scriptures that outline the principles and guidelines for designing and constructing buildings in harmony with nature and cosmic energies. Vastu Shastra, also known as the "science of architecture," is a traditional Indian system of architecture that encompasses these principles. Studying Vastu literature involves delving into various ancient texts and manuscripts that form the foundation of Vastu Shastra. Studying Vastu literature involves examining these texts, understanding the underlying principles and concepts, and applying them to architectural design and construction.

Figure 2 Vastu Core Principles

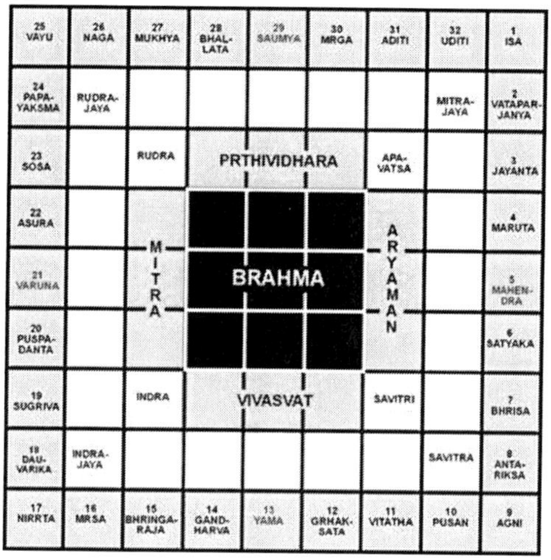

Source: Vastu Purusha Mandala All you Need to Know (housing.com)

It requires a deep understanding of Vastu Shastra's core principles, such as the orientation of buildings, the use of sacred geometry, and the incorporation of natural elements and energies. It is important to note that while Vastu Shastra holds cultural and historical significance, its principles may not always align with modern architectural practices and scientific understanding. Therefore, a critical and balanced approach is necessary when studying Vastu literature to incorporate relevant aspects into contemporary architectural design. Some of the significant texts include:

i) **Brihat Samhita:** Authored by Varahamihira, this ancient text covers a wide range of subjects, including Vastu Shastra. It includes information on site selection, soil analysis, building materials, and construction techniques.

ii) **Vastu Purusha Mandala:** This is a crucial text that describes the symbolic representation of the Vastu Purusha, an energy grid that governs the layout and proportions of a building. It provides guidelines for the placement of rooms, entrances, and other architectural elements.

Figure 3 Vastu Purush Mandala

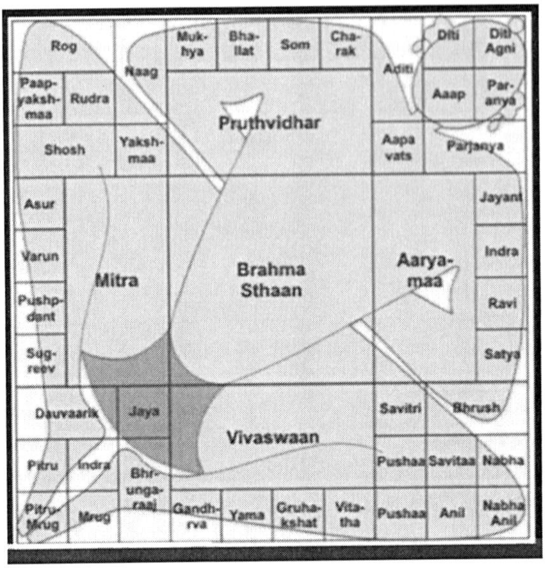

Source: Scientific Vastu | designing a house | an architect explains (architectureideas.info)

iii) **Manasara:** This comprehensive text focuses on various aspects of architecture, including town planning, building construction, and sculptural elements. It provides detailed guidelines for the design of temples, palaces, and residential buildings.

iv) **Mayamatam:** Written by Maya Danava, this text is a compilation of architectural principles and construction techniques. It covers topics such as town planning, building materials, structural design, and the symbolism behind architectural features.

v) **Vishwakarma Vastushastra:** This text is dedicated to the principles of Vastu Shastra and guides building design, layout, and the integration of natural elements. It covers both residential and commercial architecture.

vi) **Silparatna:** This text focuses on the construction of temples and religious structures. It provides guidelines on temple architecture, rituals, and the positioning of deities.

Fundamentals of Vastu Shastra

Fundamentals of Vastu Shastra revolve around the cosmic forces and the energies they produce, which impact the Earth. The foundation of Vastu Shastra is based on the five elements: Earth, Water, Air, Fire, and Space:

i) **Earth (Prithvi):** Represents stability and strength. It symbolizes a solid foundation and grounding.
ii) **Water (Jala):** Represents fluidity and purity. It signifies the flow of emotions and balance.
iii) **Air (Vayu):** Represents movement and circulation. It signifies freshness and vitality.
iv) **Fire (Agni):** Represents energy and transformation. It symbolizes warmth, enthusiasm, and purification.
v) **Space (Aakash):** Represents openness and expansiveness. It signifies the availability of space for positive energy to flow.

These elements are believed to form the basis of the universe, including the Earth and the human body. Vastu Shastra acknowledges that the universe is in a constant state of motion and requires a significant amount of energy. This energy encompasses all materials present in the universe. Humans are interconnected with nature, which is influenced by various energies and forces that affect the Earth.

Figure 4 Elements of Vastu Shastra

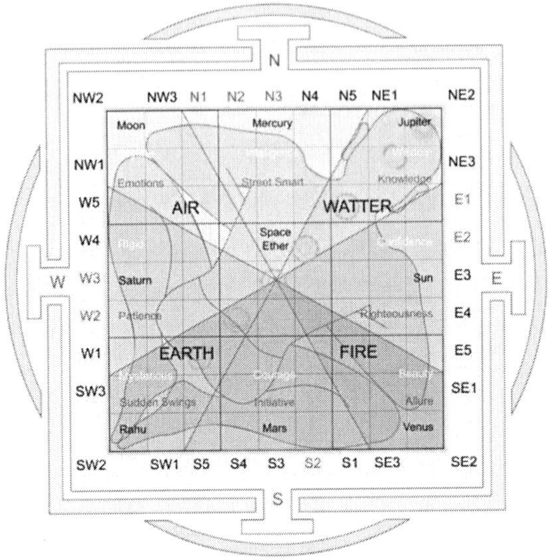

Source: Vastu Shastra: Ancient Science of Architecture | Latest Facts (squareyards.com)

Some of the energies and forces influencing the Earth include:

i) Solar Radiation: The energy emitted by the Sun impacts the Earth's environment, climate, and life forms.

ii) Magnetic Field of Earth: The Earth's magnetic field interacts with various elements and influences energy flow.

iii) Gravitational Force: The force of attraction between objects, which plays a role in shaping the Earth's structure and energy distribution.

iv) Intensity and Wind Direction: The strength and direction of the wind affect the flow of energy and environmental conditions.

Every material in the universe emits a certain amount of energy, and these energies interact with one another and with the Earth, creating a complex web of interconnected energies. Vastu Shastra recognizes the influence of cosmic forces and energies on the Earth and emphasizes the balance and harmonious integration of the five elements to create a positive and conducive living environment.

Components of Vastu Shastra

The Vastu Shastra encompasses various aspects related to the placement of different spaces and objects. It covers site selection, the relationship between open spaces and built structures, the orientation of entrances, bedrooms, kitchens, prayer rooms, store rooms, study rooms, and more. Vastu Shastra is a well-established science that offers satisfactory solutions to questions regarding the physical, climatological, and social influences on building design, suited to the present-day context. A good Vastu design involves the correct orientation and placement of spaces corresponding to the cardinal directions. With technological advancements, certain natural forces can now be controlled using mechanical means (e.g., using air conditioners for indoor air quality). This raises the question of whether Vastu Shastra is still applicable in today's context.

Summary of the directions, associated deities, effects, and recommended spaces according to Vastu Shastra:

- North: Associated with Kuber (deity of wealth and prosperity).

  Recommended spaces include the living room, seating areas, office, and entrance.

- North-East: Associated with Ishwar (deity of religion and the trinity).

  Recommended spaces include the puja room, well, and underground water tank.

- East: Associated with Indra (deity of progress and growth).

  Recommended spaces include the entrance, guestroom, verandah, and bathroom.

- South-East: Associated with Agni (deity of energy, vigour, and strength).

  Recommended spaces include the kitchen, generator, and power supply.

- South: Associated with Yama (deity of death).

  Recommended spaces include the backyard and kitchen garden.

- South-West: Associated with Nairut (demon representing purity and cleanliness). Recommended spaces include the toilet, septic tank, washing area, and water closet.

- West: Associated with Varun (deity of water).

  Recommended spaces include the overhead tank and study room.

- North-West: Associated with Vayu (deity of air/wind).

  Recommended space includes the bedroom.

- Above: Associated with Brahma (deity of spiritual knowledge).

  Recommended space is the courtyard.

- Below: Associated with Ananta (representing resources and worldly pleasures). Recommended space is the basement.

Residential Building Layout as per Vastu

i) **Parking Area:** The ideal location for a parking area is the southwest corner, facing west or south. It is advised to avoid parking in the northeast direction as it is considered inauspicious.

ii) **Entrance Of the House:** The most auspicious direction for the entrance of a home is the east, as it allows positive energy and light into the household due to the rising sun. Another suitable direction for the house entrance is the northeast.

iii) **Veranda:** The best directions to construct a balcony or veranda are the northern and eastern directions. North to northeast and east are considered positive directions, while south and southwest are considered negative directions. A veranda provides a welcoming and comfortable sitting area outside the main entrance of the house and protects it from direct rain.

iv) **Living Room or Hall:** The living room should ideally be in the north or east direction. If the house is south-facing, the living room can be located in the southeast corner. It is recommended to have windows in the north and east directions to welcome the morning sunlight. The ideal size for a living room is around 170 sq. ft or 16 sq. m

v) **Dining Room:** The dining room should be connected to the kitchen and can be located on the south, west, or east side of the house. The ideal direction for a dining room is the west. According to Vastu Shastra, the dining table should be placed in the southeast direction of the house to promote harmony and happiness during meal times.

vi) **Pooja Room:** The preferred directions for a pooja room are the northeast, east, or north. These directions are considered auspicious. It is important to avoid placing the pooja room beneath staircases or next to toilets to prevent negative energy. The recommended size for a medium-sized enclosed pooja room is at least 5x7 feet.

vii) **Kitchen:** The ideal location for the kitchen is the southeast corner of the house. It should be used for cooking while facing the east. However, it is advised not to position the kitchen directly in front of the main entrance.

viii) **Master Bedroom:** The master bedroom should be situated in the southwest corner of an east-facing home. This positioning ensures a peaceful sleep without being disturbed by cooking smells or noises. It is recommended to have square or rectangular-shaped rooms for the master bedroom, allowing other activities to take place in different areas of the house.

ix) **Bathroom/Toilets:** The placement of bathrooms is also crucial from both Vastu and general health and aesthetic perspectives. Toilets should be located in the northwest corner of the building or the northwest corner of the rooms. If this is not feasible, southeast toilets are acceptable. It is also advisable (and logical) to keep the toilets, kitchen, and prayer room in the house separate from each other.

x) **Store Room:** The store room should be placed in the northwest or southwest corner of the house. This helps prevent clutter accumulation. It is important not to locate the store room in the east or north directions. The southwest direction is suitable for storing heavy equipment.

xi) **Staircase or Lift:** For internal staircases, the southwest portion of the property is considered ideal, followed by the south and west portions. The staircase should start from the north and go towards the south. It is not advisable to have a staircase in the northeast corner as it may lead to financial losses. Staircases in any corner other than the western or southern corner are believed to bring negative effects.

Figure 5 House Plan according to Vastu

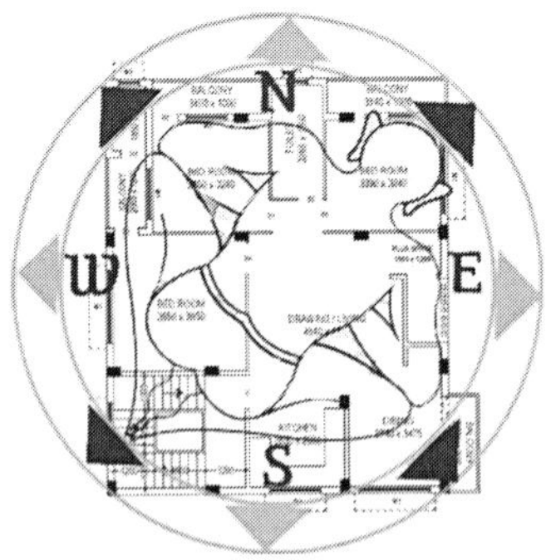

Source: Vastu Purusha Mandala All you Need to Know (housing.com)

Plants and Trees as per Vastu

i) **Bamboo Plant:** Bamboo plants are versatile, and suitable for both indoor and outdoor environments. They are associated with good health, longevity, and resilience, representing strength and modesty. It is believed that planting bamboo in the southeast region can bring wealth to the family while placing it in the east can attract good health. Bamboo's longevity is reflected in its lifespan of 400-500 years.

ii) **Catharanthus roseus (Barmasi/Sadabahar):** Catharanthus roseus, also known as Barmasi or Sadabahar, is nicknamed the "ever-blooming blossom." This plant can be placed on balconies or in personal gardens to create a cheerful ambience.

iii) **Tulasi or Basil:** Holy Basil, commonly known as Tulsi, is considered highly auspicious. It has a dual benefit as it acts as a pleasantly aromatic and energizes the entrance door. Tulsi is believed to have a tonic effect on the atmosphere, and watering it daily is said to bring financial success. Growing Tulsi in one's home or garden is believed to have spiritual healing effects.

iv) **Mint Plant:** Mint is a herb associated with enhanced understanding and communication in the realm of love and relationships. It is believed to attract prosperity and wealth. Placing fresh mint under a pillow is said to receive messages from the Divine and the Universe; placing a mint plant near a bedroom window can ward off nightmares and evil spirits. Keeping dried mint herbs near the office desk is thought to attract prosperity and abundance. Mint can also be kept around sick individuals to repel negative energy.

v) **Lavender:** Lavender is known for promoting restful sleep and calming nerves. It is used to attract love and commitment in relationships, making it suitable for the window area of a couple's bedroom.

vi) **Jade Plant:** Jade plants, with their round and succulent leaves resembling coins, symbolize wealth and abundance. They are believed to bring good fortune, prosperity, and happiness to the home. Keeping a jade plant near the cash register or cash box can improve the flow of money. Placing a jade Vastu plant near the entrance of a business is thought to bring success and prosperity.

vii) **Fern (Morpanki):** Ferns serve as natural air purifiers and are welcoming plants, making them ideal for workspaces or entrance areas. They are lush and help maintain good energy in the environment. Ferns can be placed in bathrooms or on top of bookshelves as trailing plants.

viii) **Jasmine (Mogra):** Jasmine symbolizes gratitude, love, and success according to ancient literature. It represents happiness in relationships and is known for its delicate fragrance, which reduces stress and promotes relaxation. Jasmine is considered a lucky plant for the home.

Site planning according to Vastu

When planning the site for a project according to Vastu Shastra, there are several key considerations to keep in mind.

i) **The shape of the Plot:** Preferably, choose a plot that is square or rectangular in shape. Irregular or triangular plots may disrupt the flow of energy.

ii) **Orientation:** The ideal orientation for the main entrance of the building is towards the east or north. This allows for the entry of positive energy and natural light. Avoid having the main entrance face south or southwest.

Figure 6 Building Orientation

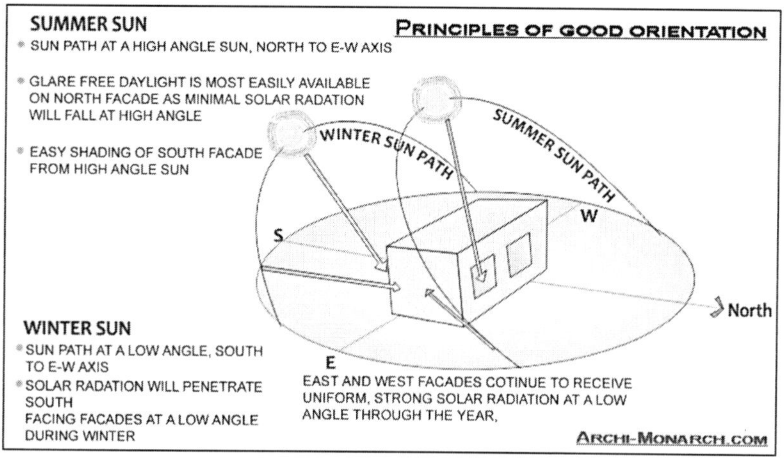

Source: Building orientation for passive design ⋆ archi-monarch

Boundaries and Fencing: Ensure that the boundaries of the plot are well-defined and in good condition. Use fences or walls to demarcate the property as this provides a sense of security and privacy.

iii) **Open Space:** Leave ample open space on the north and east sides of the plot. This allows for the free flow of positive energy and enhances the overall harmony of the site. Avoid clutter or obstructions in these areas.

iv) **Water Bodies:** If possible, include a water body, such as a pond or fountain, towards the northeast or north direction of the plot. Water elements symbolize prosperity and attract positive energy.

v) **Driveway and Pathways:** Design the driveway or pathways leading to the main entrance in a smooth, curving manner. Avoid sharp turns or irregular shapes. The pathway should be wide and well-lit, creating a welcoming approach.

vi) **Placement of Structures:** Position the main building or structures towards the southwest or west side of the plot. This helps create stability and provides a sense of strength. Leave more open space on the north and east sides.

vii) **Landscaping:** Incorporate greenery and landscaping throughout the site. Plant trees and flowers, particularly in the northeast and east areas. Ensure that plants and trees are healthy and well-maintained.

viii) **Utilities and Services:** Place utilities, such as electrical meters, generators, or water tanks, in the northeast or north direction. This helps maintain a positive energy flow and prevents any obstructions.

ix) **Parking:** Designate parking areas towards the southeast or northwest of the site. Ensure there is enough space for vehicles to move comfortably. Avoid parking in the northeast corner.

Landscaping for a Resort in Delhi-NCR according to Vastu

i) **Open Space and Flow:** Designate ample open space in the north and east areas of the resort for a free flow of positive energy. Keep these areas clean, clutter-free, and well-maintained. Avoid blocking or obstructing the flow of energy with excessive structures or landscaping elements.

ii) **Gardens and Plantings:** Create well-manicured gardens and lush green spaces within the resort. Use a variety of plants and flowers to add colour and vibrancy. Preferably, choose indigenous plant species that are well-suited to the local climate and require minimal maintenance.

iii) **Water Features:** Incorporate water elements such as ponds, fountains, or waterfalls into the landscape. Position them in the northeast or north direction to attract positive energy and create a sense of tranquillity. Ensure that the water features are clean, properly maintained, and in good working condition.

iv) **Pathways and Walkways:** Design pathways and walkways that are curving and inviting. Avoid straight and sharp-edged pathways. Create a smooth and gentle flow for guests to meander through the resort's landscape. Use natural materials such as stone or wood for the pathways.

v) **Outdoor Seating Areas:** Place seating areas strategically within the landscape to provide guests with opportunities for relaxation and enjoyment. Position seating in shaded areas with comfortable seating arrangements. Consider incorporating elements such as gazebos or pergolas to enhance the overall ambience.

vi) **Lighting:** Install appropriate outdoor lighting fixtures to illuminate pathways, gardens, and key focal points within the resort's landscape. Opt for soft, warm lighting that enhances the overall atmosphere and creates a cosy and inviting ambience.

vii) **Sacred Spaces:** Create designated areas for meditation, reflection, or yoga practice within the landscape. These spaces can be positioned in the northeast or east direction, allowing guests to connect with nature and experience a sense of serenity.

viii) **Privacy and Screening:** Use landscaping elements such as hedges, trees, or trellises to create privacy screens or boundaries where needed. This allows guests to enjoy their personal spaces while maintaining a sense of seclusion.

ix) **Eco-friendly Practices:** Emphasize sustainable and eco-friendly landscaping practices, such as water conservation through efficient irrigation systems, use of organic fertilizers, and integration of native plants that require less water and maintenance.

From the above context, it is evident that different kinds of constructions follow different kinds of patterns as suggested by Vastu.

Now, the fundamental objective with which this study was undertaken was to explore the adaptation of Vastu Shastra principles for sustainable and innovative architecture. Vastu Shastra, as discussed, is an ancient Indian system of architecture which emphasizes the harmonious integration of humans, buildings, and the natural environment. However, with the increasing need for sustainable and eco-friendly designs, there is a growing interest in incorporating Vastu principles into contemporary architectural practices. This study was proposed to examine and understand the basics of site planning by taking a resort as a case. The methodology, thus, includes a comprehensive review of Vastu literature and then a study of existing sustainable buildings that incorporate Vastu principles.

Major Findings

Site Planning of a resort case study according to Vastu:

The students of B.Arch. Semester IV were given an exercise of designing a Resort. The site given to them was Dharamshala, Himachal Pradesh. The site plan has been made according to the Vastu principles. After critically examining how to do a site planning for a resort in Dharamshala, Himachal Pradesh, adhering to Vastu Shastra principles, required careful consideration of various factors. The following were the major points as mentioned by them:

i) **Site Selection:** Choosing a site with favourable natural surroundings, such as proximity to water bodies or lush greenery. Avoiding sites with irregular or irregularly shaped plots. The site cannot be chosen due to availability constraints as the area terrain is steep.

ii) **Entrance and Orientation:** The main entrance of the resort should ideally face the east or northeast direction to allow the flow of positive energy. The orientation of the buildings should follow Vastu guidelines, ensuring the placement of rooms and facilities aligns with the cardinal directions. In this case, the East direction has been chosen as the entrance. The main buildings have been placed in the north direction

iii) **Boundary Walls:** A boundary wall around the site is important to define the property. The walls should be higher in the south and west directions compared to the north and east sides.

iv) **Open Spaces:** Leaving open spaces in the north and east directions to promote positive energy flow. Avoiding clutter or heavy construction in these areas. Open spaces are in the north and east direction to promote positive energy.

v) **Underground Water Tanks:** Placing underground water tanks in the northeast, east, or north direction of the site. Avoiding locating them in the southwest corner. The underwater tanks have been provided in the northeast direction.

Figure 7 Site Plan of the Resort

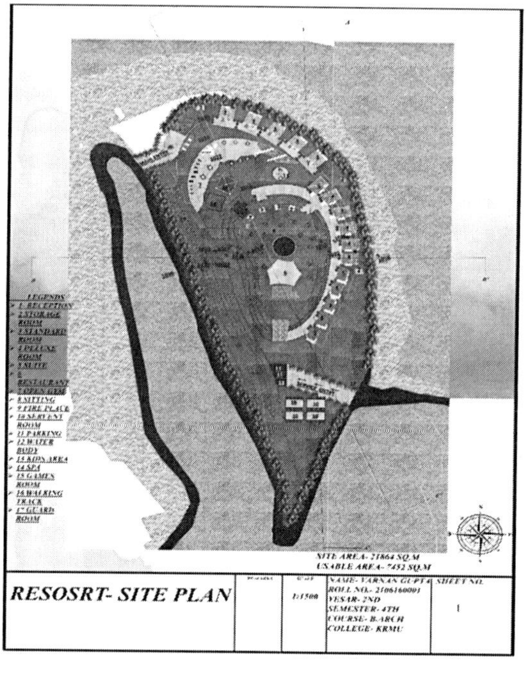

Source: Site Plan made by students of 4th semester, B.Arch.

vii) Water Bodies: Incorporating water bodies like pools, fountains, or lakes in the resort's design. Positioning them in the northeast or north direction to attract positive energy and create a serene ambience. The resort is on the river bank so water bodies were not incorporated.

viii) Landscaping: The landscapes including gardens, trees, and plants, emphasizing greenery and natural elements should be used. The indigenous plant species should be incorporated as different zones for relaxation, meditation, and outdoor activities. It was found that the landscaping has been planned according to the Vastu.

Figure 8 Zoning Plan of the Resort

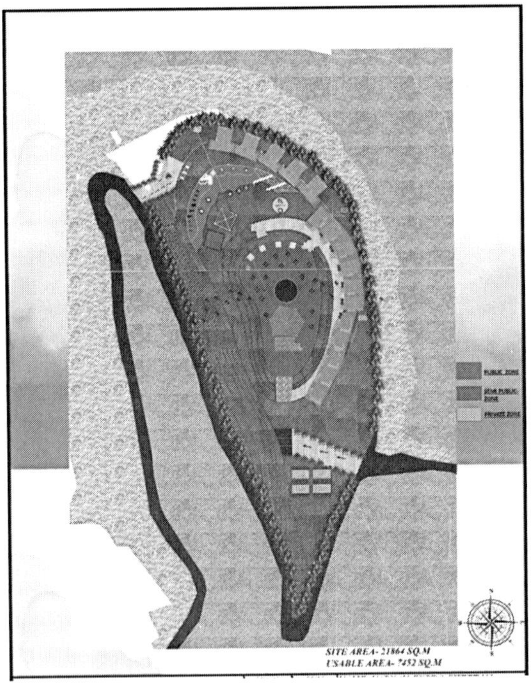

Source: Site Plan made by students of 4th semester, B.Arch

Building Layout: It is advisable to divide the resort into different zones or sections, such as accommodation, dining, recreational facilities, and administrative areas. Maintaining a logical flow between these areas while ensuring privacy and comfort for guests should be followed. As per the findings of the study, the resort was divided into many different zones for the easy flow of movement as well as the segregation between private semi-public and public spaces.

Guest Accommodations: Maximizing natural light and ventilation is important. Ideally, guest rooms should be in the east or north direction, while avoiding the southwest corner. Balconies or windows should face pleasant views and open spaces. In this study, the balconies have been provided in a way so that the people can enjoy the river view.

Dining Areas: The dining spaces, restaurants, and kitchens should be located in the southeast or northwest direction and ensure that the kitchen follows Vastu guidelines regarding the placement of cooking equipment and storage. It was seen that the Dining Areas and restaurants have been provided in the northwest direction.

Recreational Facilities: Position recreational areas, such as swimming pools, gyms, and spas, should be in the northeast or east direction. Create a harmonious and inviting atmosphere in these spaces.

Administrative Areas: Place administrative offices, reception, and conference rooms in the northeast or northwest direction. This promotes positive energy flow and enhances productivity.

Parking and Service Areas: Parking areas and service facilities, such as laundry and maintenance, should be in the southeast or northwest direction. Maintaining an organized and clutter-free environment in these spaces is important. Parking has been provided in the southeast direction.

Roads and Pathways: Ensuring that the roads or pathways leading to and within the site are wide, well-maintained, and free from obstructions. It is said that the sharp turns or T-junctions directly facing the entrance of the site should be avoided.

Vegetation and Trees: Trees and greenery are to be planted in the northeast, east, and north sides of the site to provide a positive and vibrant environment. Avoid planting tall trees in the south and west directions, as they may obstruct sunlight.

Elevation and Slopes: The site should have a gradual slope from the southwest to the northeast direction. Elevated land in the south or west should not be used, as it may block positive energy.

Conclusion

The design of the resort has been made according to the Vastu principles. The orientation of the site is a crucial aspect of Vastu. The site is aligned with the cardinal directions so as to give a positive aspect. The surrounding environment of the site should be taken into consideration. Factors such as the presence of natural elements, like hills, rivers, or forests, can influence the energy flow. The resort is on a river bank so that is becoming a focal point for the flow of positive energy into the site. Ideally, a square or rectangular shape is considered auspicious. Irregular or asymmetrical shapes can create energy imbalances. Due to the size constraint, it was not possible for the regular shape plot. The presence of water bodies, such as ponds or lakes, and the positioning of trees on the site can significantly impact Vastu energy. The landscaping has been done in abundance to provide a free flow of positive energy. The ideal entry point should be in the east or north direction to attract positive energy. The entrance to the site has been provided in the east direction for easy movement. The use of trees and plants has also been taken into consideration according to Vastu.

References

Ananth, S. *The vastu tradition.*

Barodia, P., & Shastra, V. *A holistic approach towards modern architecture.*

Bhattacharya, T. (1986). *The canons of Indian art: A study of vastu Vidya. Calcutta: Firma K. L. Mukhopadhyay.*

Chandrakar, & Parvez. (2022). *Practical application of vastu shastra in Indian residential building.*

Fazeli, H., & Goodarzi, A. (2010). The principles of Vastu as a traditional architectural belief system from an environmental perspective. *WIT Transactions on Ecology and the Environment*, 97–108. https://doi.org/10.2495/ARC100091

Hotwani, & Rastogi. (2022). *Vastu shastra: A Vedic approach to architecture.*

Kinayekar et al. (2022). *To study vastu shastra planning as per traditional Indian system and science of architecture.*

Kiran, & Subodh. (2023). *Vastu shastra in modern architecture: Exploring the intersection of tradition and innovation.*

Kramrisch, S. (1976). *The Hindu temple.* Motilal Banarsidass.

Wang, L. J., Kuzmich, A., & Dogariu, A. (2000). Gain-assisted superluminal light propagation. *Nature, 406*(6793), 277–279. https://doi.org/10.1038/35018520

Olivier, P. Encyclopedia of vernacular architecture of the world. *S.L.* Cambridge University Press. (1997).

Pandey, A. (2020). *The Ancient Indian Science of Vastu Shastra and Climate Responsive Buildings in 21st Century.*

Patra, R. (2017). *Vastu in perspective of technology.*

Rao, D. M. (1995). *Vastu Shilpa Shāstra: The Hidden Treasures of vastu Shilpa Shāstra and Indian traditions*. Saudi Biological Society Publishers.

Shukla, D. N. (1993). *Vastu Shāstra- Hindu science of architecture, II and I.* Munshiram Manoharlal.

Soni, Mishra, & Pakhale. (2019). Vastu Shastra – The concept of Sustainable Architecture Journal Of Indian Institute Of Architects, September, *1995*.

Wahaj, F. (2019). The science of vastu in architecture. https://doi.org/10.1016/0275-1062(86)90033-0

***

EXPLORING THE DEPTHS: UNRAVELING INDIAN PSYCHOLOGY

Pooja Verma

Assistant Professor, School of Education

K.R. Mangalam University, Gurugram

Nitish Kumar Minz

Student, School of Management and Commerce

K.R. Mangalam University, Gurugram

Shruti Chaturvedi

Student, School of Management and Commerce

K.R. Mangalam University, Gurugram

Abstract

This study focuses on the growth and development of Indian psychology as well as its proven value in addressing societal issues as a subfield of psychology more broadly. Indian psychology has evolved and grown significantly over the years, incorporating elements of contemporary research as well as ancient philosophical traditions and indigenous knowledge systems. This essay traces the development of Indian psychology over time, highlighting significant turning points and significant figures. It focuses on the relevance of Indian psychology in addressing the mental health needs of Indian society as it explores the distinctive contributions of Indian psychology to theory, research, and practice. This paper also discusses the difficulties and directions for the future development of Indian psychology, promoting its inclusion in the larger psychological discourse.

The difficulty in presenting Indian psychology is in maintaining the underlying metaphysics while emphasizing the practical models. As the main goal is to enrich and transform Indian psychology with the proven ability to address societal challenges, the solution to these problems is addressed throughout the article. The human mind, experience, consciousness, and self-identity serve as the foundation for the Darsana, or the Indian ways of thinking. The guidelines for researching these issues are as follows: Finding the unitary in the discrete; having a mental and spiritual meaning for every experience, its subject, and its experiencer; addressing the ontological cause of therapy rather than just the cognitive or mental component; and having values, discipline, and compassion as fundamentals are just a few of the requirements.

Keywords: Indian Psychology, Development, Advancement, Ancient Philosophy, Indigenous Knowledge Systems.

Introduction

Indian Psychology (henceforth referred to as IP) has a long history of learning about Indian civilization's cultural practices and is firmly rooted in ancient Indian literature. Its history dates back thousands of years and has been ongoing. The scope of intellectual property is broader than his academic psychology, which emerged in India in the early twentieth century under the influence of Western colonization. IP includes psychological philosophies developed within Indian civilization through careful observation, inquiry, contemplation, guidance, meditation, and sharing of inner experiences. This body of knowledge has grown, become more diverse, and, in the face of challenges and changes, continues to shape the cultural psyche of the Indian people. Although intellectual property has its roots in the Indian subcontinent, its fundamental conceptual direction is all human and tied to Eastern philosophies. It serves as a cultural discourse on worldviews and epistemology, offering an alternative to the Western logical positivist approach to psychology. Regardless of location or the cause of suffering, IP seeks to free people from captivity and suffering. a discussion of human nature and the various routes to self-knowledge and education. IP places human functioning in a space environment, illuminating private, public, and group interactions. encouraging open discourse and participation while fostering a democratic exchange of ideas.

IP is based on many idealistic and realist schools of thought, offering diverse perspectives on life, self-improvement, and interaction with the outside world. The term "psychology" is expanded to include not only the study of human behaviour but also the development of human potential. With a greater emphasis on connectivity, cohesion, and interconnection between all life forms, IP is moving away from seeing the individual as the centre of reality and towards a deeper understanding of the field. In addition to recognizing the interaction between the field (*kshetra*) and the person who knows the field (*kshetraja*), it also provides a profound understanding of human nature in the larger space-time continuum.

However, there are dangers in focusing solely on transcendental theories without considering relevant contextual experiences and practical spiritual goals. Understanding the philosophical underpinnings of intellectual property is essential to understanding its nature. The concepts of Western scientific psychology have persisted without fully being assimilated into the Indian psyche and reality because the Western tradition has dominated psychology education in India for the past century. Additionally, there have been some initiatives to connect with Indian knowledge sources, but these have been seen as separate from conventional psychology.

In totality, Indian psychology is a distinct area of research that is based on Indian traditions, philosophical tenets, and cultural norms. The book, which was developed with Western influences, presents an alternative viewpoint on human nature, individual growth, and interconnectedness. IP contributes to a broader understanding of psychology by including a wider empirical background and useful spiritual goals.

This chapter examines the evolution and significance of Indian psychology as a distinct subfield within the broader discipline of psychology. It aims to uncover its historical development, influential figures, and specific contributions to theory, research, and practice in addressing mental health concerns within Indian society. The article also delves into the challenges faced by Indian psychology and explores potential future directions for its advancement. Recognizing the importance of integrating Indian psychology into global psychological discussions, it emphasizes the delicate balance between preserving its foundational metaphysics and practical models. Employing qualitative research methods, the findings of this chapter critically evaluate the philosophical underpinnings, the impact of Western psychology, and the incorporation of indigenous perspectives to enhance the field's understanding and effectively tackle societal challenges.

Rao (2008) in his paper offered a thorough investigation of the unique features of Indian psychology. It covered a wide range of subjects, including traditional healing techniques, Indian philosophical systems, meditation techniques, cognitive processes, personality theories, social psychology, and practical applications. The authors offered a comprehensive understanding of Indian psychology that takes into account spiritual, cultural, and social dimensions by fusing ancient and modern sources. For academics, researchers, and students interested in consciousness research, cross-cultural psychology, and the distinctive viewpoints provided by Indian psychological traditions, this book is an invaluable resource. It makes the depth and complexity of Indian psychology easier to comprehend and appreciate.

Dalal (2010) in his article examined the underlying ideas and external influences that affect Indian psychology. In addition to examining the cultural, historical, and social contexts that affect psychological processes in India, he also examined the central ideas of Indian psychology, including the ideas of self, consciousness, emotions, and motivation. The article provides an in-depth analysis of Indian psychology, explanations of its distinctive traits, and helpful data for academics and professionals attempting to comprehend the psychological foundations of Indian society.

Bryde (1971) in his work gave a thorough overview of the historical developments and trends that affected Indian psychology at the time. It looks at how contemporary psychological theories and techniques have evolved in India and how they interact with the long-standing philosophical and cultural norms of the country. The self, cognition, personality, emotion, and motivation are some of the topics covered in the book within the context of Indian psychology. Bryde's (1971) work contributes to a better understanding of the current state of Indian psychology by providing insightful details about the distinctive perspectives and contributions of Indian academics and researchers in the field.

Bhawuk (2011) examined the wisdom and teachings of the Bhagavad Gita and how they apply to one's knowledge of psychology, consciousness, and well-being. The book offers priceless insights and lessons that can improve the comprehension of psychological processes, individual development, and the pursuit of inner fulfilment by drawing on the ancient spiritual wisdom of India. It provides a distinctive viewpoint on the fusion of spirituality and psychology, adding to the larger discussion on all-encompassing methods of well-being.

Bhawuk (2020) in her work mentioned the subject of the chapter as the Indian psychological concept of "lazy," which is investigated from a literary, social, and spiritual standpoint. It investigates the multifaceted nature of the hajj and its significance in influencing social interactions, romantic relationships, and individual development. The chapter illuminates the intricate interplay between shame, self-awareness, and moral development within the Indian cultural context by drawing on philosophical and cultural viewpoints. It provided important new understandings of shame and its effects on psychological health.in his piece of work investigates the connection between Indian psychology and the global psychology scene. The difficulties and opportunities faced by Indian psychology in contributing to the global conversation and adjusting to foreign research paradigms are discussed. In addition to highlighting Indian psychology's unique contributions, such as its holistic and spiritually based outlook, the article also stresses the significance of cultural context in understanding psychological phenomena. This article contributes to the ongoing discussion on cross-cultural psychology and the globalization of psychological knowledge by critically examining the connections between Indian psychology and the larger international field.

This study employs a qualitative research methodology to explore the growth and evolution of Indian Psychology (IP) as a distinctive research field. The methodology encompasses various elements, including an extensive literature review, a historical analysis, critical evaluation, conceptual framework construction, interdisciplinary approaches, and data analysis. The literature review involves thorough searches of academic databases, books, and journals to gain insights into the origins and philosophical foundations of Indian psychology. The historical analysis investigates the field's development by examining ancient Indian literature and the contributions of scholars and philosophers. A critical assessment examines the influence of Western psychology on Indian psychology and the challenges encountered in integrating indigenous perspectives. A conceptual framework has been developed to organize the diverse perspectives within Indian psychology. An interdisciplinary approach situates Indian psychology within a broader social and cultural context. Finally, data collected through these methods are subjected to qualitative analysis to identify key themes and outcomes. It is important to acknowledge certain limitations, such as relying on existing literature and providing a comprehensive overview of Indian psychology. The research aims to contribute to the ongoing discourse surrounding the integration of Indigenous psychological traditions and Western paradigms.

Major Findings

i) Evolution

Local sources did this in secret, and public perceptions of their authenticity and usefulness were not reflected in educational plans and programs. The potential for brain research and its recommended methods of classification and conceptualization existed long before socialization, and culture was excluded from the formation of mental material and constructs. For example, perceptual learning and various mental properties were kept separate from social practice. This may be due to the dynamics of creating niches in new fields and the pressure to figure out who you are within the scientific field. In the mid-1970s, some Indian psychologists, who had appreciated the applicability and relevance of their research, began to grow dissatisfied (Dalal, 1996). In the light of the current scientific model, brain research was seen by most as a natural pervasiveness, with no room for Indian or other non-Western perspectives.

Local sources did this in secret, and public perceptions of their authenticity and usefulness were not reflected in educational plans and programs. The potential for brain research and its recommended methods of classification and conceptualization existed long before socialization, and culture was excluded from the formation of mental material and constructs. For example, perceptual learning and various mental properties were kept separate from social practice.

This may be due to the dynamics of creating niches in new fields and the pressure to figure out who you are within the scientific field. In the mid-1970s, some Indian psychologists, who had appreciated the applicability and relevance of their research, began to grow dissatisfied (Dalal, 1996). Brain research, in the light of current scientific models, was seen by most as a natural pervasiveness with no room for Indian or other non-Western perspectives. Apart from this usual mission of understanding and changing human behaviour, there are distinctly contrasting perspectives. How Western cultures and non-Western cultures like India analyze, explain and understand social realities. The difference is not only related to the question being asked but is more fundamental to the ontological truths of human life.

Further complicating the comparison is the fact that while Western scholars have focused on the observed reality of human-society interaction, Indian sages have focused on the 'ideal' state of affairs. The purpose of juxtaposing the worldviews of these different societies is to examine the development of Western social psychology and its impact on the understanding of social issues and problems facing India. You can explore the knowledge base of psychosocial work in India through critical reviews. A companion piece that attempts to understand the evolution of social brain research in India as a Western enterprise. It has been established that the important historical events that shaped the field in the West had a significant influence on the development of psychosocial well-being in India. Finally, the fundamentals of the new discipline as well as the most pressing problems and frustrations facing Indian psychologists have been examined. The main goal of this chapter is to highlight how social development and psychosocial development are intertwined, making it impossible to understand one without understanding the other.

ii) Perception

In recent years, there has been a remarkable shift in attitudes and perceptions toward Indian Psychology (IP). This change can be attributed to three main factors that were considered when re-evaluating the field. First, it is increasingly clear that Western psychology is incapable of solving the complex social problems facing non-Western societies today. The positivist model, on which Western psychology is based, offers a superficial and fragmentary understanding of the complexities of human emotions, behaviour, and social dynamics. As issues like social and family violence, mental health issues, and moral decline have become more prevalent, the drawbacks of this strategy have become clear. Even Western scholars recognize the shortcomings of the individual-centred view, which fails to capture the holistic existential context of life. In addition, important aspects of the human experience such as religion, spirituality, suffering, values, reliability, creativity, love, and collectivism have been oriented by the psychological model. ignored deficit. Due to these limitations, the value of Indian psychology has been reevaluated, requiring a more profound approach.

Second, Western psychology's ability to solve current social problems has been questioned and criticized. Scholars point to the dangers of contemporary social psychology and its limitations in addressing social challenges. Protest movements such as the humanist and transpersonal movements of the 1960s arose in response to the scientism and reductionism prevailing in psychological research. Psychotherapists have also experienced identity crises, resulting in disagreements about their goals, philosophies, and moral beliefs. The importance of including spirituality and religion, which have been historically overlooked in psychology, in psychological research and theory is increasingly recognized. The limits of the mechanical and reductionist models of Western psychology are increasingly recognized in current developments, giving way to alternative perspectives such as Indian psychology.

Ultimately, the need for recognition of a more inclusive and culturally sensitive approach has contributed to changing perceptions of Indian psychology. The limits of the Western scientific framework, largely modelled on the mechanical and reductionist models of the natural sciences, have been exposed. It is increasingly recognized that a more complete and subjective understanding of human experience, including spirituality, is essential for a full understanding of psychology. This has generated renewed interest in integrating cultural and spiritual aspects into psychological research and theory.

In summary, the changing attitudes and perceptions of Indian psychology have highlighted the limitations of Western psychology in addressing non-Western social challenges, the introspection of Western psychology, and the need for a more culturally sensitive and holistic approach. It is due to gender recognition. These elements have boosted the perception of Indian psychology as an alternative paradigm that embraces more of the human experience and may provide remedies for Western psychology's shortcomings.

Indian psychology offers a distinctive viewpoint on various facets of the human experience by drawing on various facets of the Indian intellectual tradition. These traditions hold that the mind and the body are separate from consciousness. All other states—including waking, dreaming, and deep sleep—emerge from it, making it the starting point for all others. This Transcendental Consciousness, also known as Suriya, is called the "fourth" state because it supports the other three but does not have the attributes and characteristics of those states. These states are considered corrective views. In the Indian tradition, mind and matter are connected and form a continuum, unlike the Cartesian mind-body dualism. His three fundamental principles of the universe can be used to understand the interaction between mind and matter. It symbolizes sattva, creation, and enlightenment; Rajas symbolize energy; and Tamassymbolise laziness. Indian thought holds that man exists on three levels: creatures, people, and celestial bodies. Pure consciousness, the foundation of the entire universe, is associated with the divine aspect of man. Modern advances in fields such as materials science, science, medicine, and brain research are consistent with these ideas and confirm the views of the Indians. For thousands of years, these fundamental principles have shaped Indian culture and the lives of millions of people. This effect can be seen in the Indian psyche, which acknowledges all aspects of human aspiration, including material wealth (artha), contentment (kama), honesty (dharma), and profound freedom (moksha). The four-valued framework makes this clear. Man aspires to each of his four perspectives, but the two that are considered his highest aspirations - self-knowledge and freedom - are different from the other three. All aspects of human behaviour are conceptualized and understood within the framework of consciousness, which provides a clear qualitative understanding beyond the limited view of the waking state (Anand, 2016).

Conclusion

First of all, Indian psychology is a branch of psychology with strong roots in Indian culture, philosophy, and traditions. It has a long history that dates back thousands of years, in contrast to academic psychology, which was influenced by the West and emerged in the early 20th century. Ancient philosophical traditions, indigenous knowledge systems, and current research are just a few of the knowledge sources that make up Indian psychology.

Second, Indian psychology offers a distinctive and all-encompassing method for comprehending interconnectedness, personal growth, and human nature. It shifts away from the individual-centred perspective that rules Western psychology and places an emphasis on the interdependence and coherence between all life forms. Indian psychology recognizes the importance of incorporating human experiences beyond behaviour and cognition, such as spirituality, values, suffering, authenticity, and collectivism.

Third, it has been demonstrated that Western psychology cannot adequately address the complex social issues that non-Western societies face. The positivist and reductionist paradigms of Western psychology provide a fragmented understanding of social dynamics, behavioural patterns, and emotional experiences. As a result, the need for a more thorough and culturally sensitive psychology is becoming increasingly clear. Alternative frameworks and viewpoints, such as broader experiential backgrounds and practical spiritual objectives, are provided by Indian psychology. Finally, a more comprehensive understanding of psychology and addressing the needs of various societies in terms of mental health depend on the inclusion of Indian psychology in the discussion of global psychology. By encouraging an atmosphere of open discourse and participation, and facilitating the democratic exchange of ideas, Indian psychology can advance this field and contribute to its growth. It's crucial to strike a balance between the retention of Indian psychology's fundamental metaphysical and philosophical underpinnings and useful models that can effectively address social issues.

The importance of Indian psychology as a separate field within the larger field of psychology is generally highlighted by this study. This chapter demonstrates Indian psychology's integration into the global psychological debate for the benefit of society by highlighting its distinctive contributions, historical developments, difficulties, and future directions.

References

Bhawuk, D. (2011). Spirituality and Indian psychology: Lessons from the Bhagavad-Gita. https://link.springer.com/book/10.1007/978-1-4419-8110-3#:~:text=https%3A. Springer Science+Business Media. https://doi.org/10.1007/978%2D1%2D4419%2D8110%2D3

Bhawuk, D. P. *Indian psychology: Spiritual, social, and literary perspectives. The value of shame: Exploring a health resource in cultural contexts* (pp. 109–134). http://doi.org/10.1007/978-3-319-53100-7

Bryde, J. F. (1971). 'Modern Indian psychology.' This book provides an overview of modern Indian psychology, covering various topics and perspectives within the field. https://psycnet.apa.org/doi/10.1037/0735-7028.14.5.588

Bryde, J. F. (1971). *Modern Indian psychology*. ISBN 0882490273, 9780882490274.

By Elliot Aronson, T. D. (ND). *Social psychology* (9th ed). Pearson Education. ISBN 9352861515, 9789352861514.

Dalal, A. K., & Misra, G. (2010). The core and context of Indian psychology. *Psychology and Developing Societies*, 22(1), 121–155. https://psycnet.apa.org/doi/10.1177/097133360902200105. https://doi.org/10.1177/097133360902200105

Kalpna Anand, Y. K. (2016, July–September). *'Perceived Stress as Predictor of Psychological Well-being among Indian Youth.' This research article examines the relationship between perceived stress and psychological well-being among Indian youth.* ISBN: 978-1-365-39398-3.

Kalpna Anand, Y. K. (2016, July–September). Perceived stress as predictor of psychological well-being among Indian youth. *International Journal of Indian Psychology*, 7. https://ijip.in/articles/perceived-stress-as-predictor-of-psychological-well-being-among-indian-youth/#:~:text=DIP%3A%2018.01.213/20160304-,DOI%3A%2010.25215/0304.213,-abstract

Menon, S. (2005). What is Indian psychology: Transcendence in and while thinking. *Journal of Transpersonal Psychology, 37*, 98. https://doi.org/10.1017/UPO9788175968448.010

Paranjpe, A. C. (2011). Indian psychology and the international context. *Psychology and Developing Societies*, 23(1), 1–26. https://doi.org/10.1177/097133361002300101

Rao, K. P. (2008). *Handbook of Indian psychology. Cambridge university press India/foundation books*. ISBN 8175966025, 9788175966024.

***

PSYCHOLOGICAL IMPACT OF POLYTHEISM IN INDIAN SUBTEXT

Anshul Saluja

Assistant Professor, School of Education,

K.R. Mangalam University, Gurugram

Praney Surha

Student, School of Agricultural Sciences,

K.R. Mangalam University, Gurugram

Akash Garg

Indraprastha Engineering College, New Delhi

Abstract

Religion has been a major part of the Indian subcontinent, which is the birthplace of Hinduism, Jainism, Sikhism and Buddhism, with over 90% population feeling religious (Ireland, 2020). There is a myriad of concepts and beliefs bringing along with them their own philosophies which contribute to changing the individual's mindset. This chapter focuses on the origin and effects of polytheism in Hindu society and belief systems. Polytheism is a major aspect of Hinduism where the majority of people follow in India (79.8%) (Religious Composition by Country, 2010-2050, 2022) hence it will be the central focus of this study.

Keywords: Hinduism, Polytheism, Psychology, Religion.

Introduction

The concept of "polytheism" refers to the worship or belief in more than one deity. It varies fundamentally from other belief systems. In contrast to the latter, which involves holding to many faiths regardless of the number of gods they each contain, the former refers to belief in a single faith that includes a pantheon of multiple gods, each of whom has a distinct function and position in the hierarchy. Most of the world's ancient faiths are polytheistic, which was the dominant belief before Abrahamic religions arose. Taoism, Shenism, Chinese folk religion, Japanese Shinto, Santera, and most Traditional African faiths are notable examples of polytheistic religions that remain followed to date (Heinz, 2006). Polytheism brings with it a lot of distinct rituals, elaborate lore, and multiple identities for people to relate with and is acceptable to people of different backgrounds and social inclinations.

These ideas demand a lot of attention to detail to comprehend, which over decades and years have rendered them more challenging to follow and govern. Polytheism provided a range of ideas and beliefs that made it more challenging for any authoritarian to maintain control and bring the populace as one. This led to the introduction of monotheism, which offered a single deity or God to oversee all activities that had previously been divided between several sects and positions in a polytheistic approach. The foundations of monotheism can be traced back to Zoroastrians and Egypt circa 1000 BCE (Denova, 2019).

In the current modern age, the most followed religions are Christianity and Islam (Religious Composition by Country, 2010-2050, 2022) both of which originate from Abrahamic beliefs, further proving how successful the monotheistic model truly is. While most ancient polytheistic religions died out under the impact of monotheism, Hinduism stands out as a lively exception (Basuchoudhary, 2020). Of the various religions that came up through the ages in human civilisation, Hinduism is the oldest one, and it's the 3rd most followed religion in the world. People in Western and Central Asia have referred to India with the term "Hindu" for well over a thousand years. The word is derived from

Sindhu, the Indian name for Indus. From this *Sindhu* came the words Hindu and Hindustan, as well as Indus and India (Bagchi, 2017).

However, the natives of the Indian subcontinent had never before used these terms such as “Hindu” or even “India” both of which were introduced to the rest of the world by the Persian and European merchants who visited the country through the northwest crossing the Indus River. Though certain individuals ponder how Hinduism continues to thrive and is still practised by such a large number of people when other ancient religions have vanished (such as the Greek and Roman religions have been completely eradicated by Christianity which is now instead of being called religion with priests and rituals are reduced to mythology with poets and bards) is because of its constant evolution and emergence of new schools of thinking. When a religion becomes as old as 10,000 years it gives birth to a lot of different schools of thought and new ideas. In ancient India, Hinduism had 6 different systems (*shad-darsana*) *Samkhya* (rationalism), *Yoga* (philosophy), *Nyaya* (realist), *Vaisheshika* (naturalist), *Mimamsa* (philosophical realism) and *Vedanta* (Knowledge) (Nicholson, 2013).

Moreover, in Hinduism, the term used for philosophy is *Darshana* (Viewpoint or perspective), from the Sanskrit root *drish* ('to see, to experience'). This indicates that Hinduism has historically been less about complying with a particular set of practices and routine work and more about subjectivity and openness to different schools of thought, each of which offered its own interpretation of the nature of reality and how one can achieve *moksha* or freedom from the cycle of birth and death. All these systems have their own subtypes and further independent schools which have their interpretation of what is the “truth”. Hinduism even features the atheist school of thought known as the *Cārvāka* school which rejects supernaturalism and emphasizes materialism (Thomas, 2014).

All these different schools of thought which continued to be accepted in the Indian subcontinent allowed for the religion to be kept up to date and facilitated its constant evolution. The *Vishnu Purana* asserts that -the supreme goal was attained in *Satya-Yuga* by years of prolonged meditation; in *Treta-Yuga* by performing extensive yajnas; in *Dvapara-yuga* by opulent and scrupulous Deity worship; in *Kali-Yuga* the same results are easily achievable by simply chanting of the holy names of *Kesava* (Padma Purana, Uttara Khanda 42nd Chapter). Most of the ancient hymns directed towards Varuna, the more ancient Vedic deities, describe the supreme god, or Brahman in the most abstract way. Later hymns, however, are more descriptive and detailed, which hints at the evolution of abstract ideas into concrete and tangible beliefs (Phillips, 1903).

This has been the cornerstone of Hinduism's continued relevance and practice not only in India but throughout the world despite centuries of colonization, conversion, rebellions, and turmoil. This also explains how Hinduism has managed to preserve internal harmony despite having 33 to 330 million gods (Chapter 47 - Installation of Goddesses at Bahūdaka Tīrtha). According to Julius Lipner, the *Bhagavad Gītā*, composed at about the beginning of the Common Era, the first sustained textual evidence of developed thinking about devotional faith in a personal God, named Krishna was there. Hinduism has described several methods to achieve moksha one way is *jnana yoga* (liberation through knowledge) another is *karma yoga* (liberation through service) but the most famous and accepted path is *bhakti yoga* (liberation through devotion). What keeps Hinduism's contemporary polytheistic component alive today is bhakti yoga. The notion that you might now attain *moksha* and the blessings of gods without conducting prolonged prayers, sacrifices, and offerings to them, was widely embraced throughout the subcontinent. In the Vedic era, the gods were worshipped through sacrifice as a form of appeasement, in the current era Gods are worshipped out of kindness (Venkataraman,

2014). The god's position was now more personal than being divine and "supernatural". Children from an early age developed a deeper connection with a particular god and learned through their examples and stories and worshipping them in a personalised system of belief and practice.

This was especially highly needed in the time of the Mughal Empire. It was at this time when the indigenous people of this subcontinent were losing their identity and were influenced by the simplicity and benefits of Islam, many more were being forcefully converted and subjected to numerous offences (Durant, 2014). During this period, India gave birth to some influential writers and poets such as the notable *Tulsi Das* who translated *Ramayana* into the local language *Avadhi* in a poetic manner such that it could be narrated to the uneducated and the poor who had no access or the ability to read the scriptures which were gatekept by the brahmins. Like most other older religions, ancient Hinduism adhered to polytheism, which lauded natural phenomena and some natural phenomena by personifying them as gods with divine abilities and knowledge who are the guardians of their realm. For example, some of their earliest Hindu gods and goddesses are *Indra* (Weather), *Agni* (Fire), *Varun* (Air), *Usha* (Dawn), *Prithvi* (Earth), *Aditi* (Cosmic moral order), *Aranyani* (Forest), etc (Kinsley, 2005).

Contrary to what is more widely assumed, Hinduism can also be recognised as a monotheistic religion. One supreme god, who is above the hierarchy and social position of the gods who are responsible for diverse duties in the universe, was stressed by some belief systems in ancient India. According to the *Davita* School of thought, the self is the *atman* and the purpose of the self is to get connected to the *parmatma* or brahman for salvation (Fowler, 2002). The *Advaita* school of thought believes that both are the same and that the supreme god or *atman/brahman* exists within a person and discovering him is the purpose of life (Nakamura, 1990). A good supportive argument for this comes from *Kalika Purana* (14th century) which says, 'Just as rays of the sun continually come forth from the sun's disc so [the various forms of the Goddess] come forth from the body of the Goddess.' This tells us that at the core the gods are a part of the same supreme god which has taken several different forms to serve different purposes and prevent chaos and order from being maintained in the universe, with each having its own beliefs, rituals, traditions, and narratives.

The Psychological Impact of Polytheism

There is a trend in particular schools of thought and points of vision that is common in places of polytheistic belief and multi-faith systems. When these schools of thought are examined from many angles using various methodologies, such as sociology and psychology, they can offer a critical viewpoint on concerns about their worth and quality. However, doing a comparison between many systems of thought, whether monotheistic or polytheistic, would be foolish from any moralistic or upright point of view. Ramdas Lamb, a professor of religion at the University of Hawaii says, "No human has demonstrable or irrefutable proof for or against a belief in a divinity or a lack thereof. All theories regarding the divine are based on faith, supposition, and individual experience. That being the case, one should focus instead on the ramifications and practical usefulness of the various theological conceptualizations on the people who hold them as well as on the rest of the world". Therefore, in accordance with the professor's guidance, one shall solely consider the impact of polytheism in terms of its implications for the general population and their practical utility. Hinduism, a religion with features of both monotheism and polytheism in its structure, also incorporates both systems' practicalities. It obtains both the benefits and the drawbacks that are built into each system and must balance between the two alternates. The ancient author Varro in the early 50s BC defined tripartite theology as a general structure that is perfectly applicable to the majority of polytheistic religions. Varro specifically considered and mentioned Greek and Roman religions, but it also applies to ancient Egyptian and Babylonian religions, and most importantly to Hinduism, which is the focus of this discussion. The three realms of divine presence correlate to the overall framework of Varro's three theologies, namely the cosmos, the political organisation, and the myth (Johnston, 2007).

The cosmos is the first dimension, where polytheistic faiths held that the collaboration of the gods was necessary for the preservation of the entirety of the cosmos. Each celestial spirit in this system has a distinct set of duties and spheres of influence. This can involve controlling natural elements like lightning and thunder, the seasons, or facets of human nature like love, fidelity, rage, etc. Each cosmology has a hierarchical structure that, in many respects, resembles how a democracy functions in one's own society, where authority is shared among many people who then contribute to maintaining society. The experience of community, family, and state in human societies is frequently found in polytheism. It is often seen in societies where there is a distinctive social and/or political hierarchy, where individuals hold power according to their position in the social or political order, and where the primary objective of these powers is for the good of those who approach the different deities in need of assistance. The abilities of various divinities are very much like those of various governing bodies. One could choose to ignore all deities while concentrating solely on a deity who appeals to one's own traits.

Even though such people are seen to be bereft of divine assistance, it rarely comes to mind that they are being punished because of their decisions. Therefore, in many respects, polytheism is a pragmatic religious perspective that represents characteristics of a democratic system. The highest position of power in monotheism is held by a single male god, particularly as it is depicted in the Abrahamic faiths. He is all-knowing, all-powerful, and ever-present. He has anthropomorphic features, like the divine in polytheistic faiths. He requires fealty and punishes people who don't worship him only, which is contrary to what is seen in most polytheistic faiths. On a human scale, one regularly confronts such an individual in monarchies, dictatorships, and areas run by warlords, and tribal chiefs, as is present in many Middle Eastern nations nowadays. These types of structures may offer comfort for those who "belong" to the correct tribe or religious system, but an all-powerful ruler represents a danger to those who do not. Most people in such societies remain weak and powerless unless they completely adhere to those in authority and do everything they are instructed. It is accepted that this is the only way that people can survive (Lamb, 2011).

To look at this from a much more practical point of view, monotheism asserts its identity by opposing itself to polytheism, whereas no such thing occurs in polytheism. This fanatical focus of monotheism on the uniqueness of their creator and exclusivity on his mode of communication fosters within its community a tradition of intercommunal rivalry and conflict (Jaffee, 2001). Polytheism as is present in Hinduism offers a perspective that is varied and diverse in thought, that allows a plurality of identities to be formed. Hinduism contains a wide variety of sects, including those that are atheists or non-believers, agnostics, monotheists, and devotees of several different, sometimes even mythologically antagonistic deities. Nevertheless, it accepts all of them. It is having a singular form of identity and the salience of identity (Chowdhury, 2023) that makes it easier to separate the populace along simple lines of "us and them". These lines of difference often escalate to conflict, growing to acts of violence and communal riots. Intercommunal communication is also hampered by these bipartite ways of thinking. Monotheistic religions often are instilled with egocentrism

(Lochhead, 2001). They often involve judging aspects of another culture by the standards of one's own 'Culture appropriation'. Having an understanding and respect for one another's cultural beliefs is paramount for any communication being possible between different sects of people. People living in multi-faith societies (a concept integrated into Hinduism) are more accustomed to living harmoniously with people of different and diverse thought systems and cultural backgrounds (Spinner-Halev, 2005).

Additionally, there also exists an issue of inhibition that is prevalent in monotheistic religions (Verena Krause, 2021). Close-mindedness and a lack of exposure to other viewpoints obstruct the distribution of ideas and put the pursuit of knowledge on the back burner in favour of the creation of obstacles in attaining information. As is evident in the history of the medieval English Church where those with novel ideas were called heretics and put to their deaths to prevent any independent thought from arising amongst the people, lest they start opposing the church. New emerging schools of thought, without being entertained or discussed, were termed heresy because they denied the truth which was as told by the church (Cross, 1974). Due to India's history of colonisation and invasion, monotheistic Abrahamic religions arrived, resulting in widespread religious conversions. Priests and religious leaders of these Western and Middle Eastern faiths took advantage of the openness and liberal outlook of the native population that Hinduism promotes. The foundation of India's old knowledge systems and scriptures is that it has always given new concepts and ideas the benefit of the doubt and that nothing was accepted without question. Anand Neelakantan very well states in his book "Rise of Kali" (2015), "The mark of a confident civilisation is that the Indians have always celebrated stories – with debate, argument and counterargument; certainly not by accepting without dissent."

Findings

From the context presented above, it can be said that the following were some of the significant reform movements which were observed in Hinduism:

Brahmo Samaj: Introduced by Raja Ram Mohan Roy in 1828, it sought to promote monotheism and reject idol worship.

Arya Samaj: Introduced by Swami Dayananda Saraswati in 1875, it sought to promote Vedic knowledge and reject caste-based discrimination.

Ramakrishna Mission: Introduced by Swami Vivekananda in 1897. it sought to promote the idea of service to humanity in the form of worship.

Prarthana Samaj: Introduced by Atmaram Pandurang in 1867. It sought to promote monotheism and reject caste-based discrimination.

Hare Krishna Movement: Introduced by Bhaktivedanta Swami Prabhupada in 1966. It sought to promote worship and devotion to Krishna and Radha in particular.

The future however is still fairly uncertain, it is very evident how religion and its practices have been moulded to suit the current generation with the influence of foreign culture, globalisation, and fast-paced lifestyle. People can have a spiritual connection with the supernatural without engaging in complicated rituals or hours of worship; they can merely recall the name of the deity, visit a temple on occasion, and pray at home.

Conclusion

One may refer to Hinduism as the religion of the present and the future. While the other faiths were restricted in their knowledge and orthodox beliefs, the relaxation of orthodoxy is one of the ways Hinduism continually modifies itself to fit circumstances and adapt to modernity (Venkataraman, 2014). The domination by the modern Abrahamic religions for centuries, first by the Mughals for around 300 years (1526 CE to 1858 CE) and then the British for the next 100 years (1858 CE to 1947 CE), have led to a lot of new cultural changes and values. While idol worship was never the central school of thought in Hinduism in ancient India it has now become the most followed practice of worship and faith.

Bhakti yoga or devotion traditionally meant having faith in God or the deity one believes in and doing all their work or karma while being faithful to one's deity (Muller, 1884). One does not need to visit temples and carry out complex rituals to reach God; the connection is meant to be on a personal level. Hinduism, however, had to concentrate on its foundations and involve people in ritual practises to keep them engaged in their culture and tied to their roots after the advent of Abrahamic religions. As a result, idolatry and blind faith have become more prevalent as philosophers and academics have been leeched out or converted throughout the years. Such extreme fear caused Hinduism to retreat into its shell, and the tolerance that the religious teachings already instilled in its believer's minds was a further catalyst to the problem.

Hinduism has had a lot of major reforms, especially in the 18th century. New upcoming groups strived to introduce regeneration and reform to Hinduism, both in a religious or spiritual and in a societal sense (Jones, 1990). British colonisation had a huge impact on Indian society, where social and religious leaders tried to assimilate the Western culture and modernise Hindu culture (Michaels, 2004). The way for Hinduism to keep up with modernity, technological advances, and shifting cultural paradigms is to remain true to its polytheistic spirit; tolerance of differences, and ideas that seek to enchant, persuade, and, above all, make us understand, rather than make us subject to them. Thus, the way forward for Hinduism, and in fact, for any religion, is to constantly reform, and evolve one's way of thinking, to keep up with new ideas, to integrate them, to inform them of past decisions, and to maintain one's connection to spirituality.

References

Bagchi, B. G. (2017). *Hinduism- religion of nature and future.*

Basuchoudhary, A. F., Ferrero, M., & Lubin, T. (2020). The political economy of polytheism: The Indian versus the Greco-Roman religions. *Homo Oeconomicus*, 37(3–4), 183–211. https://doi.org/10.1007/s41412-020-00102-z

Chapter 47. (n.d.). ISBN: 8173861617. *Installation of goddesses at Bahūdaka tīrtha.*

Chowdhury, S. (2023). *The economics of identity and conflict. Oxford research encyclopedia of economics and finance.* https://doi.org/10.1093/acrefore/9780190625979.013.613

Cross, F. (1974). *Heresy. The Oxford dictionary of the Christian Church* (2nd ed). ISBN: 0192115456.

Denova, R. (2019). *Monotheism in the ancient world. World history encyclopedia.*

Durant, W. (2014). *The complete story of civilization: Our oriental heritage*. ISBN: 1567310125.

Fowler, J. D. (2002). *Perspectives of reality: An introduction to the philosophy of Hinduism*. ISBN: 1898723931.

Kimmerle, H. (2006). The world of spirits and the respect for nature: Towards a new appreciation of animism. In *Journal for Transdisciplinary Research in Southern Africa*, 2(2). https://doi.org/10.4102/td.v2i2.277

Ireland, S. (2020). Ceoworld magazine. https://ceoworld.biz/2020/05/16/revealed-the-worlds-most-and-least-religious-countries-based-on-religious-beliefs-2020/, *05*, 16.

Jaffee, M. S. (2001). One God, one revelation, one people: On the symbolic structure of elective monotheism. *Journal of the American Academy of Religion*, *69*(4), 753–776. https://doi.org/10.1093/jaarel/69.4.753

Johnston, S. I. (2007). *Ancient religions*. ISBN: 0674025482.

Jones, K. W. (1990). Socioreligious reform movements in British India. *New Cambridge History of India*. ISBN-10: 0521249864 (pp. 36–53).

Kinsley, D. (2005). *Hindu goddesses: Vision of the divine feminine in the Hindu religious traditions*. ISBN: 9780520063396.

Kramer, S. (2021). https://pewrsr.ch/3nXE2jN. Pew Research Center, *09* p. 21.

Lamb, R. (2011). *Polytheism and monotheism: A Hindu perspective.*

Lochhead, D. (2001). Monotheistic violence. *Buddhist–Christian Studies*. ISSN: 0882-0945, 21(1), 3–12. https://doi.org/10.1353/bcs.2001.0017

Michaels, A. (2004). *Hinduism. Past and present, Princeton*. ISBN: 9780691089539.

Muller, M. (1884). *Shvetashvatara Upanishad, the Upanishads, Part II* p. 267. Oxford University Press. ISBN 10: 0486157113.

Nakamura, H. (1990). A history of early Vedanta philosophy. Part One, Motilal Banarsidass. ISBN-10: 8120806514.

Nicholson, A. (2013). Unifying Hinduism: Philosophy and identity in Indian intellectual history. ISBN-10: 0231149875, *2–5*.

Purana, P., & Khanda, U. [42nd Chapter]. (n.d.). ISBN-10: 8120838297.

Phillips, M. (1903). *The evolution of Hinduism*. ISBN: 9780548724217.

Religious composition by country, 2010–2050. (2022). https://www.pewresearch.org/religion/interactives/religious-composition-by-country-2010-2050/. Retrieved from Pew Research Centre.

Spinner-Halev, J. (2005). Hinduism, Christianity, and liberal religious toleration. *Political Theory*, 33(1), 28–57. https://doi.org/10.1177/0090591704271472

Thomas, R. (2014). Hindu perspectives on evolution: Darwin, dharma, and design. *Sociology of Religion*, 75(1), 164–165. https://doi.org/10.1093/socrel/sru003

Venkataraman, R. (2014). *Hinduism: A complex interplay between monotheism and polytheism*.

Krause, V., Goncalo, J. A., & Tadmor, C. T. (2021). Divine inhibition: Does thinking about God make monotheistic believers less creative? *Organizational Behavior and Human Decision Processes*, *164*, 158–178. https://doi.org/10.1016/j.obhdp.2021.03.001

***

INDIAN PSYCHOLOGY AND ITS PERSPECTIVES: AN EMPHASIS ON THE CONSCIOUSNESS AND HEALTH (YOGA, AYURVEDA AND HOMEOPATHY)

Suruchi Singh

Assistant Professor, School of Humanities,

K. R. Mangalam University, Gurugram

Ayush Singh

Student, School of Humanities

K. R. Mangalam University, Gurugram

Abstract

Indian psychology is a school of thought in psychology that is based on the Indian ethos, or the unique spirit of Indian civilization. Yoga, a spirituality that honours life, and an Indian worldview based on consciousness are its cornerstones. It is a unique psychological tradition that does not have a strong materialist or reductionist bias. The psychologically relevant books discovered in classical Indian thought are referred to as Indian psychology in general. A historical perspective helps to comprehend how social institutions and processes have changed through time while also seeing the potential and difficulties that are there in promoting a more just and equitable social environment for everyone. India's collectivistic culture promotes social cohesion and interdependence. The traditional Indian joint family, which upholds the same collectivist principles, has shown to be an important asset for the care of the mentally ill.

Keywords: Consciousness, Social Environment, Mind and Body, Yoga and Asanas, Psychological Disorders, Health, Homeopathy.

Introduction

Indian Psychology (IP) has its origins in the many knowledge traditions that have been covered in detail in the literature (Shastra), as well as in the traditions, artefacts, and meanings that the people who lived in the Indian civilization (Loka) shared. It is a component of a continuing custom that has existed continuously throughout recorded history (Dalal, 2010). Since it started in India at the turn of the 20th century under the auspices of the Western domination system, Indian Psychology is distinct from and more inclusive than academic psychology (Dalal, 2010). An approach to psychology known as Indian psychology is founded on the Indian ethos or the distinctive spirit of Indian civilization. Its foundations include yoga, a spirituality that celebrates life, and an Indian worldview founded on consciousness. It is a distinct psychological tradition that does not lean too much toward materialism or reductionism. Indian psychology, in general, refers to the psychologically significant texts found in classical Indian thinking.

Academics have a passionate debate about consciousness. Depending on the expert, culture, and belief, it is conveyed differently. It is more frequently handled as common sense or a taboo in the 20th-century Western intellectual tradition than as a subject of research. As the 21st century has progressed and individuals have begun to question their existence and the value of spirituality has resurfaced, academics, scientists, and New Agers have become enthused about addressing consciousness in both academic and popular contexts. Numerous non-Western knowledge traditions, including Sufism, Buddhism, and Hinduism, are investigated in touch with the valueless Western academic norm (some refer to these traditions as a philosophy or the esoteric component of religion) (Naufanita, 2023). The social environment describes how people interact and relate to one another in their communities. People's attitudes, behaviours, beliefs, and values can all be greatly influenced by these interactions. Various elements of the social environment, including friends, family, culture, education, religion, media, and community, can be present (Dhiman, 2023).

Family is frequently seen as the most important place for socialization and is a major influence on how people behave. People learn social conventions and values in the family, which are often passed down from generation to generation. Family members act as role models for one another and have both direct and indirect effects on how one another behaves. This review article emphasizes how social context affects people's behaviour (Dhiman, 2023). In ancient times, Humans used to live in small, close-knit communities and relied on agriculture and hunting to survive. Social norms and values were heavily influenced by religious and cultural ideas, and social hierarchies were based on things like power, wealth, and lineage. New social institutions, such as governments, educational systems, and religious organizations, evolved as societies expanded and became more complicated. These institutions contributed to social order, the regulation of behaviour, and the maintenance of injustice and inequality (Dhiman, 2023).

The Industrial Revolution in the 18th and 19th centuries was a major turning point in society as quick-moving technological advancements changed how people lived and worked. New social and economic institutions as a result of urbanization and the rise of factory employment presented both opportunities and difficulties for both individuals and communities (Dhiman, 2023). The development of mass media, globalization, and technological advancements during the 20th century contributed to the social environment's ongoing evolution. Inequality and social fragmentation took on new forms as a result of these innovations, which also brought forth new modes of communication and information sharing (Dhiman, 2023). A historical perspective enables people to recognize the opportunities and challenges they have in fostering a more just and equitable social environment for all while also understanding how social institutions and processes have changed over time.

Indian psychology is a relatively new field that has its roots in Indian philosophical thought. It has aided in the creation of therapies and treatments for mental health and well-being that are culturally aware. We now have a much better knowledge of the distinctive psychological processes and behaviour of people in India as a result of recent advancements in Indian psychology. Additionally, it has aided in the creation of interventions and therapies for mental health and well-being that are culturally aware. Indian psychology has aided in the creation of interventions and therapies for mental health and well-being that are culturally considerate. It adheres to methodological pluralism and places a special emphasis on universal viewpoints that are primarily concerned with a person's inner state, are not supernatural, religious, or dogmatic, as well as applications that encourage the improvement of human conditions to promote success and well-being. The collectivistic culture of India encourages interdependence and social solidarity. The conventional Indian joint family, which adheres to the same collectivist values, has shown to be a valuable resource for the treatment of the mentally ill.

Indian Psychology and its focus on Consciousness

Awareness as such is consciousness. The Samkhya-Yoga and Advaita Vedanta systems, which are examples of Indian psychology, hold that consciousness and mind are fundamentally dissimilar. Being (sat), knowing (cit), and feeling (ananda) are the components that make up reality. The knowledge side of the cosmos is consciousness. It is the fundamental aspect of all awareness (Campus, 2022). The scientific definition of the mind is the result of brain activity. However, scientists discovered that the mind is more potent than the brain. According to Indian tradition, the mind is made up of four substances mnas, ahamkara, Citta, and buddhi. Many philosophers refer to it as the most potent tool. The ability to manage thoughts and actions through mind control enables an individual to think and act positively in every circumstance. Controlling the thoughts and emotions is so crucial. Knowing how the mind functions and how it affects the organs and senses is necessary if an individual is to be able to regulate it (Campus, 2022).

According to Indian psychology, the mind is divided into four parts:

- Manas: The sensory mind that receives information from the senses.
- Buddhi: The intellect that discriminates between objects.
- Chitta: The memory that stores past experiences.
- Ahamkara: The ego that identifies with the body.

Yoga's and Ayurveda's study of consciousness focuses on the nature and possibilities of one's awareness outside the bounds of the mind and body. Yoga is a spiritual practice that attempts to bring an individual closer to her/his actual self—pure consciousness—rather than merely being a physical workout. The foundation of all existence and the ultimate reality is consciousness. In yoga philosophy, it is also known as Brahman, Atman, or the Self.. The fundamental topic and core of who we are, consciousness is neither an object nor a phenomena. It is something we are, not something we own. The mind, which is only a tool for observation and thought, does not have any restrictions on consciousness. Buddhi (intellect), manas (memory), ahankara (ego), and Chitta (cosmic intelligence) are the four components of the mind. Meditation, pranayama, and mantra are a few of the many yogic techniques that may be used to train and develop the mind. Additionally, the body, which is only a means of expression and activity, has no bearing on consciousness. There are five sheaths or layers that make up the body: the vijnanamaya kosha (knowledge sheath), the annamaya kosha (physical sheath), the pranamaya kosha (energetic sheath), the manomaya kosha (mental sheath), and the anandamaya kosha (bliss sheath). By using asana, kriya, and mudra, among other yogic techniques, the body may be cleansed and brought into balance.

Yoga, which means union or integration, can help people access and realize consciousness. Yoga is the process of removing the limitations and impediments that keep us from becoming who one truly is. Being in harmony with oneself, others and the cosmos is another aspect of yoga. Through yoga, an individual learns to live in consciousness, which is the wellspring of freedom, happiness, and tranquillity. Through the use of both the remedies themselves and the intake and follow-up procedures, homoeopathy also aids in the awareness of patterns. While the remedies are information carriers that inspire the innate capacity for healing and create room for healing, the intake and follow-ups provide an opportunity for reflection on one's suffering and its causes.

Yoga as a part of Indian Psychology

Yoga is a method of mental and physical exercise designed to bring about spiritual enlightenment. One of the six traditional schools of Hinduism. Yoga and Indian psychology are intimately intertwined. Indian psychology is based on the Indian ethos, which is the distinctive spirit of Indian civilization. Its foundations include yoga, a spirituality that celebrates life, and an Indian worldview founded on consciousness. It has been shown that yoga is beneficial for enhancing mental wellness. It has been demonstrated to lessen stress, sadness, and anxiety symptoms. In addition to treating physical ailments, yoga is also used to treat mental illnesses like schizophrenia, bipolar disorder, and obsessive-compulsive disorder. It has been hypothesized that traditional forms of yoga, such as hatha yoga, can help alleviate mental health issues. Hatha yoga, Raja yoga, Gyan yoga, and Bhakti yoga are only a few examples of the many branches of yoga. Hatha yoga, which emphasizes physical movement, posture, and breath, is the foundation of many other forms of yoga and has been shown to have therapeutic benefits in conventional Western medicine (Bhargav, 2023). Different schools of hatha yoga, such as Ananda, Anusara, Ashtanga, Iyengar, Bikram, Kripalu, Kundalini, and Viniyoga, have different emphases and methods for treating mental health issues The Iyengar Method of Hatha yoga was developed by yogi guru B.K.S. Iyengar. The standing postures practised in this kind of yoga are designed to improve balance, core strength, and overall physical fitness (Bhargav, 2023).

Anusara yoga for depression causes a reduction in anxiety and depression as well as a reduction in stress and weariness. This kind of yoga highlights the union of outward expression and inside movement. Hatha yoga is practised by Ananda to lower stress and anxiety, intensify spiritual encounters, and enhance physical stamina and balance. This type of yoga focuses on profound relaxation and meditation. Through the practice of Ashtanga yoga postures, anxiety may be decreased, cardiovascular fitness can be increased, and flexibility can be improved. The core principles of Bikram, Kripalu, Kundalini, and Viniyoga include sweating and bodily detoxification, as well as the flowing and fusing of body, breath, and mind, the use of different mantras to direct breathing, and the fusing of different postures with chanting, breathing, and meditation. These techniques assist people with chronic health conditions in relaxing while also enhancing their physical stamina and flexibility. They are also beneficial for people who are suffering from dread and worry (Bhargav, 2023).

Numerous research has demonstrated the efficacy of Yogic intervention as a non-drug approach to treating mental disease. Yoga's effectiveness as an intervention technique for mental issues has been attested to in several publications that have been published recently. In India, yoga asanas are utilized to improve overall health and well-being. These papers offer early proof of a connection between yoga and psychological issues based on a conceptual analysis of the previous 50 years of research into the junction of yoga and Indian medicine. According to research, yoga offers several advantages, including improving cardiovascular fitness and even curing mental illnesses. The results show that yoga is useful in treating stress-related illnesses like diabetes (Deepak, 2013). Yoga has various advantages, including those related to physical exercise, breathing techniques, and mindfulness, which can be better appreciated by looking at the practice from a pathophysiological angle. Traditional yoga has been shown to promote both physical and mental wellness in people of all ages. Yoga may also play a significant role in the recovery and treatment of those who are suffering from a chronic illness, are recuperating from surgery, or are otherwise unwell owing to any ailment. Yoga provides several health advantages, such as improved strength, balance, and flexibility as well as less stress, higher quality sleep, and lessened back pain (Turmel, 2022).

Psychotherapy in Ayurveda

The systematic line of mental illnesses, according to Charaksamhita, entails Nidana Parivarjana, or the eradication of the root cause, Daivavyapasraya chikitsa, and Yukti vyapasraya chikitsa. The term "Vyapasraya" above means relying on or having faith in. The term "Daivavyapasraya" directly translates to imply any treatment that depends on the "Daivya" (Devine) or is connected to it, and it is concerned with unknowable situations that are outside the scope of reason or that cannot be established on a scientific basis, leaving it to be classified solely as a form of spiritual therapy. It includes Mantrah (Incantations), Manidharan (Precious Stones), Oushadam (Amulets), Mangalam (Propitiatory Rites), Balih (Oblations), Homah (Sacrifice), Upavasah (Fasting), Japah (Prayer), and Vratam (Vows) since it is a magico-religious practice.

Yuktivyapasraya, whose name translates to "union, connection," is quite reasonable in its approach to treating psychological illnesses (Yadav S). The literal meaning of Sattvavajaya is "conquest of mind." This treatment seems to be more logical and effective. Ayurvedic The inclusion of Sadvrittam (ideal behaviour) or a moral code is a distinctive feature of the psychotherapy known as Sattvavajaya Chikitsa (Mind Control Therapy). The psychological approach of Ayurveda known as Sattvavajaya treatment involves mind control techniques such as emotion replacement, psychophysical shocks, moral and behavioural guidelines, mental calmness, and the inhibition of some psychophysical, environmental, psychological, and volitional stresses. By embracing some temporal vagaries, such as over- or under-manifestation, a perverse manifestation of the five human senses, control of the mind, intellectual advancement, seasonal observance, and discrimination (Yadav S).

There are several techniques used in this therapy, such as progressive withdrawal from addictive behaviours and positive behaviour substitution for harmful ones. By maintaining mental equanimity such as fortitude, patience, awareness, memory, genuine knowledge, etc., one may replace emotions such as malice with love, anger with calm, greed with contentment, ignorance with knowledge, jealousy with compassion, fear with bravery, etc. This approach just guides appropriate behaviour. Insofar as it strives to replace a bad feeling like hatred with a good emotion like love, the Ayurvedic approach to psychological healing might be characterized as positive. Because of this, the sattvavajaya treatment stands out on its own (Yadav S).

Role of Homeopathy in Psychology

India has a long and vibrant history of medicine. In India, a significant body of medical knowledge has developed over thousands of years via trial and error, cultural interchange, and assimilation. Ayurveda, Unani, Siddha, Yoga, and Naturopathy are a few of these advanced systems. India has practised Ayurveda since about 4000 BC. The other systems have also existed for many centuries. Although it has German roots, homeopathy is also commonly used in India. Numerous of these systems also evaluate a person's psychological, ethical, philosophical, and spiritual well-being. They promote healthy lifestyles, which include living in harmony with the environment. The World Health Organization's definition of health is consistent with these ideas (Roy, 2015). The Government of India established the Department of Indian Systems of Medicine and Homoeopathy (ISM and H) in 1995, which was later renamed the Department of Ayurveda, Yoga and Naturopathy, Unani, Siddha, and Homoeopathy (AYUSH) in 2003. This was done in recognition of the harm that had been done to traditional systems of healing and to encourage their use (Roy, 2015). The use of holistic principles sets homeopathy apart from conventional medications. Focusing on the patient rather than the illness, taking the patient into account as a whole, removing the underlying causes of the illness rather than just treating the symptoms, restoring health to all body levels and preserving it by enhancing the body's defence mechanisms, and last but not least, using natural remedies that won't have negative effects on the body, all make homeopathy more effective than the other conventional therapies.

One of the core principles of homeopathy is that a cure is curative when it is administered based on the patient's most profound level of experience and vital feeling. There is energy at that level that is similar to non-human entities like plants, minerals, or animals. It appears to be absurd. The human component, which is meant to be there, and the non-human portion, which isn't, are like two different melodies playing inside of one person. The language of the remedy's kingdom—plant sensitivity, mineral structure, or animal survival—will be the melody that it sings. It will perfectly express itself as the substance's melody (Naude, 2010). Anxiety and depression are two psychological illnesses that can be treated with homeopathy. Additionally, several studies have demonstrated the usefulness of homeopathy in treating various psychiatric disorders such as PTSD, acute stress disorder, and trauma (Chappell, 2003). When used in therapeutic settings, homeopathic treatment can alleviate a variety of psychological conditions. According to a study's findings, homeopathy can treat a wide range of clinical conditions, including schizophrenia, autism, OCD, agoraphobia, suicidal depression, hysteria, and sleep disturbances (Johannes K, 2009). Homeopathic therapies for anxieties and phobias have been demonstrated in several studies of case analysis to be therapeutic (Guethlin C, 2010). The use of homeopathy in the treatment of psychiatric disorders is essential. A person's fundamental requirements are to live a healthy and happy life. The internal effects of homeopathic medicine individualize each patient based on their constitution. In all respects, mental health is paramount; if the mind is in good shape, so is the body, and a person leads a healthy life. In homeopathic medicine, the patient is treated, not the ailment and this is also how the medicines are prescribed. Homeopathy is a suitable therapeutic option for psychological disorders as a result.

Findings

An approach to psychology known as "Indian psychology" is based on concepts and methods that have been used for thousands of years in the Indian subcontinent. When one refers to "Indian psychology," it is implied that it is a method of psychology that is founded on beliefs and customs that have existed for thousands of years on the Indian subcontinent. It does not mean, for instance, that "psychology as taught at Indian universities" or "the psychology of the Indian people" (Joshi & Cornelissen, 2004). Yoga is a tradition that dates back thousands of years and has its roots in ancient India. It is an all-encompassing method of well-being promotion that incorporates physical postures, breathing exercises, and meditation.

The advantages of yoga practice are numerous. For instance, studies have shown that yoga can help people feel less stressed and anxious, sleep better, be more flexible and balanced, and be more physically fit overall. Yoga is significant because it fosters the wellness of the body, mind, and soul. It can boost well-being, lessen tension, and increase flexibility. It helps us become a better version of ourselves by bridging our physical, mental, and spiritual identities. Yoga poses give the body a cosmic energy boost and make it easier to achieve perfect harmony and balance. Yoga also encourages self-healing, purges toxins from the body and negative mental barriers from the mind, builds personal strength, heightens self-awareness, and aids with attention, focus, and concentration. The goal of both yoga and mindfulness is to develop a greater level of awareness, connection, or oneness between the mind, body, and spirit. Yoga cannot exist without focused awareness. Yoga and mindfulness both seek to calm the mind to foster a closer relationship with and awareness of the self. Yoga can enhance cognitive abilities including memory and learning. It develops brain regions that are crucial for memory, focus, consciousness, cognition, and language.

The ancient Indian medicinal system known as Ayurveda mainly depends on herbal remedies and other organic substances. What distinguishes Ayurveda from other medical systems is its intrinsic capacity to identify the root of a problem and treat it rather than just the symptoms. According to Ayurveda, an imbalance in the body's doshas is the primary cause of illnesses. Because it may assist us in leading a healthy, happy, stress-free, and disease-free existence, Ayurveda is still relevant today. Detoxification, pain alleviation, immune support, lifestyle optimization, stress reduction, surgery avoidance, and abstinence from prescription medicines are all possible benefits. The mind is seen by Ayurveda as a crucial component of the body which oversees the ideas, feelings, and behaviours. According to Ayurveda, the body and mind are interdependent, and neither can be healthy alone. The importance of mental health and well-being is emphasized in Ayurveda. It holds that physical and mental health are interdependent and that both are equally vital. Ayurveda also holds that an imbalance in the Doshas may be the root of mental health issues. Anxiety, sadness, and stress are among the mental health issues that ayurvedic remedies can assist with. The Doshas are meant to be balanced through ayurvedic treatments, which also aim to improve general health. Meditation, yoga, massage, herbal medicines, and dietary adjustments are all part of Ayurvedic therapy. These treatments can aid in lowering stress levels, enhancing mental clarity, and encouraging relaxation.

In homeopathy, the concept of mind and body examines the relationship between a person's psychological and emotional state and physical well-being. A holistic approach to treatment, homeopathy treats the full individual rather than simply the symptoms. According to homeopathy, the body and mind are inextricably linked and have a direct impact on one another. As a result, homeopathic treatments are chosen following the mental, emotional, and physical features of the patient as well as the illness's history and root cause. According to the "like cures like" theory of homeopathy, a chemical that creates symptoms in a healthy person can also treat those same symptoms in a sick person. Natural ingredients, such as plants, minerals, or animal products, are diluted and shaken to create homeopathic treatments. Homeopathy may cure a wide range of psychological issues, including stress, sorrow, rage, anxiety, sadness, and phobias, as well as medical conditions that have a psychosomatic cause or aggravated state, including asthma, skin conditions, ulcers, hypertension, and more. Homeopathy can also aid in the treatment of psychologically driven lifestyle illnesses including enuresis and anorexia nervosa. When choosing a remedy, homeopathy takes into account the patient's mental and emotional health. For instance, a person with agitation, dread, and thirst may want an Arsenicum album, but a person with calmness, assurance, and lack of thirst may require Bryonia alba for the same physical ailment. To discover the best treatment, homeopathy also considers the patient's personality, temperament, likes and dislikes, dreams, hobbies, etc. The goal of homeopathy is to activate the body's capacity for self-healing and to reestablish the harmony between the mind and body. Homeopathy deals with the underlying cause of the illness rather than masking or suppressing the symptoms. By boosting a person's immunity and vitality, homeopathy can also stop or lessen the recurrence of chronic illnesses.

Conclusion

The research paper focuses on the role of Indian Psychology in the sphere of health, understanding the concept of consciousness, and how the Mind can be related to the Human Body/ Psyche. The paper focuses on the aspects of psychotherapy and its relation with the Yoga Asanas, Ayurvedic Therapies also focuses on the vivid use of Homeopathy in the Indian Psychological Context and its impact on the Mind and Body concept. Currently, there has not been much advancement in studies relating to Indian psychological principles. Unity-diversity, science-philosophy, specific-integrative, technique-theory, clinical conditions-therapy, experimental-experiential, quantitative-qualitative, publish-silent, stagnant-vibrant, and other issues are some of the obstacles and conflicts that Indian researchers must contend with. The following four actions are recommended for the future: accept/enquire, identify/explore, maintain/persist, and communicate/modify.

To distinguish between ideas that are philosophical in character and those that are merely representative of and a mirror of human nature, concepts found in the many Indian philosophies must be thoroughly examined. They must be approached differently to preserve their depth and importance. To examine these, novel strategies and techniques must be created, employing, where necessary, first-person and cutting-edge scientific technology. The study employs a descriptive methodology using secondary data acquired from scholarly articles made available on Google Scholar. The author synthesizes the corpus of prior research to provide a comprehensive and up-to-date appraisal of the topic. The findings can serve as a roadmap for future studies that seek to develop the theories of sustainable ayurveda, yoga, homeopathy, and Indian psychology.

References

Avasthi, A., & A. R. (ND). Psychotherapy in the Indian context. *Journal of Clinical Psychiatry.*

Behere, P. B., & Natraj, G. S. (1984). Dhat syndrome: The phenomenology of a culture-bound sex neurosis of the Orient. *Indian Journal of Psychiatry*, 26(1), 76–78.

Bhargav, M. D. (2023). *A review on yoga usefulness to reducing anxiety, stress and depression.*

Campus, M. (2022). *Types and nature of mind according to Indian culture–an overview.*

Chappell, P. (2003). *Emotional healing with homeopathy- treating the effects*. North Atlantic Books.

Dalal, A. K., & Misra, G. (2010). The core and context of Indian psychology. *Psychology and Developing Societies*, *22*(1), 121–155. https://doi.org/10.1177/097133360902200105

Deepak, K. K. (2013). Yogic intervention for mental disorders. *Indian Journal of Psychiatry*, 55 Suppl. 3, S340–S343. https://doi.org/10.4103/0019-5545.116300

Dhiman, D. B. (2023). *How social environment influences People's behavior: A critical review.* . Available at SSRN 4417597.

Gautam, S., & Jain, N. (2010). Indian culture and psychiatry. *Indian Journal of Psychiatry*, *52*(7) Suppl. 1, 309–313. Retrieved 6 3, 2023.

https://ncbi.nlm.nih.gov/pmc/articles/pmc3146223. https://doi.org/10.4103/0019-5545.69259

Gielen, U. P., & F. J. (ND). *Handbook of culture, therapy, and healing.*

Guethlin, C., Walach, H., Naumann, J., Bartsch, H. H., & Rostock, M. (2010). Characteristics of cancer patients using homeopathy compared with those in conventional care: A cross-sectional study. *Annals of Oncology, 21*(5), 1094–1099. https://doi.org/10.1093/annonc/mdp421

Johannes, K., & Z. V. (2009). *Homeopathy and mental health care. Home links.*

Joshi, K., & Cornelissen, M. e. (2004). *Consciousness, Indian psychology and yoga. New Delhi: Centre for studies in civilizations.*

McClelland, D. (1961). *The achieving society.* Van Nostrand.

Nakamura, H. (1997). *Ways of thinking of eastern peoples: India, China, Tibet and Japan.* Kegun Paul.

Naudé, D. F., Stephanie Couchman, I. M., & Maharaj, A. (2010). Chronic primary insomnia: Efficacy of homeopathic simillimum. *Homeopathy,* 99(1), 63–68. https://doi.org/10.1016/j.homp.2009.11.001

Naufanita, H. N. (2023). Neither to the east nor the West: A multidisciplinary review of consciousness. *Journal of Strategic and Global Studies, 6*(1), 5.

(W). (2004). Hanuman Complex and its Resolution: An Illustration of Psychotherapy from Indian mythology. *Indian Journal of Psychiatry.*

Paranjpe, A. (2009). In defence of an Indian approach to the psychology of emotion. Psychological studies. psychology.net.in. (n.d.). https://psychology.net.in/what-is-indian-psychology/

Roy, M. (ND). *Integrating traditional healing practices into counseling and psychotherapy. William West.*

Roy, V. (2015). Time to sensitize medical graduates to the Indian Systems of Medicine and Homeopathy. *Indian Journal of Pharmacology*, 47(1), 1–3. https://doi.org/10.4103/0253-7613.150301

Turmel, D. C., Carlier, S., Bruyneel, A. V., & Bruyneel, M. (2022). Tailored individual Yoga practice improves sleep quality, fatigue, anxiety, and depression in chronic insomnia disorder. *BMC Psychiatry*, 22(1), 267. https://doi.org/10.1186/s12888-022-03936-w

***

BHASKARACHARYA: A FORERUNNER OF GRAVITY

P. C. Jena

Associate Professor, School of Education,

K.R.Mangalam University, Gurugram

Abstract

When one speaks about gravity, the first name that pops into the mind is "Sir Isaac Newton". In the schools, the children have been told the story of how Newton had an idea and formulated the Universal "Law of Gravitation" when an apple fell from a tree. The world believes that Newton was the first to discover the gravitational concepts. But it is a matter of startling fact that the theory of gravitation was created 1200 years before Newton by an Indian Mathematician Bhaskaracharya. The present paper tries to explore the unveiling theories of Bhaskaracharya in the field of the discovery of gravity before Sir Isaac Newton.

Keywords: Bhaskaracharya, Gurutvakarshan Shakti, Surya Siddhanta, Lilavati.

Introduction

India is considered a traditional country, but the world is unaware of its contributions to this modern world. Its theories have been used as the basis for many concepts such as weather forecasting, astronomy, astrology, aviation etc. India has developed some of the best mathematicians the world has ever seen. Among them, Bhaskaracharya was one of the prominent figures. He was an Indian mathematician and astronomer who expanded Brahmagupta's work on number systems and was born near Bijjada Bida (in present-day Bijapur district, Karnataka state, South India) in the Deshastha Brahmin family. Bhaskaracharya was the director of an astronomical observatory in Ujjain, the main mathematical centre of ancient India. His predecessors in this position included both the prominent Indian mathematician Brahmagupta and Varahamihira. He lived in the Sahyadri region. It has been recorded that his great-great-great-grandfather held a hereditary post as a court scholar, as did his son and other descendants. His father Mahesvara was an astrologer, who taught him mathematics, which he later passed on to his son Loksamudra. Loksamudra's son helped to set up a school in 1207 for the study of Bhaskara's writings.

Bhaskaracharya's work in Algebra, Arithmetic and Geometry catapulted him to fame and immortality. His renowned mathematical works called Lilavati and Bijaganita are considered incomparable and a monument to his profound intelligence. Its translation into different languages of the world testifies to its eminence. In his treatise, Siddhant Shiromani writes about planetary positions, eclipses, cosmography, mathematical techniques and astronomical equipment. In the Surya Siddhant, the force of gravity says "Objects fall on earth due to a force of attraction by the earth. Therefore, the earth, planets, constellations, moon, and sun are held in orbit due to this attraction."

Bhaskaracharya was the first to discover gravity, 500 years before Sir Isaac Newton. He was the champion among mathematicians of ancient and medieval India. His works have ignited the imagination of Persian and European scholars, who have gained fame and popularity through the investigation of his works. Before discussing the contribution of Bhaskaracharya, let us understand the basic concept of gravity. Gravity is a universal force that allows a body mass to attract other body masses. The greater the body mass, the greater is the force of gravity.

Importance of Gravity

Objects stay on Earth because of the gravitational pull. Every single body in the universe is affected by gravitational forces which also include the Earth, sun and the moon. Tidal waves are created by the gravitational pull of the moon. Sun's gravitational pull keeps all the planets in the orbit. Earth's gravity allows it to revolve around the sun. Let us get to the work of Bhaskaracharya.

The first principle of gravity was stated by "Bhaskaracharya" and not "Newton"

Bhaskaracharya stated the laws of gravity in the book Surya Siddhanta in the 11th century. Thus, the law existed even before the birth of Sir Isaac Newton (Newton was born in the 16th century). Here are some of the slokas from his book Surya Siddhanta that mention how gravitation works:

"madhye samantandasya bhugolo vyomni tisthati
bibhranah paramam saktim brahmano dharanatmikam"
[Surya Sidhantha 12th Chapter 32 Sloka]

This means that the spherical earth is at the centre of the earth in space due to the dharanatmikam shakti which prevents the earth from falling and helps it to remain stable.

"akrsta saktisca mahi taya yat svastham guru svabhimukham svasaktya
akrsyate tatpatativa bhati same samantat kva patatviyam khe"
[Sidhanta Shiromani, Bhuvanakosa, 6th Sloka]

This means that every object falls to the ground due to the earth's force of attraction. This force allows the sun, earth, moon and constellations to remain in orbit.

Bhaskaracharya wrote a treatise entitled **Lilavati** where he answers a question posed by his little daughter. In this book, he answers the curious questions of his daughter Lilavati.

This book explains that the earth has a gravitational force (**Gurutvakarshan Shakti**). There is a mutual attraction between the planets, and this allows them to stay firmly in space. He also mentioned the shape of the earth while answering his daughter's question. Bhaskaracharya stated that "what we see is not reality, the Earth may appear flat, but it is actually spherical". In addition, he explains this theory by stating "If you draw a very big circle and look at one-fourth of its circumference, you see it as a straight line. But in the true sense, it is a circle. Similarly, the earth is spherical in shape." These historical mentions are proof that laws of gravity were first discovered in India by Bhaskaracharya. His laws predate Newton's law, he did not wait for the apple to fall. Everybody knows about Newton's law of gravity, but they have no idea about "Bhaskaracharya's Law of Gravity".

Conclusion

Bhaskaracharya and his works represent a significant contribution to the mathematical and astronomical knowledge of the twelfth century. He has been called the greatest mathematician in medieval India. He calls himself a poet and it was probably Vedanti since he mentioned 'Parambrahman' in that verse. He was the champion among the mathematicians of ancient and medieval India. Some historical quotes are proof that the laws of gravity were first discovered in India by Bhaskaracharya. His laws predate Newton's law, he did not wait for the apple to fall. Everybody knows Newton's law of gravity, but they have no idea about ***"Bhaskaracharya's Law of Gravity".***

References

Burton, D. M. (2011). *The history of mathematics: An introduction* (7th ed). McGraw-Hill

PranNath. (1982). *Religions and communities of India, Vision Books, Cooke, Roger (1997). The mathematics of the Hindus,the history of mathematics: A brief course* (pp. 213–215). Wiley Interscience.

Eves, H. (1990). *An introduction to the history of mathematics* (6th ed). Saunders College Publishing.

Goonatilake, S. (1999). *Toward a global science: Mining civilizational knowledge*. Indiana University Press.

Pingree, D. E. (1970). *Census of the exact sciences in Sanskrit, 146.* American Philosophical Society.

Plofker, K. (2007). Mathematics in India. In *Katz, victor* J. The Mathematics of Egypt, and Islam: A Sourcebook. Princeton University Press.

Plofker, K. (2009). *Mathematics in India.* Princeton University Press.

Poulose, K. G. (1991). Scientific Heritage of India, mathematics, *22* of RavivarmaSamskr̥tagranthāvali, *Govt. Sanskrit college.* Tripunithura.

Sarkār, B. K. (1918). *Hindu achievements in exact science: A study in the history of scientific development*. Longmans, Green, and Co.

Seal, Sir B. (1915). *The positive sciences of the ancient Hindus, Longmans, Green and Co.*

Selin, H. (2008). *Astronomical instruments in India, encyclopaedia of the history of science, technology, and medicine in non-western cultures* (2nd ed). Springer Verlag.

Selin, H., & D'Ambrosio, U. (2001). *Mathematics across cultures: The history of non-western mathematics*, *2* of Science across cultures. Springer.

Shukla, K. S. (1984). Use of calculus in Hindu mathematics. *Indian Journal of History of Science*, *19*, 95–104.

Stillwell, J. (2002). *Mathematics and its history, Undergraduate Texts in Mathematics, Springer*.

White, L. T. (1978). *Tibet, India, and Malaya as Sources of Western Medieval Technology, Medieval religion and technology: Collected essays*. University of California Press.

SILENT NARRATIVES: STATE AND SOCIETY IN INDIA

Ruchika Yadav
Associate Professor, School of Commerce and Management, K.R. Mangalam University
Kristin Sajeev
Student, School of Commerce and Management, K.R. Mangalam University, Gurugram
Jingyasa Mohapatra
Student, School of Commerce and Management, K.R. Mangalam University, Gurugram

Abstract

The relationship between the state and the society in India has evolved. This chapter delves into the complex shade of India's political system, examining the historical roots and the mechanisms that have influenced the state-society dynamic. It focuses on understanding the concepts and systems of governance and politics that have evolved in the Indian context. This chapter aims to shed light on the characteristics and mechanisms of early Indian society and its relationship with its citizens. Furthermore, it focuses on the contribution of literary, epigraphical, and archaeological sources in reconstructing the socio-political system and understanding the relationship between the state and society. It seeks to illuminate the track of Indian society by providing valuable insights into the present-day socio-political landscape and will help deepen the understanding of the relationship between the state and society. By throwing light on the historical precedents, ideological frameworks, and mechanisms of governance, one can gain valuable insights that inform contemporary discourse and contribute to the ongoing quest for effective governance in the context of India.

Keywords: State-Society Dynamics, Governance, Politics, Socio-Political System, Literary Sources, Epigraphical Sources, Archaeological Sources.

Introduction

With its rich and diverse history, India has witnessed various forms of governance and polity, framed by different historical, cultural, and social factors. This chapter aims to shed light on the evolution of governance structures, political ideologies, overall functioning, characteristics, mechanisms, and contributions from literature and epigraphical and archaeological sources. It analyses the key concepts and system of governance and polity that have prevailed in India over time.

i) **<u>Ancient India</u>:** The era from 600 BC to 1200 AD can be considered the ancient period. One of the notable and emerging concepts of governance and polity in ancient India was 'Raj dharma', which emphasized the ethical duties and responsibilities of a ruler towards his subjects. In the Mauryan empire, Kausalya's work on the Arthashastra was described as the most precious work, it lays down two things first, on how a king can expand his territory, keep enemies at bay, enhance his external power, and amass riches; second how a king can best organize his state bureaucracy to consolidate his internal enemies, to expand the economy, to enhance his treasure through taxes, duties, and entrepreneurial activities, to keep law and order, and to settle disputes among his subjects. (Mukherjee, 2017)

ii) **<u>Medieval India:</u>** In the medieval period, there was the emergence of Islamic dynasties, which lead to a change in the governance and polity of India. The introduction of a centralized system of governance by the Delhi sultanate and the Mughal empire led to absolute powers in the hands of the ruler[king]. There was a feudal structure that included nobles and zamindars having administrative control over their regions. This period was entirely based on Islamic principles and laws.

iii) **Colonial Period:** This period has a lot of significance in the history of India. The arrival of the British marked a transformative phase in governance and polity. The British East India Company initially established trading posts but later it became a region of territorial control, and they established a colonial administrative system in which the governor-general was the highest authority. It limited Indian representation in representative bodies. The citizens had to struggle a lot for their independence and freedom.

iv) **Independence and Post-Independence:** After the independence of India in 1947 there was no authority or body of governance. That was the time when the Indian National Congress and other political movements demanded self-rule. The first thing India adopted was democracy or a democratic system of governance. Later the Constitution of India was framed and was enacted in 1950. It mentioned India as a sovereign, socialist, secular, and democratic republic. Under the Constitution, India adopted a parliamentary form of government with a prime minister as the head of the government and a president as the head of the state.

v) **Federal Structure and Panchayati Raj System:** The federal system of India divides powers between the central government and the states, where there are chief ministers and other ministers for each state. India adopted a three-tier system [Panchayati raj system] for the local regions to have their government at village block and district levels.

vi) **Current Government and Polity:** As per the current scenario India has a multiparty political system. There are also two houses of parliament, one is Rajya Sabha which is the Council of States and Lok Sabha which is the House of the People. Political parties in India have numerous ideologies and interests. The major national parties are BJP (Bhartiya Janata Party) and INC (Indian National Congress).

According to Thapar (2004), the three main sources for any discovery are literary, archaeological, and epigraphical studies. She points out that, "a major component in the construction of national identity and culture Indian nationalism is based on perceptions of early India to an astonishing degree, for some prominent nationalist historians saw Indian identity rooted in various versions of Hindu religions. `Her chapter on the politics of Northern India, circa AD 700–1200, is crucial to her interpretation of early Indian history, for this is the period referred to in many texts as "the Muslim invasion," when, according to one distinguished nationalist historian, the Muslim rulers "very nearly extinguished the Hindu culture by destroying the sources which fed and nourished it.

Bhattacharya (2003) spoke about multiculturalism and pluralism in the contemporary world. He talked about the notion of "governance of multicultural societies" covering a wide range of geographical and historical situations. Moreover, it is often used interchangeably with the term "pluralism". He stated that plural society had a lot of significance in the pre and post-colonial periods.

Khan (2001) stated that Aurangzeb's religious policy is thought to have provoked a Hindu Reaction that destroyed the unity built by Hindus and their successors. It is possible to argue that, besides being influenced by the freedom movement's motive for political unification, this characterization reflected the Mughal political system and administration. To historians like Irvine and Sarkar, the decline was because of the personal deterioration of the kings and nobles. Desai (2005) examined the relationship between a strong expansion between the 1860s and early 1940s, in Kerala, India, under indirect British rule. The author argues that the early welfare policies in Kerala were implemented in a dependent colonial context. Attention was focused on Kerala as the model of creating state policies and social development. No single work has attempted to understand the significance of its prior legacy of welfare.

On these lines, the major objective of this chapter is to examine the dynamic relationship between the state and society in India, with a focus on governance, polity, and the evolution of this relationship over time. The study aims to explore the various mechanisms through which the state interacts with society, including policymaking, public administration, and political processes. By analyzing historical and contemporary contexts, the research seeks to understand the impact of state-society relations on governance outcomes, social cohesion, and citizen participation. Additionally, it aims to identify key challenges, opportunities, and potential strategies for strengthening the state-society relationship in India, considering the diverse cultural, political, and socioeconomic factors influencing this dynamic.

To get the answers to these questions, an interdisciplinary approach to analysis that combines historical research, policy analysis, and sociological inquiry to explore the relationship between the state and society in India has been adopted. This involves examining primary sources such as government documents, legal frameworks, and political speeches, alongside secondary literature such as scholarly articles, books, and policy reports. By conducting comparative analysis and contextual understanding, this study aims to shed light on the evolving dynamics of governance and polity in India across different historical periods, political regimes, and cultural contexts. To gain a deeper understanding of the political transitions and socio-economic factors influencing the formation of states in contemporary India, it also includes a thorough analysis of primary sources like historical documents, governmental records, and speeches of notable leaders. To assess the effects of empires, colonial control, and nationalist movements on the political landscape of the Indian subcontinent, the study also uses a comparative analysis. Thus, to provide a thorough picture of the development of Indian states and politics throughout history, the research technique blends qualitative analysis, literature evaluation, and historical interpretation. It also highlights the historical and contemporary dynamics between the state and society in India, emphasizing the need to consider colonial legacies, socio-economic factors, and civil society engagement for inclusive and responsive governance.

Findings

This research delves into the intricate dynamics between the state and society in India, exploring the governance, polity, and evolving relationship between the two entities over time. The examination of historical and contemporary perspectives offers valuable insights into the socio-political fabric of the nation. Additionally, this research effort provides a comprehensive understanding of the evolving dynamics between the state and society in India. It highlights the impact of historical, political, and socio-economic factors on governance and the challenges and opportunities that have emerged over time. By examining these findings, policymakers and scholars can gain valuable insights into fostering more inclusive and responsive state-society relations, contributing to the overall development and well-being of the nation.

Features and Mechanisms of Early Indian Society

The early Indian society included various features and mechanisms that shaped its structures and functions. The varna system was one of them; the varna system was like the caste system and was based on a social hierarchy which classified individuals into 4 varnas namely Brahmanas who were the priests and scholars; second, the Kshatriyas who were the warriors and rulers; the Vaishyas who were the merchants and the farmers and the last were the Shudras or the lower caste who were expected to serve the rest three. Next was the jati system which referred to sub-caste or occupational groups. The jatis are the groups that were based on a person's occupation or profession. Another mechanism of the earlier Indian societies was the Vedic religion that was influenced by the Vedic traditions and scriptures called the Vedas the society was organized around ritual sacrifices and worshipping different types of deities. Also, in ancient times, there were no nuclear families and most of the families were joint families. The societies were predominantly agrarian and village communities from the basic unit of social and economic organization. The local governance was ensured by the village councils that included the panchayats known as the *sabhas*. Many people even followed Dharma which mentioned the duties and responsibilities based on one's caste, age, gender and stage of life and ashram system was also very common at that time and divided into 4 types of ashrams brahmacharya, grihastha, vanaprastha, and sannyasa. These features and mechanisms evolved and changed over time.

Contribution from Literature, Epigraphical, and Archaeological Sources

Literary epigraphical and archaeological sources play a crucial role in understanding the mechanism of early Indian society because they provide valuable insights into understanding the political socio-economic aspects of ancient Indian society as well as the relationship between the society and the state. Here are some contributions from literature epigraphical and archaeological sources.

i) **Literary Sources**: The literary sources include works of scholars' philosophers and they provide information about the early Indian society there are various types of literary sources like the Vedas. It includes the Rigveda, Yajurveda, Samaveda, and Atharveda, all these Vedas speak about religious practices and among them 'Rigveda' is the oldest religious text in

Hinduism. Apart from Vedas, there are various other literary sources like Dharma shastras which are texts that include Manusmriti and Arthashastra which lays down laws, governance, and codes. The Mahabharata and Ramayana are epic poems that provide information about the governance system and the political structures and it's one of the best literary sources available. The teachings of Buddha and Mahavira in the Buddhist and Jaina text provides knowledge about societal structures and ethical principles.

ii) **Epigraphical Sources:** The epigraphical sources refer to those sources that are found on rock pillars, plates of copper or even cave walls. One of the major epigraphical sources is the rock edicts of Ashoka including inscriptions by the Mauryan emperor Ashoka which reveal his policies, religious beliefs and efforts towards social welfare it also includes his teachings about dhamma. Other inscriptions include inscriptions by the Gupta dynasty which was considered a golden age in ancient Indian history it also provides information regarding the governance and patronage of art and culture. Other than this other cave inscriptions are also knowledgeable in providing insights about the state and society inscriptions found in cave complexes like Ajanta and Ellora which signify the religious practices as well as the beliefs the people followed.

iii) **Archaeological Sources:** The contribution from the archaeological sources includes various artefacts, coins, city ruins etc. During the Harappan civilization, various excavations at Harappan sites like Mohen-jo-Daro and Harappa have rebuilt urban planning and development of that time and also talks about the Indus Valley civilization and during the Mauryan empire archaeological finds at Patliputra and Sarnath have also provided information about the urban life during the Mauryan. The archaeological sources also include various monuments like the Buddhist and Hindu monuments like the Sanchi stupa and Konark sun temple provide the religious practices and beliefs of that time.

Evolution of Indian States During Ancient India and Medieval India

1. In ancient Indian history, there were states alongside empires. India gained independence in 1947, before that period India saw many transitions concerning political structure, governance, and the role of states within the federal system.
2. During the ancient period, India witnessed the rise of several powerful empires such as the Maurya Empire (321-185 BCE) under Emperor Ashoka, the Gupta Empire (320-550 CE), and the Mughal Empire (1526-1857 CE). These empires exerted significant control over large territories with centralized authority as well.
3. Alongside these powerful empires, there were many smaller states and kingdoms which had their own rulers and governing systems. One example can be the kingdom of Magadha, these states engaged in conflicts with others and also with powerful and larger empires. It can be said that the image of ancient India was characterized by a very complex interplay of states regional powers and imperial entities.
4. The arrival of the Mughals had a lasting impact on various aspects of Indian society including administration, governance, culture, politics, architecture, etc. The Mughals under the leadership of emperor Akbar and his successors brought a large of the Indian subcontinent under a single centralized administration. This led to an expansion of the Mughal's political stability, encompassing a vast territory.
5. From the mid-18th century to 1947, British rule lasted for nearly 200 years which had a significant and lasting impact on the territorial and political landscape of the Indian

subcontinent. British East India Company which came with the initial motive of trade, gradually expanded its power and influence and established political control. They introduced policies and practices favouring their economic interests, leading to the exploitation of India's wealth and essential resources. The traditional Indian industries like textiles, handicrafts, etc. declined due to heavy taxes imposed by the British. Eventually, India became a large supplier of raw materials for British industries. These industries were highly machinery-equipped which produced a large number of goods and cheaper prices. With this British introduced the permanent settlement system, ryotwari and mahalwari systems which increased their revenue extraction from agricultural land by following oppressive practices.

6. They followed the strategy of "Divide and rule" to strengthen their control. Which led to the exploitation of existing religious, social, and regional divisions. The most powerful and deliberate strategy to create divisions between Hindus and Muslims was the partition of Bengal in 1905.
7. British rule gave birth to a strong nationalist movement in India. Many leaders like Mahatma Gandhi, Jawaharlal Nehru, Subhash Chandra Bose, and others fought against the Britishers for the independence of India. This freedom struggle led to widespread protests, civil disobedience movements, and the eventful attainment of independence in 1947 for India. It's fair to say that the legacy of British rule continues to shape India's social, economic, cultural, and political background to this day.
8. During ancient and medieval times, India faced political fragmentation, with numerous small and large kingdoms and empires. Within this political landscape, princely states merged as independent or semi-independent entities as it was not directly governed by the British but by an Indian ruler.

These states had their administrative systems, revenue-collecting systems, and judicial systems. There were around 565 princely states at the time of independence and around 562 of them were integrated with India through the efforts of Sadar Vallabhai Patel. The era of princely states ended with independence in 1947. Jawaharlal Nehru didn't want the independent India to accept the "divine right of kings." He declared any state not joining the constituent assembly would be treated as an enemy state. There were cases of Jammu and Kashmir, Hyderabad state, Junagarh, and Kalat which led to long disputes between the countries. With the emergence of the Mughal Empire and later the British Raj, the authority and autonomy of princely states went through significant changes.

Formation of States and Politics in Contemporary India

1) In contemporary India, it was a very complex and evolving process in the formation of states and politics which is shaped by historical, linguistic, and socio-economic factors. Today the political landscape of India is characterized by a federal system with a parliamentary form of government but before this India had to undergo several harsh transitions.
2) During the 1950s to 1960s reorganization of states on linguistic lines took place which was one of the most significant developments. Before that states were recognized or defined by administrative boundaries. India is a country with diverse linguistic and cultural identities aimed at the creation of linguistic states. This led to the formation of states such as Maharashtra, Karnataka, Tamil Nadu, and others.
3) Today India follows a federal system of governance where the power and resources are divided between the central government and states. Over the years, there have been debates and discussions about the extent of power-sharing and creating a balance between the centre and the state. The relationship

between them has evolved, with states demanding more autonomy and resources which resulted in the formation of regional political parties and regionalism which is playing a significant role in Indian politics till now. Akali Dal party is the second oldest in India, after Congress, which was founded in 1920.

4) There was a rise of these regional parties in India which has been a prominent feature of Indian politics. Parties like the DravidaMunnetraKazhagam (DMK) in Tamil Nadu, Telugu Desam Party (TDP) in Andhra Pradesh, Shiv Sena in Maharashtra, Trinamool Congress (TMC) in West Bengal, and many others have gained influence and importance in their respective states. As they champion local and regional issues which strengthen the shape of state politics.
5) During the 1990s, when no single party got a clear majority in Lok Sabha, many national parties came into an alliance with many regional parties to form a government at the centre. Which led to a new culture of sharing power and respect for the independence of state governments. This led to the trend of coalition governments. This trend was supported by the judgment of the Supreme Court which gave state governments power and made it difficult for the central government to dismiss them arbitrarily. Thus, it can be said that federal power sharing is far more effective today than it was in the early years.
6) Social and economic factors like caste-based politics, identity politics, and regional aspirations have also influenced the politics of Indian states. It plays a crucial role in state-level elections and government formation.
7) In totality, the evolution of Indian states and politics is an ongoing process, shaped by various socio-political factors. The dynamics continue to evolve as new challenges and opportunities arise, requiring adaptability and innovation in

the Indian political system. The ancient and medieval times have served as a complex interplay of powerful empires and regional power, further growing into linguistic states in the present. The Mughal and the Maurya's influence on the governess influence the culture, politics, and the state of society in present India. As a result, of the collision of societal changes and politics the state of India aims to be diverse and unique internally in modern times.

Conclusion

Based on the study of state and society relations, as well as literary, epigraphical, and archaeological sources, it is evident that India has undergone various forms of governance and polity throughout its history, transitioning from monarchial to democratic systems. As a diverse country, India encompasses people from different backgrounds, classes, creeds, and genders, who follow distinct rituals and worship different deities. However, they are bound together by a sense of unity and patriotism. Literary, archaeological, and epigraphical studies have played a crucial role in identifying the country's flaws and governing it effectively.

The development of administrative structures and social hierarchies has fostered a better relationship between the state and its citizens. The country and its leaders have consistently endeavoured to introduce innovative approaches to governance, enabling adaptation and evolution in the face of challenges. India's constitution and democratic framework serve as a significant benchmark for other nations. Nevertheless, India continues to face challenges such as corruption, injustice, gender inequality, communal riots, and more. Overcoming these issues requires sustainable planning and decisive action.

Before progressing further, it is essential to enhance the knowledge regarding effective governance and uphold the values of justice and equality. Achieving this goal necessitates a comprehensive understanding of rich history and polity, coupled with a dedicated commitment to progress. By working collectively towards making India a better place, characterized by good governance, equality, and zero discrimination, a brighter future for all can be created.

References

Bhattacharyya, H. (2003). Multiculturalism in contemporary India. *Int. J. Multiculturalism*, *5*(2), 151–164. ISSN 1817-4574.

Desai, M. (2005). Indirect British rule, state formation, and welfarism in Kerala, India, 1860–1957. *Social Science History*, *29*(3), 457–488. https://doi.org/10.1017/S0145553200013018

Khan, I. A. (2001). State in the Mughal India: Re-examining the myths of a counter-vision. *Social Scientist*, 29(1/2), 16–45. https://doi.org/10.2307/3518271

Mukherjee, S. (2017). Book review: Patrick Olivelle (trans.), King, Governance, and Law in Ancient India: Kautilya's Arthasastra—A New Annotated Translation. *Indian Historical Review* P. Olivelle (trans.), 44(1), 134–136. https://doi.org/10.1177/0376983617694671

Thapar, R. (2004). Early India: From the origins to AD 1300. https://www.abebooks.com/9780520242258/Early-India-Origins-1300-Thapar-0520242254/plp?cm_sp=plped-_-1-_-isbn. University of California Press.

***

SHAPING INDIA: A STUDY OF STATE AND SOCIETY INTERACTIONS

Anshul Saluja

Assistant Professor, School of Education,

K. R. Mangalam University, Gurugram

Nitish Kumar Minz

Student, School of Management and Commerce,

K.R. Mangalam University, Gurugram

Abstract

The history of India is examined in this essay, from its prehistoric civilizations to colonial domination to the birth of contemporary India after independence. It clarifies the various social systems in Indian society, including those influenced by caste, religion, language, gender, and class, which add to the complexity of interstate ties. and friendly.

The goal of this study is to examine the elements that influence how the Indian state and society interact. The research employed an interdisciplinary strategy that included primary and secondary sources, qualitative and quantitative techniques, and comparative analysis. In addition to contributing to the discussion on the social dynamics of the country, efficient governance, social inclusion, and sustainable development, it strives to give a thorough grasp of the Indian nation and society. In addition, the historical overview, Indian state structure, dynamics of Indian society, state-society relations, challenges, and opportunities are highlighted as key areas of research in the document.

The study's key conclusions and recommendations are then provided, highlighting the significance of bolstering democratic institutions, decreasing economic and social inequality, managing communities, and fostering sustainable development. The study contends that India may map a route to a more inclusive, egalitarian, and sustainable future by concentrating on these areas.

Keywords: State-Society Relations, Historical Background, Social Structure, Caste, Religion and Governance.

Introduction

Due to its diverse population and extensive cultural history, India offers a difficult relationship between the state and society. India's historical trajectory, which has been characterized by the rise and fall of empires, the influence of several religious and philosophical traditions, and struggles for independence and self-rule, has had a profound impact on the dynamics of state-society relations in India. India's historical, cultural, and social context strongly support the relationship between the state and society there. From the ancient Indus Valley Civilization through the Mauryan and Gupta Empires, the state has been crucial to the governance of the many civilizations that have emerged. India's state-society dynamics underwent a substantial change with the arrival of colonial authority as new political, economic, and social institutions were imposed by outside powers. new partnership. Following its independence, India saw the birth of a democratic state that would satisfy the aspirations and needs of a diverse populace. The connection between the state and society, though, presents both possibilities and difficulties in modern India. This connection is made more difficult by the intricacies of societal boundaries based on caste, religion, language, gender, and class as well as the ongoing interaction between traditional and modern ideals.

The major objective of this chapter is to examine India's state and society with an emphasis on their interconnections, interdependence, and effects on governance and development. This chapter aims to evaluate the historical setting, look at the framework of the Indian state, and recognize the complex social structure inside Indian society. It aims to describe the social, political, economic, and cultural aspects of the interaction between the state and society.

This study's vast reach includes both conventional and cutting-edge viewpoints. Considerable historical periods in India will include prehistoric cultures, medieval kingdoms, colonial authority, and post-independence India. The many social groups, communities, and institutions that make up Indian society will be addressed regarding caste, religion, language, gender, and class throughout the course.

Philips (2021) in his book explored the social, historical, and cultural influences on India's governance and societal systems as it digs into the complexity of that country's political scene. The book's contributors addressed a variety of subjects, including state-society interactions, political institutions, societal divides, identity politics, governance issues, and policy consequences. The book offers a detailed view of India's political and social realities by using a multidisciplinary approach. For academics, researchers, and policymakers attempting to understand the complexities of India's varied and changing political and social fabric, it is an invaluable resource since it critically explores power dynamics, societal transformations, and policy developments in the Indian context.

Basole (2019) gave a thorough overview of the Indian labour market and working conditions. With an emphasis on the informal sector, the study analyzed several job-related factors, such as salary trends, unemployment rates, and employment growth. It drew attention to the difficulties that employees confront, including poor pay, underemployment, and job instability. The paper explores the problems of social and gender inequality in the workforce and offers policy suggestions to solve these challenges. The study is an essential tool for policymakers, scholars, and organizations interested in comprehending the dynamics and difficulties of employment in India since it draws on a substantial amount of data and applies thorough analysis.

Basham (2021) investigated the political theories and ideas that influenced ancient Indian culture. He talked about the varna system (caste system), raj dharma (duties of rulers), and the principles of dharma (moral obligation) as essential elements of classical Indian political thinking. Basham investigated how these concepts affected ancient Indian society's social organization, system of government and power relationships. He examined the function of kingship, political administration, and the dynamic between rulers and their subjects. Basham gave helpful insights into the political climate of ancient India and its ongoing impact on modern Indian society through a thorough analysis of ancient Indian literature and historical records.

Singh (2020) examined how caste affects how the democratic system works and how power is distributed. He looked at how caste-based politics affects political parties, campaign tactics, and decision-making procedures. The difficulties that social hierarchies, inequality, and caste-based discrimination provide to the values of democracy and social justice are examined by Singh. He offered a detailed view of the socio-political environment of North India based on extensive research and empirical data, illuminating the complexity of caste relations and their influence on the democratic process. For scholars, policymakers, and anyone else interested in comprehending the intricacies of Indian culture, the book adds to the scholarly conversation on caste, politics, and democracy.

To comprehend the historical setting, Indian state structure, and societal motives, qualitative approaches like document analysis are utilized on historical records, government papers, political materials, and academic publications. These sources will provide valuable information on the development of relations between states and societies. In addition, qualitative interviews and focus group discussions were conducted with key stakeholders, including government officials, policymakers, civil society organizations, and community perspectives, to gather first-hand perspectives on the dynamics of the Indian national society.

History Overview

i) **Ancient and Medieval India:** India's state and civilization have origins that go back to the early and late medieval periods. Powerful kingdoms and empires like the Mauryas, Guptas, and Cholas rose to prominence in ancient India, establishing centralized systems of government and social institutions. During this time, the state was crucial in upholding law and order, collecting taxes, and carrying out justice (Bithin, 2019).

ii) **Colonialism and its Impact:** The arrival of European colonial powers, especially the British, marked a transformative period in Indian history. The British East India Company gradually established control over various areas and eventually assumed political power. Colonization brought about significant changes in state-society relations, with the British implementing policies that served their economic and administrative interests (Allouche, 2019). Colonialism disrupted existing social structures, exploited resources, and introduced new administrative and legal systems. It also led to the emergence of social and political movements that challenged colonial rule and asserted Indian identity (Pernau, 2019).

iii) **Independence and the Formation of Modern India:** When India was released from British colonial authority in 1947, the fight for independence came to a successful conclusion. As India begins the process of nation-building and the creation of a contemporary democratic state, this is a crucial turning point in the interaction between the state and society (Kothari, 2019). The authors of India's constitution envisioned a nation that upheld social justice, secularism, and democracy. The state is responsible for defending the rights and interests of its people and fostering a diverse society. To rectify historical disparities and uplift the disadvantaged in society, the construction of democratic institutions, the decentralization of authority, and the implementation of social welfare programs were all key components in the formation of modern India.

Indian State Structure

i) **Constitutional Framework:** The Indian state operates within a constitutional framework that provides fundamental principles and guidelines for governance. The Constitution of India, adopted in 1950, defines the structure, powers, and functions of the various organs of the state and respects the rights and freedoms of the citizens (Khosla, 2020).

ii) **Executive, Legislative and Judicial Branches:** The separation of powers between the executive, legislative, and judicial departments underpins the functioning of the Indian state. The president and prime minister are in charge of the executive branch, which is in charge of carrying out policies and managing the government. Parliament, which is in charge of passing laws and advancing public interests, is part of the legislative branch. The Supreme Court is in charge of interpreting and enforcing the law (Khosla M. &., 2021).

iii) **Bureaucracy and Administration:** The Indian bureaucracy plays an important role in the functioning of the state. The bureaucracy consists of civil servants responsible for implementing government policies, providing public services, and maintaining administrative efficiency (Taub, 2022). The administrative system is hierarchically structured, with many departments and ministries at different levels of government.

The Dynamics of Indian Society

i) **Diversity and Pluralism:** Indian society is characterized by its diversity and pluralism (Gallegos-Riofrío, 2022). It is home to many religions, languages, cultures, and ethnicities. The state has recognized and promoted diversity through its constitutional provisions and affirmative action policies, which promote harmony and social inclusion.

ii) **Gender and Social Relations:** Gender dynamics play an important role in Indian society. Despite efforts to promote gender equality and women's empowerment, challenges persist in areas such as access to education, economic opportunity, and gender-based violence. Social relationships are influenced by traditional norms and practices, with patriarchy often shaping power dynamics.

iii) **Class and Economic Disparities:** India is marked by significant economic disparities and social stratification. The country has a diverse socioeconomic background, with a significant portion of the population living in poverty (Chancel, 2019). Class divisions, income inequality, and unequal resource allocation pose challenges to inclusive development and social cohesion.

iv) **Social Movements and Activities:** Indian society has been shaped by many social movements and activists. These movements have advocated for various causes, such as social justice, caste equality, environmental protection, and human rights. They have played an important role in challenging power structures, raising awareness, and influencing political decisions (Andrée, 2019). Understanding the dynamics of Indian society provides insight into the complexities and challenges facing the state in addressing social issues, promoting inclusive development, and ensuring coherence. social connection. This section sets the stage for a comprehensive analysis of state-society dynamics in India.

State-Society Relations

i) **Democratic Governance and Citizen Participation:** The relationship between the state and society in India is shaped by democratic governance and citizen participation. The democratic system provides opportunities for citizens to participate in political processes, voice their opinions, and hold the state accountable. This section explores the dynamics of civic participation, electoral politics, and the role of civil society in shaping relationships between state and society.

ii) **Policy on Social Protection and Social Development:** The Indian state has introduced many social welfare policies aimed at promoting social development and improving the welfare of its citizens. This includes initiatives in areas such as education, health, poverty alleviation, and rural development (Sahoo, 2008). This section examines the impact of these policies on the relationship between the state and society and analyzes the challenges and successes of implementing social protection programs.

iii) **Identity Politics and Community Tensions:** Identity politics and community tensions are important factors influencing state-society relations in India. Divisions based on religion, caste, ethnicity, and language sometimes lead to conflicts and challenges to social harmony (Subramanian, 2002). This section delves into the complexities of identity politics, the role of political parties, and the state's efforts to manage and mitigate community tensions.

Challenges and Issues

Governance and Corruption: One of the major challenges facing the Indian state is governance and corruption. The effectiveness and efficiency of government institutions, transparency, and accountability mechanisms have a direct impact on the relationship between the state and society. This section explores challenges related to governance and corruption and analyses the implications for socio-state dynamics (Rose-Ackerman, 2005).

i) **Community Tension and Social Unrest:** Community tensions and social unrest pose significant challenges to state-society relations in India. Conflict and violence stemming from differences in religion, caste, and ethnicity can strain social cohesion and impact state functioning (Bharti, 2022). This section examines the causes and consequences of community tension and explores strategies to promote harmony among communities.

ii) **Inequality and Social Justice:** Addressing inequality and promoting social justice are essential aspects of the relationship between the state and society. India struggles with significant disparities in income, access to resources, and opportunities. This section analyzes the challenges related to inequality and social justice and discusses policy measures to ensure a more just society (Subbiah, 2021).

iii) **Urbanization and Environmental Sustainability:** Rapid urbanization and environmental sustainability pose complex challenges for the Indian state. Pressure on infrastructure, resource depletion, pollution, and climate change impact both the functioning of the state and the welfare of society. This section explores the effects of urbanization and environmental sustainability on relations between the state and society and discusses strategies for sustainable development (Prajapati, 2021).

Prospects and Recommendations

Strengthening Democratic Institutions: To improve relations between the state and society, strengthening democratic institutions is very important. This involves reforms in areas such as electoral processes, political party systems, and institutional mechanisms for citizen participation and accountability.

Promoting Social Cohesion and Inclusiveness: The Indian state should focus on promoting social cohesion and inclusion by addressing identity-based divisions and promoting dialogue, tolerance, and understanding among communities. This includes initiatives aimed at bridging social distances, promoting cultural diversity, and creating a sense of national identity.

Economic Disparity Settlement: To improve the relationship between the state and society, it is essential to address economic disparities and promote inclusive growth. This can be achieved through targeted policies aimed at poverty reduction, job creation, equitable resource allocation, and skills development.

Sustainable Development and Environmental Protection: The Indian state must prioritize sustainable development and environmental protection. This involves adopting policies and practices that promote sustainable urbanization, resource management, renewable energy, and ecological conservation. By addressing these challenges and taking recommended actions, the Indian state can strengthen state-society ties, promote inclusive development and ensure a sustainable and sustainable future. harmony for its citizens.

Major Findings

This research paper examined the state and society in India, exploring the historical overview, structure of the Indian state, the dynamics of Indian society, the relationship between state and society, challenges and problems, and prospects. During the analysis, several key findings emerged:

1. A historical overview highlights the development of India from ancient times, and medieval times to the impact of colonial rule and the formation of modern India after

independence. 2. The structure of the Indian state includes the constitutional framework, executive, legislative, and judicial branches, as well as bureaucracy and administration.

2. The dynamism of Indian society was explored, emphasizing the diverse and diverse nature of the country, the importance of social and gender relations, and the existence of disparities in terms of gender. class and economy, and the role of social movements and activism.

3. The relationship between the state and society was examined, highlighting the importance of democratic governance and citizen participation, the impact of social protection and social development policies, as well as challenges posed by identity politics and community tensions.

Conclusions and Future Orientations

The findings of this study have several implications for the state and society in India. They highlight the strengths and weaknesses of existing state-society relationships and identify areas for attention and improvement. Based on these implications, future directions can be considered:

first.

Strengthening democratic institutions: Efforts should be made to improve the functioning of democratic institutions, promoting transparency, accountability, and citizen participation in decision-making.

Fight against economic and social disparities: Policies must be developed to close income, resource, and opportunity gaps, ensuring a more inclusive and equitable society.

Community stress management: Measures must be taken to resolve identity conflicts and promote harmony among communities through dialogue, tolerance, and understanding.

Promoting sustainable development: Environmental sustainability should be a priority, with an emphasis on sustainable urbanization, resource management, and ecological conservation.

By pursuing these future orientations, the state and society in India can move towards a more inclusive, just, and sustainable future. Stakeholders must collaborate and work to address the identified challenges and implement recommended actions for the betterment of the country and its citizens.

References

Alasuutari, H. (2020). *Tackling inequity in education during and after COVID-19.*

Allen, M. E., Mabry, E., Mattrey, M., Bourhis, J., Titsworth, S., & Burrell, N. (2004). Evaluating the effectiveness of distance learning: A comparison using meta-analysis. *Journal of Communication*, *54*(3), 402–420. https://doi.org/10.1111/j.1460-2466.2004.tb02636.x

Allouche, J. (2019). State building, nation making and post-colonial hydro politics in India and Israel: Visible and hidden forms of violence at multiple scales. *Political Geography*, 75. https://doi.org/10.1016/j.polgeo.2019.102051

Andrée, P. C. (2019). *Civil society and social movements in food system governance* p. 216. Taylor & Francis.

Basham, A. L. (2021). *Some fundamental political ideas of ancient India. Politics and society in India*. Routledge.

Basole, A. (2019). *State of working India.*

Bharti, S. (2022). Corporate social responsibility in India: International arena and social development. *Corporate Social Responsibility in India*, 51–96.

Bithin, T. (2019). *History of environmental conservation. Ancient and medieval periods*.

Chabbott, C. S., & Sinclair, M. (2020). SDG 4 and the COVID-19 emergency: Textbooks, tutoring, and teachers. *Prospects*, *49*(1–2), 51–57. https://doi.org/10.1007/s11125-020-09485-y

Chancel, L., & Piketty, T. (2019). Indian income inequality, 1922–2015: From British raj to billionaire raj? *Review of Income and Wealth*, 65(S1), S33–S62. https://doi.org/10.1111/roiw.12439

Crawford, J. C., & Cifuentes-Faura, J. (2022). Sustainability in higher education during the COVID-19 pandemic: A systematic review. *Sustainability*, *14*(3), 1879. https://doi.org/10.3390/su14031879

d'Orville, H. (2020). COVID-19 causes unprecedented educational disruption: Is there a road towards a new normal? *Prospects*, *49*(1–2), 11–15. https://doi.org/10.1007/s11125-020-09475-0

Devercelli, A. (2020). *Supporting the Youngest Learners and Their Families in the COVID-19 (coronavirus) response*. World Bank.

Gallegos-Riofrío, C. A.-T. (2022). *Chronic deficiency of diversity and pluralism in research on nature's mental health effects: A planetary health problem. current Research in Environmental Sustainability*.

Giannini, S. (2020). *Three ways to plan for equity during the coronavirus school closures. World education blog*.

Azevedo, J. P., & A. H. (2021). Simulating the potential impacts of COVID-19 school closures on schooling and learning outcomes: A set of global estimates. *World Bank Research Observer*, *36*, 1–40.

Joo, Y.-J. B.-J. (2000). Self-efficacy for self-regulated learning, academic. *Educational Technology*, *48*(2), 5–17.

Kaffenberger, M. (2020). Modeling the long-run learning impact of the Covid-19 learning shock. *International Journal of Educational Development*, 0738–0593.

Khosla, M. &. (2021). The three faces of the Indian state. *Journal of Democratic*, 111–125.

Khosla, M. (2020). *India's founding moment: The constitution of a most surprising democracy*. Harvard University Press.

Kim, J. S., & Quinn, D. M. (2013). The effects of summer reading on low-income children's literacy Achievement From Kindergarten to Grade 8. *Review of Educational Research*, *83*(3), 386–431. https://doi.org/10.3102/0034654313483906

Kothari, S. (2019). *Social movements and the redefinition of democracy. India briefing* (pp. 131–162).

Leal Filho, W. B.-B., Brandli, L. L., Lange Salvia, A., Rayman-Bacchus, L., & Platje, J. (2020). COVID-19 and the UN sustainable development goals: A threat to Solidarity or an Opportunity? *Sustainability*, *12*(13), 5343. https://doi.org/10.3390/su12135343

Lewin, K. M. (2020). Contingent reflections on coronavirus and priorities for educational planning and development. *Prospects*, *49*(1–2), 17–24. https://doi.org/10.1007/s11125-020-09480-3

Meisam Ranjbari, O. (2021). Three pillars of sustainability in the wake of COVID-19: A systematic review and future research agenda for sustainable development. *Journal of Cleaner Production*, *6526*, 0959.

O'Connor, C. A. (2020). Economic recovery after the COVID-19 pandemic: Resuming elective orthopedic surgery and total joint arthroplasty. *Journal of Arthroplasty Suppl.*32eS36.

Pernau, M. (2019). *Emotions and modernity in colonial India: From balance to fervor*. Oxford University Press.

Pham, L. L. (2019). Does e-learning service quality influence e-learning student satisfaction and loyalty? Evidence from Vietnam. *International Journal of Educational Technology in Higher Education*, *16*(1), 1–26.

Philips, C. H. (2021). *Politics and society in India*. Routledge.

Prajapati, H. R. (2021). Social, economic and environmental indicators of urban sustainability in India. *SSRN Electronic Journal*. https://doi.org/10.2139/ssrn.3883833

Chawla, R. (2019). Determinants. *Journal of General Management*, *6*(1), 78–89.

Rose-Ackerman, S. (2005). The challenge of poor governance and corruption. Especial 1 DIREITO GV. *Law Review, 207*.

Sahoo, S. (2008). Globalization, social welfare, and civil society in India. *Journal of Comparative Social Welfare*, 24(2), 133–141. https://doi.org/10.1080/17486830802231073

Sharma, N. D. (2020). All India Ophthalmological Society-Eye Bank Association of India consensus statement on guidelines for cornea and eye banking during the COVID-19 era. *Indian Journal of Ophthalmology*, 1258.

Singh, J. (2020). *Caste, state, and society: Degrees of democracy in North India*. Taylor & Francis.

V. D. Soni. (2020). *Global impact of e-learning during COVID-19. SSRN*.

Starkey, K. (2020). Turning our education crisis into opportunity: Lessons from high-performing. *Forbes*.

Subbiah, A. K. (2021). *A study on role of enforcing minimum wage policy in promoting equality and social justice in an economy: A case of Indian economy* [Doctoral Dissertation]. National College of Ireland.

Subramanian, N. (2002). Identity politics and social pluralism: Political sociology and political change in Tamil Nadu. *Commonwealth and Comparative Politics*, 40(3), 125–139. https://doi.org/10.1080/713999599

Taub, R. P. (2022). *Bureaucrats under stress: Administrators and administration in an Indian state*. University of California Press.

Tomasik, M. J. (2020). Educational Gains of *In-Person vs. Distance Learning* in Primary and Secondary Schools: A Natural Experiment during the COVID-19 Pandemic School Closures in Switzerland. *International Journal of Psychology*.

Weeden, K. A., & Cornwell, B. (2020). The small-world network of college classes: Implications for epidemic spread on a university campus. *Sociological Science*, *7*, 222–241. https://doi.org/10.15195/v7.a9

Wang, X., Li, G., Malik, S., & Anwar, A. (2022). Impact of COVID-19 on achieving the goal of sustainable development: E-learning and educational productivity. *Economic Research-Ekonomska Istraživanja*, *35*(1), 1950–1966. https://doi.org/10.1080/1331677X.2021.1927789

Xin-yu Wang, G. L. (2022). Impact of COVID-19 on achieving the goal of sustainable development: E-learning and educational productivity. *Economic Research*, *35*(1), 1950–1966.

Zhong, R. (2020). The coronavirus exposes education's digital divide. *The New York Times*, *18*.

***